The History and Ethics
of Authenticity

The History and Ethics of Authenticity

Meaning, Freedom and Modernity

Kyle Michael James Shuttleworth

BLOOMSBURY ACADEMIC
LONDON • NEW YORK • OXFORD • NEW DELHI • SYDNEY

BLOOMSBURY ACADEMIC
Bloomsbury Publishing Plc
50 Bedford Square, London, WC1B 3DP, UK
1385 Broadway, New York, NY 10018, USA
29 Earlsfort Terrace, Dublin 2, Ireland

BLOOMSBURY, BLOOMSBURY ACADEMIC and the Diana logo are trademarks of
Bloomsbury Publishing Plc

First published in Great Britain 2021
This paperback edition published in 2022

Copyright © Kyle Michael James Shuttleworth, 2021

Kyle Michael James Shuttleworth has asserted his right under the Copyright,
Designs and Patents Act, 1988, to be identified as Author of this work.

For legal purposes the Acknowledgements on p. ix constitute an extension
of this copyright page.

Cover design by Charlotte Daniels
Cover image: *The Wanderer Above the Sea of Fog* by Caspar David Friedrich, c. 1817
(© Niday Picture Library / Alamy Stock Photo)

All rights reserved. No part of this publication may be reproduced or transmitted
in any form or by any means, electronic or mechanical, including photocopying,
recording, or any information storage or retrieval system, without prior
permission in writing from the publishers.

Bloomsbury Publishing Plc does not have any control over, or responsibility for, any
third-party websites referred to or in this book. All internet addresses given in this
book were correct at the time of going to press. The author and publisher regret any
inconvenience caused if addresses have changed or sites have ceased to exist,
but can accept no responsibility for any such changes.

A catalogue record for this book is available from the British Library.

Library of Congress Cataloging-in-Publication Data
Names: Shuttleworth, Kyle Michael James, author.
Title: The history and ethics of authenticity: meaning, freedom and modernity /
Kyle Michael James Shuttleworth.
Description: London; New York: Bloomsbury Academic, 2020. |
Includes bibliographical references and index.
Identifiers: LCCN 2020029957 | ISBN 9781350163423 (hb) | ISBN 9781350186408
(paperback) | ISBN 9781350163461 (epdf) | ISBN 9781350163454 (ebook)
Subjects: LCSH: Authenticity (Philosophy) | Ethics.
Classification: LCC B105.A8 S68 2020 | DDC 170–dc23
LC record available at https://lccn.loc.gov/2020029957

ISBN: HB: 978-1-3501-6342-3
PB: 978-1-3501-8640-8
ePDF: 978-1-3501-6346-1
eBook: 978-1-3501-6345-4

Typeset by Deanta Global Publishing Services, Chennai, India

To find out more about our authors and books visit www.bloomsbury.com and
sign up for our newsletters.

*'"Know thyself" was written over the portal of the antique world.
Over the portal of the new world, "Be thyself".'*

~ *Oscar Wilde;* The Soul of Man Under Socialism

Contents

Acknowledgements	ix
Introduction: A prelude to the problem(s)	1
0.1 What is authenticity?	1
0.2 Why freedom, meaning and modernity?	7
0.3 A structural overview	9

Part One The problem and the resolution

1 The problem(s) of modernity	15
1.1 What is modernity?	16
1.2 Enlightenment: Maturity and freedom	19
1.3 Counter-Enlightenment: Nihilism and disenchantment	26
1.4 Embracing one's fate	35
2 Variations on the concept of authenticity	39
2.1 Articulating authenticity	40
2.2 Alternative ethical ideals	42
2.3 The socio-ethical turn	46
2.4 Sartre's existential authenticity	50
2.5 Taylor's ethic of authenticity	54
3 Dimensions of socio-existential authenticity	60
3.1 What determines our sense of authenticity?	61
3.2 How can we ensure our ideal is achievable?	66
3.3 Where do our choices derive from?	68
3.4 What validates our choices?	71
3.5 Meaning	78

Part Two Challenges for authenticity

4 Can the Enlightenment project be completed? ... 85
   4.1 The project of modernity ... 86
   4.2 Completing the project ... 95
   4.3 Ethics or morality? ... 104

5 Is the 'self' a fiction? ... 113
   5.1 The subjection of individuality ... 114
   5.2 From power to subjection ... 119
   5.3 Technologies of the self ... 123
   5.4 Foucault's Nietzsche ... 130

6 Are all modern ethics emotive? ... 137
   6.1 Modern culture of emotivism ... 138
   6.2 Emotivism and authenticity ... 145
   6.3 Practices, narrative and tradition ... 151
   6.4 Criticisms of MacIntyre's virtue ethics ... 159

7 Finding meaning in freedom ... 168
   7.1 Picking up the spear ... 169
   7.2 Finding meaning in freedom ... 174
   7.3 Can one be authentic within contemporary society? ... 178
   7.4 Concluding remarks ... 190

Bibliography ... 193
Index ... 205

Acknowledgements

The contents of this book represent the culmination of over a decade of philosophical enquiry and thought. Although I began this particular project as a doctoral student and brought it to completion as Visiting Research Fellow at Queen's University Belfast, many of the ideas contained within occurred to me prior to undertaking philosophy as an academic endeavour. My personal motive for studying philosophy was to come to terms with the modern world as a fluid, dynamic and shifting concept; to discover what it means to live well; and to understand my place within such a conceptual framework. With this book I have sought to satisfy these concerns by articulating modernity as a philosophical problem and the ethics of authenticity as a response.

Whilst this book may bear my name alone, human beings do not develop independently of one another. We are, rather, as I argue, dialogical beings who owe our identity to the many cultural contexts and communities to which we belong. With this in mind, it would be ignorant to believe that the completion of this book could have been achieved in isolation. First and foremost, I owe an immense debt of gratitude to my doctoral supervisors: Keith Breen and Cillian McBride. Both of whom pushed me in directions which I was initially reluctant to go and whose advice and encouragement made this project far more successful than I alone could have imagined or achieved. I am also obligated to the examiners of my viva voce, Jonathan Webber and Fabian Schuppert, who pushed me beyond my comfort zone, forcing me to think on my feet and testing the commitment to my ideal (which I hope was maturely conceived!)

I am simultaneously appreciative and apologetic to the audiences of countless conferences and workshops to whom I subjected work in progress and who offered valuable, and much appreciated, constructive criticism on early chapter drafts. The primary outlet for my research was the immensely beneficial Friday Ethics Workshop at Queen's and its regular attendants: Cillian McBride, Keith Breen, Tom Walker, Jeremy Watkins, Josh Milburn, Hanhui Xu, Suzanne Whitten and Michael Whitten. I am also thankful to my friends and fellow members of the Sartre Society UK (Jonathan Webber, T Storm Heter, Maria Russo) and the European Network of Japanese Philosophy (Hans Peter Liederbach, Yusa Michiko, Inutsuka Yu, Morisato Takeshi), where I not only received valuable feedback on presentations but also developed many of my ideas during intervals and coffee breaks.

I also owe special thanks to Gaven Kerr who encouraged me to pursue doctoral research whilst I was still an undergraduate student, and whose friendship has endured as long as my formal philosophical training. Last but not least, I am grateful to my parents and grandparents: Margaret Shuttleworth, Alan Shuttleworth, the late Rita Parkinson and Joseph Parkinson – who encouraged and helped cultivate my intellectual curiosity. Finally, my best friend Sayaka Shuttleworth for her infinite patience and belief in my ability to bring this book to completion, especially when my own confidence began to falter.

皆さん本当にありがとうございました

K.M.J.S.

Introduction
A prelude to the problem(s)

0.1 What is authenticity?

The first documented concern with the authenticity of a work of art dates to the nineteenth century and two almost identical paintings of Raphael's portrait of Pope Leo X, located in Florence and Naples, respectively. On a visit to the late pope's family in the 1520s, the Marquis of Mantua perceived the painting, became enamoured and requested it for his own collection. The Marquis's request was granted, and the painting was brought to the artist Andrea del Sarto to construct a suitable frame. Whilst in his possession, Sarto made a duplicate of the painting which was deemed to be aesthetically on par with the original. The duplicate was then presented to the Marquis, who upon being informed that it was not painted by Raphael nevertheless praised the painting in terms of the artist's own merit. However, attitudes towards duplicates changed in the nineteenth century. As Jonathan Keats articulates,

> whilst Andrea del Sarto was still venerated in the 1800s – ranking just a tier below Raphael and Michelangelo – skill was no longer valued as highly as authenticity. Whether the Pope's damask looked realistic was secondary to whether Raphael had painted it. Experts made a living assembling and documenting provenance. Eventually, Naples was humbled by scholarly consensus that Florence had the original painting. (2013: 3)

In this regard, the authenticity of a work of art refers to an artistic creation which can be verified in terms of provenance and by connoisseurs who possess expertise in the techniques and mind-set of the artist in question. Here an epistemological distinction is made between an original and a replica which has been produced with the intention of deceiving others. With the increase of modern technology, skill is no longer required to replicate works of art, and forgery has become much more prevalent. One reason why reproductions are deemed inferior is because they lack the history of the original. According to Walter Benjamin, 'even the most perfect reproduction of a work of art is lacking in one element: its presence in time and space, its unique existence at the place where it happens to be' (1999: 124). This historical element is precisely that which makes an object authentic in his account. As Benjamin continues, 'the authenticity of a thing is the essence of all that is transmissible from its beginning, ranging from its substantive duration to its testimony to the history which it has experienced' (1999: 125). The authenticity of art pertains to not only paintings but also music and in particular the genres of punk rock and hip-hop.

In 1975 a group of working-class lads from London debuted under the stage name 'The Sex Pistols'. Their political messages of anti-establishment and disenfranchisement soon came to epitomize punk culture. However, questions surrounding their legitimacy arose. When the group's manager Malcolm McLaren first encountered the soon-to-be lead vocalist, John 'Johnny Rotten' Lyndon, Lyndon had orange hair and was wearing a Pink Floyd t-shirt to which he had prefixed 'I hate'. And although Lyndon was a substandard vocalist, McLaren invited him to join the group on account of his unique sense of style. Another iconic member of the band, John 'Sid Vicious' Richie was originally introduced as a bassist but was deemed incompetent – indeed, Richie only featured on one track on the iconic *God Save the Queen* album, which was eventually dubbed over – nevertheless Richie was not introduced for his musical talent, but for his arrogant, outspoken attitude which caused frequent controversy, and thus publicity, at their shows. Despite the questionable recruitment of members, and whether the group was manufactured by McLaren, the issue of authenticity arose in relation to the backgrounds of the members themselves. As Peter York makes explicit, 'because of punk's creation myth – that it was all about alienated, working-class youths breaking through – the authenticity debate arrived immediately after with the most literal-minded Jacobin interrogation. Every punk band had to face a new line of questioning. How genuinely working class were they?' (2014: 42).

In hip-hop, rap artists place a premium on 'keeping it real' by remaining true to the customs and values of the cultural community within which they were raised. One of the first and most prominent rap groups to provide a social commentary on the gangster lifestyle prevalent within American ghettos was N.W.A. However, the group's song writer O'Shea 'Ice-Cube' Jackson did not personally partake in the violence-fuelled culture conveyed in his lyrics. To maintain an air of authenticity, Eric 'Easy-E' Wright, who was renowned for his street-sense, was introduced as a frontman for the group. After disagreements over royalties, Jackson departed from the group to pursue a solo career though was branded a traitor by the remaining members on their succeeding album *Efil4zaggin* (1990). Jackson riposted on the song 'No Vaseline' by claiming they 'moved straight out of Compton, living with the whites' (1991). Referencing their hit song and eponymously titled debut album, Jackson questioned his ex-group's authenticity by inferring they have forgotten their origins and distanced themselves from the black community. In Kembrew McLeod's account, claims of authenticity in hip-hop arise in response to artists finding themselves within the mainstream of a culture they oppose. In McLeod's own words, 'they preserved this identity by invoking the concept of authenticity in attempting to draw clearly demarcated boundaries around their culture' (1999: 136). Thus, for punk rock and hip-hop, as with art, the question of authenticity is a question of provenance: Is the disadvantaged rhetoric real, are the artists disenfranchised as their lyrics portray, and are they pretending to be something they are not?

One common concern at the heart of the discussion of authenticity in popular culture relates to the development of mass society and the subsequent loss of traditional identity. This concern is aptly expressed by José Ortega Y Gasset in *Revolt of the Masses* (1930), where mass society is presented as a threat to individuality and free thought.[1] In his own words,

> the mass crushes beneath it everything that is different, everything that is excellent, individual, qualified and select. Anybody who is not like everybody, who does not think like everybody, runs the risk of being eliminated. And it is clear, of course, that this 'everybody' is not 'everybody'. 'Everybody' was normally the complex unity of the mass and the divergent, specialized minorities. Nowadays, 'everybody' is the mass alone. (1994: 14–15)

In contemporary culture, the rejection of mass society is perhaps best expressed by the rise of hipsters, who can ironically be identified by their plaid shirts, quirky facial hair, retro electronics and fixed-gear bicycles – as satirized within Chris Morris's Channel 4 comedy *Nathan Barley* (2005). And although it has become fashionable to mock the conformity of these non-conformists, their rejection of mainstream values is fuelled by the pursuit of authenticity.

As attested by Ico Maly and Piia Varis, 'what is absolutely crucial – and global – in defining a hipster is the claim to authenticity, uniqueness and individuality. Being a true hipster is about "being real", and not "trying too hard". "Being real", however, demands identity work, and being a hipster comes with very strong

---

[1] Interestingly, Sigmund Freud published his *Civilisation and its Discontents* in the same year, which also focused on the clash between the desire for individuality and freedom and civilization's demand for conformity in modern society.

and reoccurring identity discourses that all focus on authenticity' (2015: 8). This pursuit of authenticity in response to mass society has led to a progressive counterculture which seeks to impede the corrosive effects of globalization by reviving traditional practices. That is, the hipster's desire to be authentic has led to the preservation and utilization of traditional ways of life. This, however, is not to be confused with nostalgic, blood and soil sentiment – the stark cold reality of pre-war Britain was urban squalor, consumption, indentured labour and zero prospects. Rather, as David Boyle makes explicit, 'authenticity doesn't just mean reliving the past: it means using it to find new ways of living – maybe even new kinds of progress. The most authentic isn't necessarily the most true to the past; it could be the most creative or the most human' (2004: 44). It is precisely in this respect that hipsters excel.

Through their use of typewriters instead of the latest MacBook, and opting for vintage clothing rather than the latest trend in fashion, the rise of hipsters can be understood as a response to mass society, generic produce and a rejection of capitalism. Against factory work and mass production, which threaten the loss of traditional skills, we have also seen the return to handmade produce, ranging from hand-died silks and wallpaper printing to the promotion of independent business such as microbreweries. There has been a backlash against the mass production of food in the form of complaints against artificial produce which has been genetically modified and produced with synthetic flavours. This has led to the rediscovery of local produce with an emphasis on organic, free-range, gluten-free and vegan alternatives to promote sustainable lifestyles. A further concern is the loss of local identity, which has been seen in the replacement of corner shops with superstores, rendering every major city identical in terms of commercial output. In response, we have seen the emergence of bare brick bars and restaurants decked out with distressed furniture and architectural salvage as has become a cliché in Shoreditch, London. Thus, whilst hipsters may wear vintage clothes, utilize retro electronics and participate in bygone past-times, they have also had a significant impact upon local communities through their pursuit of authenticity.

Why has the concept of authenticity become so prevalent? According to Andrew Potter,

> absent from our lives is any sense of the world as a place of intrinsic value, within which each of us can lead a purposeful existence. And so we seek the authentic in a multitude of ways, looking for a connection to something deeper in the jeans we buy, the food we eat, the vacation we take, the music we listen to, and the politicians we elect. (2010: 264)

David Boyle expresses a similar sentiment:

> our demand for authenticity is partly a response to living in a fake, constructed world, to being manipulated over the airwaves at every moment of the day, to the way virtual communication is cutting out human contact. It is partly a simple reaction against modernity. But it is also something else: it's a demand for a different kind of life in the century ahead when, for the first time since the industrial revolution, questions about how we are intended to live – and how we should live – become central again. (2004: 282)

It is in this sense that we will take up the concept of authenticity in this enquiry – not in terms of provenance, or uniqueness in reaction to mass society, but in relation to oneself.

The importance of authenticity in relation to oneself is reflected within the plethora of self-help guides and spiritual gurus which claim to possess the secret to unlock our true selves.[2] This literature advocates leading an 'authentic' life as the means to increased happiness and meaning. And although this does not express the concept of authenticity per se, it nevertheless demonstrates the demand for self-realization. The market has also responded to this demand, offering personalized products and commodities which propose to enable self-discovery and realize our inner being.[3] This message is perpetuated by billboards, commercials and online bloggers promising that the product in question provides the means to achieve self-actualization. Through marketing and consumerism, we can thus detect a reciprocal shaping of capitalism and authenticity. Society urges us to actualize our potential, to become what we are and capitalize upon our unique abilities and attributes. However, these supposed spiritual aids and marketplace creations merely gesture towards an innate sense of self, without saying anything substantial about what it is to be authentic. What is it precisely, then, that they are attempting to articulate?

In general terms, authenticity indicates genuineness and a sense of being true to oneself. One way to conceptualize our 'true self' is through the metaphor of childhood, recalling how children possess strong characteristics and opinions, aspiring to a particular calling which resonates with them. This notion of who we really are, and what we truly want, is often said to become obscured by the

---

[2] Examples of influential self-help guides include Dale Carnegie's *How to Make Friends and Influence People* and Stephen Covey's *The 7 Habits of Highly Effective People*, both of which became best sellers.
[3] For example, the British-based gym Fitness First uses the motivational slogan 'be yourself, only better'. Moreover, in Lancome's advertisement for their perfume *La Vie Est Belle*, Julia Roberts is depicted breaking free from chains whilst at a formal dinner, suggesting that the perfume epitomizes independence and individuality.

social ordering and demands imposed upon us by others. In this regard, we can thus conceive of who we truly are by articulating that which is at our core when stripped of the pretence of one's social roles. One can thus conceive of one's true self as constituted by one's own-most values, abilities and interests. In short, we like to think that our authentic self is constructed by actualizing those abilities which are uniquely our own. There are, however, various theories which attempt to articulate this state of existence by advocating alterative understandings of that which our true self consists of and how to achieve authenticity. On the one hand, there are advocates who claim that we possess an individual essence which is discovered through introspection. On the other, there are those who reject any sense of human essence, and instead argue that we are what we determine ourselves to be through self-creation. Nevertheless, in each of these approaches, authenticity refers to an individual mode of existence, and one which is self-determined.

If authenticity is an individual mode of existence, then surely any attempt to formally define it will result in inauthenticity. That is, if we attempt to reduce authenticity to a formula which anyone can apply, then it seems to follow that such a formula will lead to a generic existence which is neither uniquely one's own, nor authentic. By offering an analysis of that which constitutes an authentic existence, our intention is not to provide instruction on how one ought to act, but to explain the conditions which lead to an inauthentic existence and how to determine whether one's existence is indeed authentic. What we will present is the *form* of authenticity, as opposed to the content. Thus, far from constructing a framework to adhere to, the purpose is to provide a diagnostic tool which will enable us to identify aestheticism and egotistical self-indulgence and demarcate these from an authentic existence. Furthermore, a formal account of authenticity avoids the presuppositions of an underlying metaphysical approach; that is, to claim that we have an authentic self which is our own suggests that we possess an individual essence. However, by offering a formal account of authenticity we are able to avoid relying upon any such underlying essentialism of normative ideals.

The aim of this book will be to make a positive contribution to the contemporary literature on authenticity. Although there has been a resurgence of academic interest in the phenomenon of authenticity, as will be demonstrated in Section 2.4., there is still room for growth and development. The particular contribution which this book is intended to make, and the problem which it will address, is to determine the extent to which an ethic of authenticity is capable of responding to the increase of negative freedom and loss of meaning within contemporary European society. That is, the central focus of this book will be to concern ourselves with the manner in which authenticity is simultaneously capable of addressing the increase of negative freedom and providing the individual with a meaningful mode of existence within the wake of a post-metaphysical society. The question that both motivates this enquiry and which this book intends to address is therefore: To what extent can authenticity provide a compelling resolution to the problems of freedom and meaning which pervade modern existence?

0.2 Why freedom, meaning and modernity?

The traditional view of philosophical problems is that they are distinguished by the fact that they are eternally relevant and engage with topics which lack an obvious, straightforward response. Reading Platonic dialogues, it is difficult to conceive of intellectual progress in the Occidental tradition because we are still unable to provide an explanation to the metaphysical, epistemological and ethical problems raised within. It is for this reason we can appreciate Alfred North Whitehead's famous exclamation, 'the safest general characterization of the European philosophical tradition is that it consists of a series of footnotes to Plato' (1978: 39). Having mapped the intellectual terrain of human understanding, Plato's predicaments became those which subsequent theorists have attempted to resolve. However, after 2,600 years of engagement, there is very little which one can contribute to these debates. Anything which could have been said has doubtlessly already been proposed. Thus, many traditional issues appear as but dry, dusty philosophical problems which have been over-analysed with no real significant contributions.

This conception, however, was challenged by the onset of modernity, which brought about a radical overhaul of existing social orders. Although the project of modernity was developed with the intention of achieving immense progress and resulted in a variety of social and political developments, it nevertheless brought a host of new problems with it. Modern theorists advocated that the end goal of human civilization was absolute autonomy and actively pursued the realization of this ideal. What ensued from the Enlightenment's endeavour was the breakdown of social hierarchies which were prejudiced against certain social classes and the undermining of corrupt political institutions that took advantage of those they were designed to protect. Although these orders and institutions were challenged with the intention of increasing freedom, which was taken to be a positive contribution to human civilization, there were, nevertheless, negative consequences of the Enlightenment's utopian ideal.

The onset of modernity caused seismic intellectual activity which disrupted the metaphysical grounds of human existence. The rational pursuit of freedom saw social hierarchies and religions as an impediment to progress, and it was this particular perspective which led to the secular dismissal of religion and the scientific rejection of Aristotelian metaphysical biology, which had advanced the belief that human nature possessed a natural *telos*. Although the rejection of these beliefs led to an initial increase in freedom, there were also unforeseen consequences. The breakdown of social hierarchies challenged our role within society and led to a loss of a shared communal goal, affecting how we conceive of ourselves, and subsequently, how we conduct ourselves ethically. The rejection of religion resulted in the loss of a natural end to our existence, to transcend the material world and discover our true nature, which was to be achieved by living in accordance with God's word. In each of these cases, the reverent pursuit of freedom brought about a loss of raison d'être. Freedom thus came at the cost of meaning. However, even the modern achievement of autonomy has been relinquished. That is, the freedom which the Enlightenment had actively pursued was consequently lost by the introduction of bureaucratic procedures.

It is this particular problem – the loss of meaning brought about by the pursuit of freedom – which we will engage with in this book. One may, however, object that there are more pressing philosophical problems, such as the increasing inequality which seems to be perpetuated by modern economic systems, and racial/sexual discrimination against ethnic/gender minorities. In this respect, one could argue that the problem of meaning is but a bourgeois ideal for those with no other concern than to vanquish boredom. On the contrary, it will be upheld that meaning is necessary to living a fulfilled existence. This position is made explicit by Abraham Maslow who, in his hierarchy of needs, postulates that humans have five states of psychological development: physiological, security, love, esteem and self-actualization.[4] It is the final sphere, self-actualization, which Maslow takes to be the pinnacle of psychological development and where he locates the need for meaning (1990: 370–96). Thus, whilst it may be argued that there are more fundamental issues which ought to be addressed, such as those of security for the impoverished, and esteem for minorities, the question of meaning is one which can be understood as an end goal which all human beings consciously pursue. Thus, far from an empty ideal pursued by those who

---

[4] The desire for meaning is also perpetuated in the sociological studies of Marx through his notion of alienation and Durkheim with *anomie*. A sense of meaninglessness is also portrayed in the great works of twentieth-century literature, as demonstrated through Dostoyevsky's underground man in *Notes from Underground*, and Kafka's K in *The Trial* and *The Castle*.

have found satisfaction in the fulfilment of basic needs, the drive for meaning is an intrinsic aspect of healthy psychological development.

0.3 A structural overview

In order to address the problems of freedom and meaning, and to determine the extent to which an ethic of authenticity can respond to these, our enquiry will be divided in two parts. The first part will be explicatory, outlining the problem and proposed resolution. Here we will explain the origin of the decrease of freedom and loss of meaning, noting the socio-historical conditions which led to not only the problem but also the emergence of authenticity as an ideal. In this way, our book will address the question from a hermeneutic standpoint. That is, we will discuss the emergence of authenticity in relation to a historical problem and maintain that it only makes sense within this context. We will also explicate the concept of authenticity much more thoroughly, explaining the ways in which it has developed and seek to make a contribution to the various traditions by constructing our own approach.

In Chapter 1, we will begin by presenting a historical framework within which to situate the problems of modernity. After offering a general account of the intellectual trajectory of modern European society, we will then narrow our understanding by focusing specifically on the Enlightenment as 'the project of modernity'. In order to address our primary research question, we will attempt to determine the problems which modernity poses in terms of freedom and meaning. We will then turn to address the Enlightenment's effect on the pre-modern framework, the vicissitudes it induced and the consequences of the Enlightenment's failure. In order to demonstrate these, we will consider the counter-discourse of Friedrich Nietzsche and Max Weber, who illuminate the outcome of the Enlightenment project. Having determined the negative implications, we will then present our particular approach to modernity.

Within Chapter 2, a comprehensive account of authenticity will be presented, by drawing out the intricacies of this concept. We will begin with a preliminary account of authenticity, defined as a distinctly modern phenomenon, which emphasizes individuality and that is understood in relation to inauthenticity. We will then expand upon this by comparing and contrasting authenticity with the alternative ethical ideals of sincerity, integrity and autonomy. We will also discuss contemporary approaches and illustrate that they reject the existential approach to authenticity, and instead advocate a socio-ethical inspired account.

In order to understand why this occurred, we will consider Sartre's existential approach. However, it will be argued that we can understand Taylor's socio-ethical approach as a development of existential authenticity.

With a thorough understanding of the phenomenon of authenticity, we will then be in a better position, in Chapter 3, to develop a concept of authenticity which builds upon the existing literature. Our intention here is to construct a theory which merges the social and existential approaches outlined in the previous chapter. Here it will be determined that there are six dimensions to the socio-existential approach to authenticity: choice, commitment, maturity, becoming what one is, intersubjective consciousness and heritage. It will then be argued that a further consequence of these six dimensions is a meaningful existence. We will also offer a preliminary elucidation of how the concept of authenticity is capable of addressing the problems of freedom and meaning. And as there will be outstanding issues, such as the concern that authenticity has become commodified, we will then turn our attention to considering alternative approaches to the problems of freedom and meaning.

The second part of this book will offer an analysis of alterative contemporary theorists who problematize modernity in terms of freedom and meaning. Here we will focus on Jürgen Habermas, Michel Foucault and Alasdair MacIntyre. These theorists have been chosen because they each attempt to engage with the intellectual failure of the Enlightenment and devise a resolution similar to authenticity; however, each undermines our account in a specific way. In each instance, we will consider the challenge which these accounts pose to authenticity, defend our account and argue that these approaches are insufficient to resolve the problem of meaning. However, our strategy will not be as simple as to defend and counter-strike, but through engagement with these thinkers our aim is to develop our concept of authenticity. That is, through being challenged we can detect weaknesses and overcome flaws by assimilating aspects of the theorists in question.

Chapter 4 will focus on the modernist response to the problem of freedom and meaning, as advocated by Jürgen Habermas. Although he recognizes the problems which have been caused by the failure of the Enlightenment project, Habermas nevertheless believes reverently that the project can be completed. That is, he argues that the outstanding, unfulfilled potential of the Enlightenment, if completed, would provide the means to resolve questions of freedom. In his account, the problems are a consequence of the colonization thesis that systems imperatives have been imposed upon the lifeworld. Habermas's approach is to restrict power/instrumental reason to systems and increase communicative reason within the lifeworld. However, it will be argued that Habermas's dualist conception of system and lifeworld is unrealistic because power cannot be restricted to system spheres. Furthermore, his theory of discourse ethics is subject to a performative contradiction. Namely, he prioritizes morality over ethics, though morality itself depends upon a prior conception of the good. However, Habermas's strength, and that which we will take from our engagement, is that resistance to the colonization thesis provides the continued possibility of an authentic existence.

In Chapter 5, we will consider the postmodernist response developed by Michel Foucault. Unlike Habermas, Foucault accepts the failure of the Enlightenment and the metaphysical ruins that surround him rather than attempting to complete the project. However, he believes that within modern society the subject has come to be produced by discourses of power. The consequence of his book is that, if there is no individual subject then none of our choices are our own; as such, we cannot live an authentic or meaningful life. However, Foucault later relinquishes this claim and attempts to develop a means of recovering subjectivity from this dominating force. He attempts to achieve this aim by drawing upon the Stoic-inspired ethic 'care of the self' which he believes has not been affected by discourse. However, although he offers a response to social domination through the ethic of care, his approach does not say anything explicit with regards to the problem of meaning. Nevertheless, we will draw out the implications of his ethic of care and suggest that despite being morally insensitive, to the extent that his approach cannot inhibit one from impinging upon the autonomy of another, his account can nevertheless be shown to provide a sense of unity. From our encounter, it will be claimed that Foucault enables us to develop our understanding of inauthenticity in terms of power relations.

The penultimate chapter offers an analysis of Alasdair MacIntyre's pre-modernist response, which focuses upon the negative ethical implications of the Enlightenment. In MacIntyre's account, the breakdown of hierarchies and the rise of modern society, which ensued from rationalization, lead to the loss of a unifying communal good and the emergence of emotivism– that is, our moral point of view is determined by our emotions alone. However, rather than accepting our existential condition, MacIntyre argues that in order to overcome emotivism we ought to revive the Aristotelian virtue ethics tradition. This, however, challenges our concept of authenticity on two grounds: (i) MacIntyre's account would suggest that authenticity is a manifestation of emotivism, and (ii) if teleology can be restored, as MacIntyre intends, then our concept of authenticity becomes redundant. In order to defend our concept of authenticity, we will challenge MacIntyre's concept of tradition, which underpins his virtue ethics, and demonstrate this is an unrealistic resolution for the reason that it is steeped in nostalgia. However, the aspect which we will take away from our experience with MacIntyre is his sense of narrative quest, which will enable us to further articulate the sense of unity inherent within our concept of authenticity.

In Chapter 7 of this book, we will bring together those aspects which we have learned and assimilated from the aforementioned theorists. Namely, we will attempt to explain how we may resist the colonization thesis, the relations of power with which theories of authenticity must contend and how we can acquire a unified sense of self through conceiving of authenticity in terms of a narrative quest. We will also demonstrate how our socio-existential concept of authenticity is capable of resolving the problems of freedom and meaning and complete our account by demonstrating that it provides a better resolution than the alternative theorists considered. Having defended our theory, we will then turn to consider practical and social problems to authenticity. In particular, we will consider whether our current economic structure inhibits one's ability to realize one's authentic self. We will also question the implications of social media upon our ability to live authentically, and what potential problems this may pose in the future. Having defined the key concepts, justified our choices and provided a structural framework of our book, let us now proceed.

Part One

The problem and the resolution

1

The problem(s) of modernity

With the onset of modernity and establishment of new systems and structures, new challenges simultaneously emerged. Perhaps the biggest challenge with which modern individuals were required to contend was the freedom which ensued from the collapse of pre-modern hierarchies. Those who perceived this as progress pursued freedom fervently as a rational end. However, the unforeseen consequence of the unbridled pursuit of autonomy was the ironic restriction of freedom, the very thing which propelled their efforts. The failure to establish a rational end led subsequent theorists to form a counter-discourse, rejecting the continuation of the attempt to provide a rational foundation for human existence. Those who opposed the Enlightenment recognized that the rejection of absolute values, upon which to orientate oneself, led to the concern of nihilism, that life is fundamentally meaningless. The focus of this chapter will be to present that which we intend to engage with within this monograph. Rather than focusing on modernity as a problem, namely, what modernity is, and whether this has ended and we are now living within a postmodern era, we will concern ourselves with the philosophical implications of the onset of modernity. Specifically, the aim will be to determine the problems that modernity poses with regard to freedom and meaning.

In order to achieve our aim, we will begin with a brief analysis of modernity, articulating that which early modern thinkers believed themselves to be attempting to achieve (Section 1.1). Here we will discuss the intellectual developments which separate modernity from pre-modernity and focus on that which MacIntyre has termed the 'Enlightenment project' (2010: 36). We will then turn our attention to determining the key concepts which came to be indicative of modernity (Section 1.2). Focusing specifically on the philosophical programmes of Immanuel Kant and Georg Wilhelm Friedrich Hegel, it will be illustrated that the concepts of maturity and autonomy are those which defined the Enlightenment project. Having provided an overview of modernity, attention will then be turned towards the negative consequences of the Enlightenment (Section 1.3). Here two specific problems will be raised and elucidated. The first problem, as explicated by Friedrich Nietzsche, is that of nihilism, that life is fundamentally meaningless. The second problem, which is raised by Max Weber, is disenchantment, which was a consequence of increased rationalization, which decreased the individual's ability to actualize their freedom. Having determined the problems which modernity poses, with regards to freedom and meaning, we will then articulate the approach to modernity which will be upheld in this book (Section 1.4). Here we will note that our particular disposition will be one of acceptance, that is, rather than attempt to explain away the problem, we will confront it directly.

1.1 What is modernity?

In order to address the problem of modernity it is necessary to first provide a context within which to situate our investigation. Historically, modernity is understood by its distinct division from the medieval era. As Robert Pippen explicates, 'Modernity, as the name suggests, implies a decisive break in an intellectual tradition, an inability to rely on assumptions and practices taken for granted in the past' (1991: 10–11). In this preceding period, the social system was feudal, the economy agricultural and the countries were controlled by monarchs or emperors. However, each of these components was gradually replaced. Society became capitalist, the economy industrial and the policies of state eventually came to be determined by democratic vote. With the implementation of these institutions, practices and traditions, the modern age was essentially born. The establishment of each of these elements, however, was not simply a matter of replacing one theory with another. On the contrary, what we now recognize as the 'modern world' is the result of 300 years of enquiry and development in various fields of science, economics and philosophy. Western modernization is a complex process, and as such there exist various historical narratives that account for its emergence and development. Furthermore, the attempt to offer a linear account of the intellectual developments which shaped contemporary society would be a considerable undertaking, and one best left to historians.[1]

---

[1] For a well-developed historical account of the emergence of the modernity, see Jonathan Israel, *A Revolution of the Mind: Radical Enlightenment and the Intellectual Origins of Modern Democracy*

However, in order to proceed, a rough historical account must be given to contextualize our investigation and determine the problems which modernity poses with regards to freedom and meaning. Recognizing the restrictions which are imposed by a philosophical enquiry, the account offered here will be limited to that of the Enlightenment. The reason for restricting our enquiry to this concrete historical event is because the Enlightenment came to define the modern era, intellectually. Although there were various Enlightenments, both regionally and within the various disciplines, in what follows, we will offer a précis of the key ideas and historical events which came to define the modern age.[2]

One underlying belief which resonated throughout Enlightenment thought was that the expansion of knowledge via reason and scientific understanding would lead to epistemological progress. This perspective was a result of the likes of Francis Bacon, who in his *Novum Organum* (1620) advanced an alternative to the 'stagnant' Aristotelian method. In his own words, Bacon claimed, 'knowledge must be sought from the light of nature, not fetched back out of the darkness of antiquity' (2009: I.CXXII). Bacon's development of the inductive method was designed to reap truth and enable humankind to understand God's creation. This was further fortified by Isaac Newton, who in his *Philosophiæ Naturalis Principia Mathmatica* (1687) suggested that nature was governed by laws and that the natural world could be explained and understood through rational principles such as cause and effect.[3] Within his scientific tour de force, Newton claimed 'the economy of nature requires us to make gravity responsible for the orbital force acting on each of the planets'.[4] Believing that the world was rational and beneficent, and that nature was essentially good, the idea spread that people possessed the potential to improve themselves and their environment. The outcome of this social awakening was that for the first time in history, individuals not only expected their future society to be significantly different to

---

(Princeton: Princeton University Press, 2009), and Norman Hampson, *The Enlightenment: An Evaluation of Its Assumptions, Attitudes and Values* (London: Penguin Book, 1990).

[2] See Jonathan Israel, *Democratic Enlightenment: Philosophy, Revolution, and Human Rights 1750-1790* (Oxford: Oxford University Press, 2013) in particular, part II where Israel discusses the Scottish, Austrian, German, Italian and Spanish Enlightenments.

[3] There is an anecdote that Edmund Haley (who discovered the eponymous comet) asked Newton to calculate the path that an object (such as a planet) would follow under the influence of a force that moved as the inverse square of the distance from the centre, and that *The Principa* was the result of his calculation. See Peter J. Bowler and Rhys Morris, *Making Modern Science: A Historical Survey* (Chicago: University of Chicago Press, 2005), 46.

[4] *The Principia: Mathematical Principles of Natural Philosophy*, ed. I. Bernard Cohen and Anne Whitman (Berkeley, CA: University of California Press, 1999).

that in which they were raised but also actively worked towards achieving this ideal.[5]

The Enlightenment was achieved not solely through advancements in science but also in politics.[6] In France, men of letters, such as Diderot, Voltaire and Rousseau, collaborated in order to compose the *Encyclopédia ou dictionnaire raisonne des sciences, des arts, et des metriers*.[7] The aim of their collective effort was to increase public understanding and produce a more virtuous and happier population.[8] Not only did these free thinkers seek to enlighten citizens, but they also drew awareness to corrupt institutions such as the then-repressive Catholic Church, their ineffective monarchy and the officials in charge who abused their positions. Advocates of the Enlightenment believed that it pointed the way towards political reform and sought to establish a system based on its principles. The Enlightenment thus culminated with the French Revolution in 1789, which 'replaced a decaying and obsolete social and political order with rational institutions' (Mah 1990: 4). By applying these scientifically derived principles to society, it was believed that human civilization would progress towards a more liberal state.

From the accounts thus far discussed, what can be determined is that the Enlightenment was the consequence of a dual process. First, there is the scientific sense of having a veil removed from one's eyes. In this account, the Enlightenment sought to obtain a greater understanding of the universe. This was achieved by Francis Bacon, who established induction as the scientific method, and Isaac Newton's discovery of natural laws. Here the belief in progress spurred on the increased 'rationalization' of the natural world, that is, the demystification of nature, and how one ought to understand it (Weber 2005: 30). Secondly, there is the ethical and political sense, in which one was enlightened insofar as one had a burden lifted from one's shoulders. Through historical movements, such as the French Revolution, political enlightenment brought about the realization of a free legal, political and personal order, within which people were encouraged

---

[5] For an excellent history of the development of modern science and its influence on technological developments, see Peter J. Bowler and Rhys Morris, *Making Modern Science: A Historical Survey* (Chicago: University of Chicago Press, 2005).

[6] See Stephen Eric Bronner, *Reclaiming the Enlightenment: Toward a Politics of Radical Engagement* (Columbia: Columbia University Press, 2004).

[7] Encyclopaedia, or a Systematic Dictionary of the Sciences, Arts, and Crafts.

[8] In the entry on encyclopaedia, Diderot himself defines 'The aim of an Encyclopédia is to bring together the knowledge scattered over the surface of the earth, to present its overall structure to our contemporaries and to hand it on to those who will come after us, so that our children, by becoming more knowledgeable, will become more virtuous and happier; and so that we shall not die without earning the gratitude of the human race'. The Open University, *The Enlightenment*. Milton Keynes (The Open University, 2013), p. 13

to live mature, individual lives. Thus, through the dual process of scientific and political enlightenment, what occurred was the erosion of the feudal-social hierarchy and creation of the de jure free individual. This in turn led to the loss of a stabilizing sense of tradition through the development of science and rationalization. Having defined modernity in terms of the Enlightenment, we will now turn our attention to determining the key philosophical concepts which came to be indicative of modernity.

1.2 Enlightenment: Maturity and freedom

Perhaps the best expression of the moral–ethical attitude that permeated Enlightenment thought is to be found within the work of Immanuel Kant. In his short essay, 'An Answer to the Question: What is Enlightenment?'[9] Kant offers a reflective account which seeks to understand this intellectual movement from within the confines of its own framework. The importance of this short text, and the precision with which Kant succinctly expressed the Enlightenment ideal, is recognized by not only the advocates of the Enlightenment but also its critics.[10] Here Kant famously claimed that enlightenment is '*man's emergence from self-incurred immaturity*' (2009: 1). In order to appreciate the significance of this claim, it is important to understand that which is inferred by 'immaturity'. Within his essay, Kant employs this term in a dual sense. First, on an individual level, from the literal definition of one who is emotionally and intellectually undeveloped. Here one's immaturity is a result of one's choice to remain dependent upon others. Secondly, Kant's understanding operates on the social level, which is explained with the figurative notion of a paternal society. In this sense, one does not necessarily choose to remain dependent, but is provided for by one's society and has no need to use one's understanding and no occasion to think for oneself. Kant claims that we not only depend upon such authorities for guidance and direction, but these very authorities, which he refers to as 'guardians', portray maturity as troublesome and dangerous. The guardians, by whom he means elders of the church, officers in the military and governmental civil servants, thus make themselves necessary to the masses by controlling them

---

[9] Kant's paper was published in Berlinische Monatsschrift in response to a question posed in a footnote of an article by Johann Friedrich Zollner, a pastor, theologian and educational reformer.
[10] For example, see Michel Foucault's *What Is Enlightenment* in *the Foucault Reader*, edited by Paul Rabinow (New York: Pantheon Books, 1984), 32–50.

through fear.[11] For these reasons, Kant claims, it is difficult to extricate oneself from immaturity. Furthermore, it is difficult for one to think for oneself if one has never before been afforded the opportunity to do so. There are, however, a few individuals who through 'their own cultivation of their spirit' have liberated themselves from dependence upon others (2009: 2). Kant states that, as a result of these independent thinkers' influence, it is inevitable that the public will eventually begin to think for themselves. Like the slave liberated from Plato's cave who returns in order to enlighten the others, independent thinkers who have matured will also want the masses to think for themselves.[12] However, he warns us that, if influenced by guardians who are incapable of enlightenment, the public may impede their own progress by maintaining these social, political and cultural beliefs, and cause themselves to remain immature.

Due to the guardians, who uphold traditional values and introduce these to the masses, the process of enlightenment is a slow, gradual one. Furthermore, Kant claims that it cannot be achieved by social revolution. He urges that although a revolution may displace despotism, avarices and oppression, it is incapable of imparting thought. It will simply replace the prejudices which harness the great unthinking masses.[13] The only way for enlightenment to be achieved, in his account, is for individuals to challenge conventions and teach the masses to think for themselves. The motto of the Enlightenment, he claims, is '*Sapere aude!* – Have courage to make use of your own understanding' (2009: 2). The goal of the Enlightenment, for Kant, is thus to mature intellectually by liberating ourselves from social authorities. The process of Enlightenment is therefore a dual one, necessarily depending first upon individual and then social pursuit. Whilst it is the individual's responsibility to free themselves, in order for society to advance towards greater freedom, this self-liberation must also be embraced by society as a whole.

---

[11] This is a recurrent theme throughout the history of philosophy. Compare it, for instance, with Heidegger's account of *das Man* in *Being and Time*, who control individuals through fear in order to preserve themselves. *Being and Time*, trans. John Macquarrie and Edward Robinson (Oxford: Blackwell Publishing, 2010), 298. This concept can also be traced back to Plato, who advocates the 'noble lie' regarding the origin of social classes in order to ensure social harmony. See *Republic* Book 3 414e-15c.

[12] *Republic*, trans. Robin Waterfield (Oxford: Oxford University Press, 2001).

[13] Ironically, this was written prior to the French Revolution, which many German intellectuals took to be the pinnacle of the Enlightenment. Furthermore, as Harold Mah argues, many Germans desired, 'to incorporate Germany's new cultural identity into a general discourse of modernity as defined by the French Revolution.' (1990: 4) Although Kant later came to celebrate the French Revolution as an achievement in enlightenment, his perspective here can be understood as a result of his belief that one has a duty to uphold civil laws, which revolution directly violates. See Hannah Arendt, *Lectures on Kant's Political Philosophy* (Chicago: University of Chicago Press, 1989).

It has been illustrated that Kant's understanding of the Enlightenment was the personal and political acquisition of maturity. However, maturity is not only an end in itself but also a means to an end. By taking personal responsibility he believed that society would progress towards an end goal. The *telos* towards which he envisioned the Enlightenment to be orientated was one of increased freedom or autonomy. As Pippen makes explicit, 'the modern question of independence became itself a philosophical issue in Kant, the reflective attempt by reason to determine the rules of its own activity, to set for itself its ends, to determine its own limits' (1991: 118). This, it was believed, was the end which was inherent in human civilization itself. Kant, however, did not believe that he lived in 'an *enlightened age*, but an *age of enlightenment*', within which this process of maturity was simply underway (2009: 2). In order to hasten an enlightened state, his essay not only offered an explanation but also proposed what he believed to be the means to maturity. According to Kant, the necessary condition for the Enlightenment of the masses is freedom to make use of one's reason, which he believed would enable both the individual and society to cultivate increased freedom.

Although Kant proposes maturity as a means to autonomy, Georg Wilhelm Friedrich Hegel takes this one step further, claiming that autonomy is the rational end of human civilization. In his *Philosophy of History*, Hegel presents an account of the historical development of human consciousness as a highly complex, yet rational process.[14] In his thought, the attainment of freedom in the modern world is the end goal of history, though more importantly for Hegel, this is a result of the temporal unfurling of what he refers to as 'absolute Spirit'. He explains this concept in relation to matter, which is logically that which it is furthest removed from. He states that 'just as gravity is the substance of matter, so also can it be said that freedom is the substance of Spirit' (2001: 31). However, since Spirit in itself is universal and abstract it cannot emerge in existence through its own efforts. The emergence of existence's actualization rather depends upon man's will. Although 'World Spirit' seems to suggest an otherworldly being, Stephen Houlgate claims it 'is not some cosmic consciousness beyond our own that uses us for its own ends; it is simply humanity itself coming to a clean understanding of its own freedom and transforming the social and political world in the process' (2008: 28).

---

[14] Hegel's lectures on the philosophy of history were presented at the University of Berlin between 1821 and 1831, the notes from which (including those of his students) were first published by Eduard Gans six years after Hegel's death in 1837. See Charles Hegel's Preface in *Philosophy of History*, trans. J. Sibree (Ontario: Batoche Books, 2001).

In the *Philosophy of History*, the dialectical development of freedom is explained alongside corresponding historical epochs.[15] Each of these contains a certain level of freedom, which is brought forth through the actions of a specific group of people. Hegel names these vehicles of Spirit 'world historical individuals'. And although these heroes of history strive towards their own ends, Hegel claims that they unconsciously do so on Spirit's behalf. As pawn pieces upon Spirit's chessboard, they are subjected to what Hegel calls 'the cunning of reason' (2001: 105). It is thus as a result of the individual's implementation of new political and social institutions that Spirit becomes actualized and human freedom increases. In other words, 'the more people develop spiritually, the more they become conscious of themselves; and the more they become conscious, the more they become free' (Luther 2009: 70). In his account, Hegel divides history into three specific stages, the childhood of the Oriental world, the adolescence of the classical and medieval eras, and the maturity of the modern age.

In the Oriental world, consciousness was unreflective insofar as individuals were unaware of themselves as autonomous. Only one person possessed subjective freedom, the ruler, before whom everybody else was equal in servitude. This early stage is the childhood of history in two senses: chronologically, it is the infancy of history in the modern conception; and figuratively, because the ruler fulfils a paternal role in relation to his subjects, 'who like children [. . .] can gain for themselves no independent and civil freedom' (2001: 123). Thus, ordinary subjects in the Oriental world possess neither political freedom nor rational thought. In Hegel's account, China and India are considered to be 'stationary', standing outside of history, and it is in Persia where world history first begins. In China and India, the rulers were considered to be deities, and as such, the subjects were obedient to their divine laws. In Persia, however, the laws were based on the teachings of Zoroaster, which meant that both the ruler and his citizens were subjected to the same rules and principles. This then provided the potential for freedom, but since consciousness only existed in one individual this could not be realized. Thus, because political liberty, moral freedom and consciousness were absent, society could not progress.

After the fall of the Persian Empire, historical Spirit passed from the vanquished into the consciousness of the victorious Greeks, who had defeated

---

[15] In each of Hegel's systems, be it the philosophy of *Phenomenology*, *Logic*, or *Right*, dialectic is the means by which everything proceeds. Although the dialectic is often referred to as Hegel's 'method', I side with Stephen Houlgate in the claim that it is not a method per se, since it is not something which Hegel himself employs, but rather a pattern which he observes as emerging immanently from considering pure indeterminate Being. See Houlgate's *Opening Hegel's Logic*, Ch. 2.

the Persians at the battle of Marathon. Here we find the first emergence of freedom, according to Hegel, which was dispersed through the medium of the democratic *polis*.[16] However, although the Greeks enjoyed individual freedom, it was only the citizens of the *polis* who were reflected in public life, whilst foreign residents and slaves were excluded. Thus, in the Oriental world only one was free, but with the actualization of consciousness in Greece, some then became free. Subjective freedom thus appears for the first time in ancient Greece, but it remains unreflective insofar as the Greeks are unable to conceive of themselves apart from their *polis*. It is here that Hegel suggests the first actor on the world stage makes his appearance. Disrupting the harmony of the Greek *polis*, Socrates introduced reflection, and critical thought, turning attention away from the *polis* and towards universal truth.

The World Spirit then passed to Rome where, like Persia, the people are still subordinated to the sovereign will of the emperor. However, Hegel maintains that individual freedom is recognized and exists as a fundamental notion within the Roman political constitution. Thus, as the actualization of Spirit, the Greek concept of individuality lives on. It is here, for Hegel, that the first conception of the 'person' emerges, defined as the subject of rights. With the rights to property, for example, freedom becomes legal. Despite this, the individual freedom to form one's own identity and ideas is suppressed by the Roman state. Due to this tension between the ideal of individuality and the absolute power of the government, citizens are only able to discover freedom through philosophical contemplation. Hegel makes reference to the philosophical systems of the Stoics, Epicureans and Sceptics,[17] which despite their metaphysical diversity all have 'the same general purport, viz., rendering the soul absolutely indifferent to everything which the real world had to offer' (2001: 318). This desire to retreat into oneself, to escape from reality, is a necessary consequence of the dominating external power of the state. What these contemplative philosophies achieve is freedom of thought; however, for Hegel this is a negative approach because thought made itself its own object and did not enable Spirit to advance.

In the medieval world, Hegel argues that Christianity provides the solution to this problem, of turning inwards to achieve freedom, offering a medium

---

[16] A *polis* is a small independent city-state, of which Hellenic (fifth century BC) Greece was constituted and to which its inhabitants pledged loyalty and claimed citizenship.
[17] The inadequacies of these philosophical approaches are illustrated in *Phenomenology of Spirit*, wherein Hegel refers to them, in his discussion of the freedom of consciousness, as stages of the unhappy conscience. See Sections 197–207.

between the individual and the state. In his view, 'since the emergence of Christianity, history has been a continuous unfolding of the principle of subjective freedom in the state' (2001: 319). Individuals are trapped in the natural, material world, until they recognize themselves as spiritual beings which Christians understand to be their true nature. In Hegel's account, the individual and the state first come to be reconciled through the world historical individual, Jesus. This is implemented by the community of his followers who came together to form the church. However, Spirit is unable to progress until the religious freedom of self-consciousness, as mediated through the church, becomes one with society. This, however, cannot be actualized in the Western Roman Empire, and passes into the Byzantine Empire, within which the church becomes a political power. This is a bipartite process, and is achieved 'first [through] the settlement of doctrine; and secondly [by] the appointment to ecclesiastical offices' (2001: 339). However, here Christianity becomes stagnant and remains so until the Byzantine Empire collapses, and the doctrine of Christ is adopted by the Germanic people.[18]

World Spirit reached maturity in the modern era beginning with the Protestant Reformation, which Hegel considers to be the first key event since the Roman age. Here the Germanic Spirit becomes the Spirit of the new world, as the bearer of the Christian principle. In the preceding period the Catholic Church had become internally corrupted, no longer treating God as a spiritual being, but as something material. This corruption was exemplified in the 'remission of sins' which Catholic priests had begun to offer in exchange for money.[19] This was instrumental in causing Martin Luther to protest against the church, who by doing so recovered the spirituality of Christianity, according to Hegel. Moreover, the removal of the priest as a medium between the individual and God allowed the World Spirit to progress, to obtain consciousness of its own freedom, and create the modern conception of selfhood. As a result of this, obedience to the laws of the state became the principle of human conduct. This in turn led to the rationalization of the state. And since man's consciousness had become rational, for Hegel, it was also necessary that institutions also become rational in order for individuals to freely accept and support them (2001: 441).

---

[18] Timothy C. Luther, in *Hegel's Critique of Modernity*, suggests that Hegel, 'uses [the term] Germanic people very broadly, encompassing all the Christian nations of Europe' (2009): 87.

[19] 'The *remission of sins* – the highest satisfaction which the soul craves the certainty of its peace with God, that which concerns man's deepest and inmost nature – is offered to man in the most grossly superficial and trivial fashion – *to be purchased for mere money*.' *Philosophy of History* (2001): 414.

This principle of rationality was carried forth into the Enlightenment, where the empirical method created a new conception of man and nature. Through the advance of scientific reason the world came to be known as conforming to rational and law-governed principles. Initially, it was believed that God had created the world upon principles of reason, and as such, discovering rational explanations was an attempt to become closer to Him. However, as a consequence of the search for universal principles, the natural world became devoid of divine mystery, and the sole pursuit of human enquiry was reduced to scientific reasoning. This distance which was created from religion then in turn created the free will, which is 'that by which Man becomes Man, and is therefore the fundamental principle of Spirit' (2001: 443). However, although people became fully aware of themselves as individuals, they lost sight of the community. Merely concerned with individual liberation, people began to perceive of the world as nothing other than objects to be understood, rather than as the manifestation of reason. Thus, although free will emerged, it merely appeared as an isolated individual will (2001: 443).

The next major event in Hegel's account was the French Revolution, which occurred as a result of the *philosophes* criticizing French social institutions. More specifically, they targeted the dominant class and their insatiable greed which was fuelled by government funding and public taxation. The significance of the revolution for Hegel was the emergence of 'the recognition of the principle that Thought ought to govern spiritual reality' (2001: 447). However, the revolution failed to empirically establish the subjective will of the many as that of the general will. The Revolutionary Terror then followed, in Hegel's account, because abstract philosophical principles were put into practice without any regard for the people. The role of reason was misunderstood and applied in isolation from the community and its citizens. For Hegel, this problem of reconciling the community and the individual was one which he believed his contemporary time to be tasked with. He then concludes his history by reiterating that the path of history is none other than the unfolding of the concept of freedom, the prerequisites of which are self-governing according to conscience, and the rational order of social and political institutions.

What Hegel presents in his *Philosophy of History* is a historical narrative of subjective and objective freedom, emerging and unfettering themselves from the various bonds which ensnare and inhibit them. It expresses not only their emergence but also their development and intertwining through the course of history, the goal of which was to establish themselves in the unified state of what Hegel refers to as absolute freedom. Hegel thus follows from Kant insofar as he conceives of the world as becoming increasingly rational, with the end goal as human freedom.[20] As previously discussed, for Kant the modern world was an age of Enlightenment, which had not yet reached its final stage of maturity. Hegel, however, takes the analogy of maturity one step farther, suggesting that the entire human history of the world has been a process of maturity towards the present. However, freedom is not a choice for Hegel, despite the individual's effort, but a predetermined path, which world historical individuals advance on behalf of the World Spirit.

Thus, what we can conclude from our exchange with Kant and Hegel is that the key philosophical concepts which came to define the Enlightenment were maturity and autonomy. It is particularly the latter concept, autonomy, which came to encapsulate the moral–ethical attitude of advocates of Enlightenment. What this entails, according to Pippen, is 'the possibility that human beings can regulate and evaluate their beliefs by rational self-reflection, that they can free themselves from interest, passion, tradition, prejudice and autonomously "rule" their own thoughts, and that they can determine their actions as a result of self-reflection and rational evaluation, an evaluation the conclusions of which ought to bind any rational agent' (1991: 13). Having determined that it was ultimately autonomy as an end, which is definitive of modernity, we will now turn our attention to the negative consequences, as outlined in the counter-discourse. Here we will illustrate that the unforeseen consequences of the project of modernity were that it restricted the freedom it promised and resulted in the loss of personal meaning.

1.3 Counter-Enlightenment: Nihilism and disenchantment

In Nietzsche's account, the yearning for maturity and freedom which underpinned Enlightenment philosophy was frustrated by the course of modernity. Whilst his contemporaries hailed their era as one of immense progress, Nietzsche rhetorically questions, 'is the nineteenth century, especially in the closing decades, not merely a strengthened, *brutalised* eighteenth century, that is to say a century of *decadence*?' (1971: 103). Moreover, aside from rejecting that

---

[20] Hegel and Kant's concepts of freedom vary. In the *Philosophy of Right* Hegel provides a thorough analysis of existing concepts of freedom and outlines his own belief. For an in-depth analysis of the variance between Kant and Hegel's notions of freedom, see Timothy C. Luther's *Hegel's Critique of Modernity*, Ch. 4; Alan Patten's *Hegel's Idea of Freedom*, Ch. 3; and J. P Stern's *Understanding Moral Obligation: Kant, Hegel, Kierkegaard*.

the Enlightenment had achieved that towards which it had focused its effort, Nietzsche rejected the concept of progress itself.[21] In his perspective, rather, '"mankind" does not advance, it does not even exist. The overall aspect is that of a tremendous experimental laboratory in which a few successes are scored, scattered throughout all ages, while there are untold failures, and all order, logic, union, and obligingness are lacking' (1968: §90). Thus, whilst his contemporaries were preoccupied with determining the rational end towards which human civilization was naturally inclined, Nietzsche saw their acts as none other than exercises in futility. Although cultural criticism is a theme which pervades his entire *oeuvre*, his critique of modernity is perhaps best expressed with a famous parable from *The Gay Science*.

The passage begins with the tale of a madman who, during daylight, runs to the marketplace with a lit lantern and incessantly announces his search for God. However, as those around him lack faith in God's existence they ridicule his search and sarcastically mock him. In reaction to this, the madman meets their condescending gibes with the disdainful exclamation not only that is God dead but also that we have killed Him. He then launches into a seemingly absurd stream of consciousness, quizzing their motives for unchaining the earth from the sun and demanding to know our destination.[22] Here he is making an obvious allusion to the Baconian Project and scientific desire to know all of nature completely. After this abrupt outburst, the madman ends his spiel by shattering his lantern on the ground, symbolically suggesting that we remain in the dark. Having regained composure he expresses the prematurity of his announcement and warns them that they are not yet aware of the consequences of their act: 'I come too early', he then said,

> my time is not yet. This tremendous event is still on its way, wandering; it has not yet reached the ears of men. Lightning and thunder need time; the light of the stars needs time; deeds need time, even after they are done, in order to be seen and heard. This deed is still more remote to them than the remotest stars – and yet they have done it themselves! (1991: §125)

Although many commentators have focused on the proclamation of God's death, it is not this which ought to be the primary feature and focus of the parable.

---

[21] In his middle period Nietzsche actually advocated Enlightenment as a remedy to romanticism; however, this greatly changed in his later thought. For a thorough account of the development of Nietzsche's attitude towards the Enlightenment, see Graeme Garrard, 'Nietzsche for and Against the Enlightenment', *The Review of Politics*, 70, no. 4 (Fall 2008): 595–608.

[22] This is clearly in reference to the Copernican Revolution, which saw the shift from a geo-centric model of the universe to a helio-centric one.

This is evident when one considers the madman's confrontation with those who do not believe in God. If his intention was to simply advocate atheism, then surely, he would address theists rather than atheists, to whom God's existence had not lost all validity. As such, the madman's claim, that God is dead, is clearly intended to be understood as a cultural reflection rather than a crusade against Christianity. The secularization of society is therefore something which Nietzsche here recognizes rather than advocates. As Albert Camus eloquently puts it, 'Nietzsche did not form a project to kill God, he found Him dead in the soul of his contemporaries' (2004: 37). The most important aspect of the parable, rather, is that which the madman seeks to convey to the crowd – namely, the unforeseen consequence of their rejection of religion.

In an attempt to illustrate the logical implications of the death of God, Nietzsche asserts 'now that this faith has been undermined, how much must collapse because it was built on this faith, leaned on it, had grown into it – for example, our entire European morality' (1991: §343). His claim, precisely, is because Western ethics is grounded upon Christian precepts, the rejection of religion necessarily entails the loss of morality. This critique also includes Kant's attempt to construct an autonomous ethical ideal based upon freedom and maturity. In targeting those whose scientific convictions rendered their acceptance of religion as untenable, yet who continued to live according to Christian laws, Nietzsche can thus be seen to undermine Kant and his fellow advocates of Enlightenment.

This is further evident in *Twilight of the Idols*, where Nietzsche elucidates by explaining 'when one gives up Christian belief one thereby deprives oneself of the *right* to Christian morality. [. . .] Christianity is a system, a consistently thought out and *complete* view of things. If one breaks out of it a fundamental idea, the belief in God, one thereby breaks the whole thing to pieces' (1971: 69). The madman's intention is thus to illustrate that those who believe it possible to be moral without being religious either are self-deceived or have failed to systematically evaluate their own values. More importantly, that behind this façade, European culture lacks a sound moral foundation. The implication of this for the Enlightenment is that any attempt to construct a modern moral theory is destined to fail.

In Nietzsche's prognosis, the ultimate consequence of the cultural death of God was the advent of nihilism. This refers to the belief that human life is fundamentally meaningless. Upon accepting that European morality is without foundation, one comes to the realization that existence is absurd, and that there is no purpose to life. Thus, the liberation promised by the Enlightenment delivered all too well on its promise for Nietzsche. That is, although it achieved the freedom it sought, this freedom undermined the ability to live ethically. His thoughts on nihilism are assembled in *The Will to Power*, which is a compendium of notes initially intended to form a monograph, but hastily assembled with little academic merit by his sister.[23] Here Nietzsche notes that one of the key advantages of Christian morality was that 'it granted man an absolute value, as opposed to his smallness and accidental occurrence in the flux of becoming and passing away' (1968: 9). Thus, in providing human existence with a natural teleology, Christian ethics also granted meaning to human existence. However, to depart from God's moral law is to forgo natural teleology and, subsequently, a meaningful life. Thus, in rejecting Christianity, the ultimate consequence of the atheism of those in the marketplace was the onset of European nihilism.

In order to determine who this charge is aimed towards, it is necessary to question who the atheists in the marketplace are supposed to represent. In *Thus Spoke Zarathustra*, Nietzsche discusses a group of individuals whom he refers to as the 'last men'. They are given this title due to their belief that humanity had reached its end. However, drawing attention to the loss of natural teleology, Zarathustra attempts to inform them that 'man is something that shall be overcome', and that 'what is great in man is that he is a bridge and not an end' (1996b: 12–15). Here Nietzsche is referring to the thinkers of the Enlightenment who advocated that humanity had an end goal and that this had been achieved. This is further elucidated in *The Genealogy of Morals* where Nietzsche emphasizes 'our faith in science is still based on a metaphysical faith – even as we knowers of today, we godless anti-metaphysicians, still take our fire from the blaze set alight thousands of years ago, that faith of the Christians, which was also Plato's faith, that God is truth, that truth is divine' (2008: 112). However, as evident in Nietzsche's critique of modernity, the freedom that the Enlightenment so deeply desired, and achieved through the rejection of religion, has had profound implications on modern society.

The same critique can be held against the atheists of the marketplace who reject religion, believing they had acquired greater freedom. In both cases that with which Nietzsche is engaging is the negative consequence of freedom – namely, freedom from all values and the descent into nihilism. The claim that the thinkers of the Enlightenment caused the problem of meaninglessness is further suggested with his claim that 'the faith in the categories of reason is the cause of

---

[23] Although *The Will to Power* cannot be taken seriously in presenting any coherent overall argument, this does not detract from that which the aphorisms and passages themselves infer.

nihilism. We have measured the value of the world according to categories *that refer to a purely fictitious world*' (1968: 13). Here he can be seen to be blaming the thinkers of the Enlightenment for the onset of nihilism, who believed reverently in the fiction of progress and advocated that the end goal towards which human civilization is orientated was one of autonomy. However, in their pursuit of freedom they rejected religion, which had provided the pillars of ethics and purpose. In Nietzsche's critique of modernity, the problem of nihilism is therefore a consequence of the freedom pursued by the Enlightenment, which increased freedom at the expense of human meaning.

A further consequence of the dogmatic pursuit of autonomy as a rational end is explicated in the thought of Max Weber. Whilst Weber's account of modernity contains a degree of pessimism, to categorize it as such would be to misrepresent his perspective. His perspective of modernity, rather, is more accurately defined as one of deep ambivalence.[24] Although he is usually placed on the negative scale of the dichotomy between cultural pessimism and optimism, it does a severe injustice to his thought to apply such a simplistic label. Whilst Weber's writings do indeed display a degree of disdain for certain modern practices, he also acknowledges that modernity offers various redeeming features which previous eras could not. He notes, for example, the modern development of rationalization – which will be discussed in greater detail later – is capable of providing increased autonomy to the individual. Thus, whilst there is a loss of unity, there is also an increase of personal freedom, though only for a lucky few. Weber's multifaceted understanding of modernity is encapsulated in his concepts of 'rationalization' and 'disenchantment' and as such, it is to these concepts which we will now turn.

In *The Protestant Ethic and the Spirit of Capitalism*, Weber focuses on three forms of rationality.[25] The first of these, *substantive* rationality, refers to goal-orientated rational action in the context of ultimate ends. The second, *theoretical* rationality, refers to mastery of reality through abstract concepts. The third, *formal* rationality, relates to the domination of life spheres through rational organization of life according to uniform rules and principles, such as economics, law and science. It is the latter of these, however, which is the most important for Weber and upon which he fixes his gaze. Within his enquiry, he notes that formal rationality has come to dominate Occidental culture and sets his sights

---

[24] For an in-depth discussion of the debate, see Steven Seidman's 'Modernity, Meaning, and Cultural Pessimism in Max Weber', *Sociological Analysis* 44, no. 4 (1983): 267–78.
[25] See Stephen Kalberg, 'Max Weber's Types of Rationality: Cornerstones for the Analysis of Rationalisation Processes in History', *American Journal of Sociology* 85, no.5 (1980): 145–79.

on determining the reason for this. This process of 'rationalization', however, despite its promise, resulted in the subsequent denial of freedom.

In order to determine why, Weber analysed the Protestant work ethic, the remnants of which he claimed still dominated everyday life. In his analysis, Weber revealed that the ascetic attitude of the Puritans, that 'every hour lost is lost to labour for the glory of God', caused them to naturally amass substantial sums of capital (2005: 104). The psychological attitude which perpetuated this perspective was the fear of damnation. Although Lutherans and Calvinists believed that they were predestined to go to heaven or hell, they continued to labour reverently, as a sort of psychological shield. That is, since salvation came through God's grace, their labour in the service of God had no bearing upon their fate. This belief in pre-destination also espoused *contemptus mundi*, or contempt for the world, because it was believed that the Puritan's true calling was spiritual. However, despite the decline of Christianity, the spirit of Protestantism came to define modern capitalism and the modern social order, leading individuals to labour with the same intensity and fervour, but with the sole end of capital acquisition. In Weber's own words, 'the search for the Kingdom of God commenced gradually to pass over into sober economic virtue; the religious roots died out slowly, giving way to utilitarian worldliness' (2005: 119).

That is, the ascetic accumulated material wealth as a consequence of proving one's devotion to God, but when the religious role receded, the accumulation of wealth became an end in itself. As Weber beautifully puts it, 'the care for external goods should only lie on the shoulders of the "saint like a light cloak, which can be thrown aside at any moment". But fate decreed that the cloak should become an iron cage' (2005: 123). Through this notion of an 'iron cage', Weber metaphorically encapsulates the consequence of increased rationality upon modern society.[26] Namely, the outcome of a social order bound to technical and economic conditions of machine production, which has led to 'mechanized petrification' and determines the lives of individuals within it, leading to a growth in senseless bureaucracy and consumerist hedonism. Weber quotes Goethe in relation to the latter two effects upon individuals, whom he understands as 'specialists without spirit, sensualists without heart' (1991: 124).

---

[26] The standard translation of *Stahlhartes Gehäuse* as 'iron cage' by Talcott Parsons is that which English-speaking scholars have come to accept; however, a literal translation would be 'shell as hard as steel'. See Peter Baehr, 'The "Iron Cage" and the "Shell as Hard as Steel": Parsons, Weber, and the Stahlhartes Gehäuse Metaphor in the Protestant Ethic and the Spirit of Capitalism', *History and Theory* 40, no. 2 (May 2001): 153–69

Thus, unlike Puritans, who wanted to work in a calling, we are forced to work in a calling which is limited to specialized work. It is for these reasons that the primary assertion of *The Protestant Ethic and the Spirit of Capitalism* is that this Protestant work ethic became the essential feature of the modern economic structure.

Although Weber offers a genealogy of the rise of the modern economic and social order, what is important for our inquiry is his description of the rational process which Occidental society underwent. What Weber revealed was that the Puritan belief that everyone has a calling, and that one must labour in order to earn God's grace, espoused a form of rationality absent in previous Christian denominations. This widespread practice and hostility towards more mystical-based belief then opened the flood gate to increased rationality in religion. Ironically, whilst religion supported rationalization, it was this very ideal that would lead to religion's eventual demise. As religion is inherently irrational in character, from a scientific perspective, the demand for increased formal rationality began to corrode its very core. What then ensued was an iron cage of capitalism and bureaucracy – namely, 'when asceticism was carried out of monastic cells into everyday life, and began to dominate worldly morality, it did its part in building the tremendous cosmos of the modern economic order' (1991: 124).

Although Weber notes that rationalization created the modern socio-economic conditions, what is more important is the consequence this process has had upon Occidental culture. In his short essay 'Science as Vocation', Weber addresses this issue much more fully. As science adhered to strict rational laws and principles it denounced that which did not conform to the scientific standards of empirical verifiability. This resulted in what Weber termed 'the fate of our times [. . .] the disenchantment of the world' (1991: 155). In an attempt to lay bare the fundamental facts of the universe, science accepted as true only that which could be proven by repeatable experiments. The result was that myths and cultural practices which did not possess scientific standards were either dismissed or replaced with reason and logic. By 'disenchantment', Weber means the unveiling and rejection of cultural practices which were often explained in terms of 'magic' and had remained shrouded in mystery. As Christianity was unable to conform to the level of rationality which it advocated, it was ironically unravelled by that which it had helped create. One consequence of the rational rejection of religion was the loss of a unifying ethic. Without this unity, human life became compartmentalized, with individuals fulfilling competing roles, leading to internal conflict due to an unstructured plurality of values. This is explained by Weber in terms of the growth of moral–ethical 'polytheism', which he likens to ancient Greece, within which one could choose from many causes and gods to follow.[27]

A further consequence of the loss of a unifying purpose for Weber was that it rendered human existence meaningless, a side effect which is also noted by Nietzsche. Weber gives the example of Abraham, who having obtained a sense of achievement through his actions could die happily. As Weber explains,

> Abraham, or some peasant of the past, died 'old and satiated with life' because he stood in the organic cycle of life; because his life, in terms of its meaning and on the eve of his days, had given to him what life had to offer; because for him there remained no puzzles he might wish to solve; and therefore he could have had 'enough' of life. (1991: 140)

However, in a rationalized society that advocates a process of perpetual progress, one's contribution can never truly be meaningful since all acts are means to an end rather than ends in themselves. That is:

> Whereas civilized man, placed in the midst of the continuous enrichment of culture by ideas, knowledge, and problems, may become 'tired of life' but not 'satiated with life.' He catches only the most minute part of what the life of the spirit brings forth ever anew, and what he seizes is always something provisional and not definitive, and therefore death for him is a meaningless occurrence. And because death is meaningless, civilized life as such is meaningless; by its very 'progressiveness' it gives death the imprint of meaninglessness. (1991: 140)

In science, for example, what one contributes is destined to be surpassed and made obsolete. In response to this, Weber questions, 'why should one do something which in reality never comes to an end?' (1991: 138). Thus, the consequence of disenchantment is a culture with no objective means to ground one's convictions, which in turn had led to the loss of meaning for human life. As Keith Breen quite rightly notes, 'Weber is concerned not just with the loss of freedom in modernity, but also with the meaninglessness of a rationalised world, its having become thoroughly disenchanted' (2012: 13).

Like nihilism, disenchantment refers to the loss of meaning within European society. However, how these two concepts are demarcated is not immediately

---

[27] In ancient Greece almost every other day was a religious festival, dedicated to one particular deity. However, rather than participating in all of these festivities, one chooses whichever God's one felt best represented oneself. See Michael H. Crawford and David Whitehead, *Archaic and Classical Greece: A Selection of Ancient Sources in Translation* (Cambridge: Cambridge University Press, 2010).

apparent. Thus, it is important to determine whether there is any substantial difference between these, or if they are simply two articulations of the same problem. The first thing to note is that both are the result of rationalization. For Nietzsche, the Enlightenment project led to the cultural death of God, which in turn undermined European morality and deprived modern life of meaning. Thus, for Nietzsche, nihilism is the logical consequence of the secularization of society. In Weber's account, the application of rationality to culture not only undermined its Christian foundation but also led to the subsequent rejection of practices which did not conform to the empirical method. It was this sequence of events which Weber sought to categorize with the concept of disenchantment. Thus, rather than representing the same phenomenon, they allude to two separate events. Disenchantment refers to the event which Occidental culture has undergone, whilst nihilism is the consequence of that process. Nietzsche and Weber therefore offer two independent, but compatible, accounts of the consequences of rationality, which the Enlightenment advocated. Furthermore, for both thinkers, the negative consequences of the Enlightenment were a result of its misguided belief in progress towards the realization of real freedom.

Having determined the problems of modernity which have been induced by the pursuit of autonomy, we may now address the opening question: what problems does modernity pose with regards to freedom and meaning? What has thus far been determined from Weber's account is that there are two main problems. First, the loss of meaning which is compounded by compartmentalization, or the growth of moral–ethical 'polytheism'. Secondly, the promise and failure of formal rationalization to deliver individual freedom. Like Nietzsche, Weber believed that rationalism had caused the modern world to become objectively meaningless and dedicated his academic career to determining the reason for this. However, whilst Nietzsche traced the trajectory of the cultural death of God, Weber offered a genealogical explanation of the rationalization of religion itself.[28] Both thinkers were also concerned with the consequences of the emergence of individual freedom. Whilst Nietzsche conceived of this as a vast open sea, Weber argued that although this is what rationality suggests in theory, what it offers in practice is an 'iron cage', within which one is confined to limited freedom, but freedom nevertheless.

---

[28] For an account of Weber's method as genealogical, see chapters 5 and 6 of David Owen's *Maturity and Modernity: Nietzsche, Weber, Foucault and the Ambivalence of Reason*.

1.4 Embracing one's fate

The cover of this book is adorned with Friedrich Casper David's *Wanderer above the Sea of Fog*.[29] Perched upon an outward standing crag, the wanderer seems to have reached the end of his journey. It appears as though he has gone as far as he can go, unable to proceed despite having travelled such a long distance. His hair is windswept by the howling gusts at the peak, sending forth a chill from the summit. Clouds convey the great heights which he has ascended and those which he must descend in order to carry on. An uncertain path lies before him. The closest visible landmarks are further outstanding crags, offering no more vantage than his current location. There is no apparent end point, only a long and arduous journey. The multitude of peaks fades into the horizon, and if there is a final destination, it is far beyond, obscured from sight. Such an image portrays human insignificance and conjures forlorn hope and an air of abandonment. Nevertheless, the wanderer's head is not lowered in defeat, but held high, facing forward. His posture – signified by his elevated leg and hand on hip – suggests determination and resolve. His walking stick symbolizes stability. The outcrop of trees is indicative of life and implies hope. One must imagine the wanderer's gaze fixated on the vistas in his periphery and the determination to push forth regardless of the tumultuous task which awaits him.

Painted during the peak of romanticism in 1818, David's wanderer symbolizes the key romantic tenants: individuality, turning one's back on the scientific advances of the Enlightenment and the desire to return to nature. However, despite epitomizing the romantic ideal, this image also encapsulates the spirit of this book. The problem of freedom and meaning which will be addressed is symbolized by the wanderer himself and by the vast empty space which confronts him. That is, there is neither an established path, leading to a set destination, nor an end in sight. The wanderer is a solitary individual who must determine, chart and navigate his own course. Within a post-teleological context, where there is no natural teleology or objective moral values, we must decide for ourselves and bear responsibility for our choices. Our attitude towards the problem is also characterized by the wanderer's posture; despite the colossal task that confronts us, we nevertheless possess the resolve to venture forth into unknown intellectual terrain. Thus, David's wanderer has been chosen for the reason that

---

[29] The German title of the painting 'Der Wanderer über dem Nebelmeer' wanderer can also be translated as hiker.

he accurately conveys the leitmotifs of freedom and meaning, and the attitude towards them which will be endorsed herein.

The particular position which will be upheld is one which accepts the socio-historical conditions of modernity. That is, we will adhere to a realistic approach, of coming to terms with our existential condition and attempt to overcome it from within modernity itself. Our attitude is thus in contrast to the attempt to continue the project of modernity, to reject it completely and engage in postmodern discourse, or attempt to reinstate a premodern framework with which to undermine the problem. We will, however, explore these alterative attitudes in Part II of our investigation. Our particular approach is upheld by the likes of Nietzsche, Weber and the existentialists. Habermas sees Nietzsche as rejecting the Enlightenment project completely, and according to whom, '[Nietzsche] renounces a renewed revision of the concept of reason and *bids farewell* to the dialect of enlightenment' (1987b: 86). However, on this line of argument we will side with Robert Pippen, who claims that 'Nietzsche is trying to hold the Enlightenment to its own standards, to share its own "self-contradiction"' (1991: 84).

The Nietzschean response to the problem of modernity is an acceptance of what he terms the 'horizon of the infinite'. That is, he does not deny the Enlightenment's achievements, but acknowledges the consequence that one may no longer lay claim to that which came before. Nietzsche frames the freedom which the Enlightenment achieved as a directionless voyage in which one cannot return to one's place of departure and in which there is no destination towards which one is orientated. As he exclaims, 'we have forsaken the land and gone to sea! We have destroyed the bridge behind us – more so, we have demolished the land behind us!' Even if it were possible to return, Nietzsche warns against over-idealized, romantic yearnings for a previous way of life, which are not what one may imagine them to be, as he continues, 'woe, when homesickness for the land overcomes you, as if there had been more freedom there – and there is no more "land"!'(1991: §124).

The Nietzschean perspective thus suggests a realistic coming to grips with humanity's existential condition. More than this, he asserts, 'I want to learn more and more how to see what is necessary in things as what is beautiful in them - thus I will be one of those who make things beautiful. *Amor fati*: let that be my love from now on!' (1991: §276). His position, therefore, is not only to accept one's fate, but to love it. Nietzsche's account is thus in contrast to that espoused by Habermas, who wants to continue the Enlightenment; Foucault, who sought to overcome it; and MacIntyre, who advocates returning to an ethical model which predated it. Nietzsche would associate each of these with the 'last men', whose response was one of self-deception, choosing to ignore the problem rather than embrace it. This is exemplified in a famous aphorism where he presents the Buddhist-esque concept of eternal recurrence.[30] Here the reader is asked to imagine that a demon has cursed one to eternally relive one's life and then asked whether one would be able to praise the demon as divine. It is the ability to say 'yes', to embrace the judgement upon one's life and accept it wholeheartedly which Nietzsche deems the best response. As he rhetorically asks, 'how well disposed would you have to become to yourself and to life to long for nothing more fervently than for this ultimate eternal confirmation and seal?' (1991: §341). The Nietzschean response is to create a new goal beyond ourselves, rather than to restore and preserve that which went before.

Although Max Weber was ambivalent in regarding that which the Enlightenment had achieved, like Nietzsche, his response to modernity is one of acceptance. Weber understood that the unity of existence which pre-modern social order provided was no longer attainable. However, rather than attempting to re-establish unity he recognized that modern life was now defined by plurality and embraced this. What is meant by 'plurality' is aptly explained by a quote from a lecture which he presented at the German Sociological Association: 'in comparison to men in other societies, modern man is a *vereinmensch* [formed by the many voluntary associations to which he belongs].'[31] Although bureaucratization has come to impinge upon all aspects of social life, Weber determines a way in which the individual could exercise influence. In a social order of restricted freedom, Weber believed that it was still possible to find meaning through vocational specialization. What he is here pointing towards is the meaning one can derive by subjectively surrendering oneself to a cause.[32]

A similar attitude was advocated by the existentialists, who in reacting to the problem as outlined by Nietzsche, and how they themselves experienced it, sought to provide a response to the modern individual's existential predicament. This is evident in Jean-Paul Sartre's famous maxim, 'existence precedes essence' (2007: 20). What this meant is that, accepting the logical consequences of the predominant secularization of European society, there is no essential thing which human beings

---

[30] For an examination of the comparison of Nietzsche's eternal recurrence and the Buddhist concept of *samsara*, see Guy Welborn, *The Buddhist Nirvana and Its Western Interpreters* (Chicago: University of Chicago Press, 1975): 187.

[31] Quoted in Steven Seidman, *Liberalism and the Origins of European Social Theory* (Berkeley: University of California Press, 1983): 267 from *Gesammelte Aufsatze zur Soziologie und Sozialpolitik* (Tubingen: Mohr, 1924): 442.

[32] 'Science as Vocation', in *From Max Weber: Essays in Sociology* (Oxford: Oxford University Press, 1991).

are. Moreover, if there is no God, no creator who designed us to fulfil a purpose, then it follows that there is no purpose to human existence. However, according to the existentialists, the loss of natural teleology does not necessitate that one's life cannot be imbued with subjective meaning. Within each of these three responses to modernity underlies a courageous and confrontational attitude to modernity, one willing to not only directly engage with the problem but also embrace one's fate, and it is this particular perspective which will underpin our approach.

1.5 Summary

Within this chapter, our intention was to determine what problems modernity posed with regards to freedom and meaning. We began with a brief synopsis of the intellectual developments which constitute modernity and narrowed our focus to the Enlightenment. We then turned our attention to the conceptualization of the aims of the Enlightenment, which we found inherent within Kantian thought. Here we determined the concept of maturity to be indicative of the project of modernity. Although Kant believed that the actualization of maturity would lead to increased freedom, Hegel took this line of argument one step further. His claim was that absolute autonomy was the implicit, rational end of human civilization. However, when we turned our attention to the counter-discourse of Nietzsche and Weber, we discovered that the modern disposition towards autonomy was decidedly more ambiguous and ironic than beneficial. Nietzsche recognized that the rejection of the pre-modern framework led to nihilism, and Weber discovered that rationalization resulted in unfreedom and disenchantment. We thus came to understand the modern predicament to consist in the restriction of freedom and the loss of meaning.

Although the primary focus of this chapter has been to elucidate the problems of modernity, we also expressed our particular approach to these predicaments. Our attitude towards the failure of the enlightenment project and subsequent restriction of freedom and loss of meaning was to embrace our fate. Understanding the problems in context, the responses elicited by the counter-Enlightenment, and positing our initial attitude then provides the necessary grounds for our discussion of authenticity in the following chapter. That is, by explaining the issues to be addressed, and the arguments, we have provided the general context for the concept of authenticity to have emerged and make sense. With our disposition made explicit, we will now turn to articulating our proposed approach.

2

Variations on the concept of authenticity

Having addressed the problem with which this book is to be concerned, that modernity has decreased freedom and led to a loss of meaning, the aim of this chapter will be to present the solution which will be espoused. The idea which we intend to espouse is 'authenticity'. As an idea, authenticity is superficially simple yet definitively elusive. Although 'authenticity' has been defined in terms of 'originality' and 'self-realization', and expressed through the imperative 'be true to oneself', what is actually inferred by these terms is obscure and often left unsaid. Fostered within an individualistic culture, it seems intuitive that one has one's own particular mode of being; however, one confronts difficulty in attempting to articulate exactly what it means to be authentic. One is confronted with various strands of thought, which take one on alternative tangents and far from the process of simply being oneself. The issues with which one must engage include whether there can be such a thing as a 'true self', whether one creates or discovers oneself and what precisely provides the means to be authentic. How then to best approach the task of explicating the concept of authenticity?

In order to achieve our aim, we will begin by setting forth a general overview of the concept of authenticity, which will permit us to further develop our own concept within the course of our enquiry (Section 2.1). Here we will explain authenticity as a distinctly modern concept and discuss the various aspects of this complex ideal. We will then proceed to further define authenticity in relation to alternative ethical ideals (Section 2.2). Authenticity will be compared and contrasted with the ethics of sincerity, integrity and autonomy. In the third section we will consider the social turn of authenticity (Section 2.3). What this entails is that modern advocates of authenticity have turned away from existentialism and towards social thought for inspiration. In order to understand why existential authenticity fell out of favour, we will turn to discuss the existentialist approach (Section 2.4). Here we will focus on Jean-Paul Sartre and attempt to elucidate the flaws in his account. In the fifth and final section we will then turn to an ethic of authenticity (Section 2.5). Focusing on Charles Taylor, it will be argued that rather than providing an alternative to the existential approach, Taylor can instead be understood to develop this tradition.

2.1 Articulating authenticity

In general terms, the phenomenon of authenticity implies individuality, originality and being true to oneself. However, as discussed in the introduction, the concept of authenticity initially appears relatively intuitive, but quickly descends into obscurity. There are various approaches, and multiple interpretations of the aspects of authenticity. We will discuss the intricacies in the following sections, expanding it in contrast to alternative ideals. Here, however, we will begin by discussing the fundamental features of authenticity. Within this section it will be claimed that on a basic level, the concept of authenticity emphasizes individuality, is understood in relation to inauthenticity, and is a distinctly modern concept.

The first aspect of authenticity which will be discussed is its emphasis on individuality. That is, to be authentic is to be truly oneself, to choose for oneself, as opposed to accepting what one has become unreflectively. Søren Kierkegaard epitomizes this particular feature in his notebooks, where he claims that the purpose of his enquiries is 'to find a truth which is true for me, to find the idea for which I can live and die' (2015: §A75). His reason for this individualistic approach is because he realized that many people who are born into specific cultural practices accept them unquestionably. This belief is inherent in his attitude towards the Christian church, within which he believed that many so-called practitioners had not themselves chosen to be Christian. In order to explain this, he employed a travel metaphor depicting two men who had arrived at the same location, however, whilst one had mounted a horse and consciously travelled there, the other had fallen asleep on the back of a hay cart and arrived through no will of his own (2009: 261). For Kierkegaard, one's faith had to be freely and consciously chosen. To freely choose it is necessary to reflect upon oneself, induce an element of doubt and embrace that which one determines to be self-evident. It is therefore the examined and self-chosen life which could be said to be authentic for Kierkegaard. This, however, raises the question, from where does one derive one's sense of individuality?

This leads us to a second feature that authenticity is a relative concept insofar as it is defined in relation to inauthenticity. To be inauthentic is to adhere to the herd and to derive one's beliefs, opinions and values from externally imposed norms. Authenticity, on the other hand, suggests the contrary of determining one's own values for oneself. One does not need to live according to social goals, of learning to drive by eighteen, of going to university, or pursuing a conventional career, working 9 to 5 within an office. This is made explicit by Martin Heidegger, who claims that our existence is inauthentic for the most part. In the mode of existence which he terms 'everydayness' one does not choose oneself, but rather one's values, beliefs and desires are determined by *das Man*, or 'the One'. Heidegger defines this mode of everydayness by stating, 'we take pleasure and enjoy ourselves as *das Man* take pleasure, we read, see, and judge about literature and art as *das Man* see and judge' (2010: §127). The particular mode of existence which is dominated by *das Man* thus suggests social conformity. Authenticity is thus characterized by its attitude towards uncritical acceptance. As Jacob Golomb succinctly puts it, 'one knows what one is only after realising what one is not' (1995: 201). Although there are approaches that are almost anarchistic to the extent that they call for a radical rejection of conformity to social norms, there are also subtler theorists who simply suggest that we do not accept values uncritically.[1] Nevertheless, authenticity is determined in relation to inauthentic existence which is not chosen by ourselves.

Can this concept also be retrospectively applied to the likes of Socrates who quite clearly meets the condition of having not acted in accordance with social convention? Not quite. The reason is because the concept of authenticity is a modern ideal and one which is inextricably linked to individuality. Although Socrates may have gone against the social norms, and that which was expected of him as an Athenian citizen, he nevertheless acted in terms of the social norms definitive of the *polis* and expected of all citizens. Thus, whilst he may have been charged with corrupting the youth, he believed that his philosophical midwifery, of helping those pregnant with possibility to conceive of truth, was beneficial for the *polis*, as he so boldly claims at his trial (2003). Even Diogenes's revolutionary claim to be cosmopolitan does not exempt him from the social recognition his fellow Greeks adhered to, for to understand oneself as a 'citizen of the world' is still to understand oneself as part of a larger social collective (1948: VI.II.§63). As Charles Guignon makes explicit, 'certainly Socrates and St. Augustine, among other pre-modern thinkers, had a vivid sense of the importance of self-knowledge and a commitment to being true to oneself in what one says and does.

---

[1] The spectrum of advocates ranges from Kierkegaard's radical rejection of society to socially conceived approaches like that of Charles Taylor.

But they lacked the experience of the self as a bounded centre of experience and action with no defining connections to anything distinct from itself' (2008: 279).

Rather, to be authentic requires that one understand oneself as an individual and determine one's values for oneself, rather than derive these from one's society. Insofar as it is premised upon the concept of individuality, authenticity is a distinctly modern theory. As noted in our historical survey of modernity, individuality as an idea emerged alongside the breakdown of traditional social hierarchies. Thus, pre-modern subjects cannot be characterized in terms of authenticity because prior to modernity this phenomenon did not exist conceptually. Having offered a preliminary account of authenticity – that it is an individual, relative and distinctly modern concept – it will now be compared with the alternative ethical ideals of sincerity, integrity and autonomy. The reason for doing so will be, firstly, to differentiate authenticity from other modern ideals to which it bears a resemblance, and, secondly, to further define authenticity in relation to these.

2.2 Alternative ethical ideals

The first ethical ideal with which authenticity will be contrasted is that of sincerity. In our everyday understanding, to be sincere is to express one's heartfelt convictions, or at the very least, to not attempt to deceive others with regard to one's true intentions. In *Sincerity and Authenticity*, Lionel Trilling demarcates the decline of sincerity as an ethical ideal and the emergence of authenticity as a more prevalent ideal. Trilling offers a genealogy of sincerity, though he determines that 'the word as we now use it refers primarily to a congruence between avowal and actual feeling' (1972 [2009]: 2). What this means is that sincerity carries connotations of frankness and expression of one's innermost beliefs. In his explication of sincerity, Trilling cites Polonius famous lines from Shakespeare's *Hamlet*: 'to thine own self be true / And it doth follow, as the night the day / Thou canst not then be false to any man' (1972 [2009]: 3). For Trilling these three lines epitomize what it is to be sincere – namely, the avoidance of being false to others by being true to oneself.

Although one must first discover one's true self, on a sociological level, one is then required to portray this to others, as opposed to presenting a false image of oneself. This concept is also intricately linked with one's social status, or role within society. That is, to be sincere is to understand one's place within society and to act in accordance with this. As Trilling claims, 'society requires of us that we present ourselves as being sincere, and the most efficacious way of satisfying this demand is to see to it that we really are sincere, that we actually are what we want our community to know we are' (1972 [2009]: 10–11). However, the breakdown of traditional structures has problematized this, since if there is no role with which to identify then there is nothing to act sincerely in accordance with.

Although the idea of being true to oneself seems congruous with authenticity, there are two distinct differences. First, sincerity requires that one be oneself for the benefit of others, whilst to be authentic is solely for one's own sake. Thus, as Trilling notes, '[sincerity] does not propose being true to oneself as an end, but only as a means' (1972 [2009]: 9). Secondly, from a negative standpoint, one is understood to be insincere if one does not act in accordance with one's social status, or the expectations of society. 'In short, we play the role of being ourselves, we sincerely act the part of the sincere person, with the result that a judgement may be passed upon our sincerity that it is not authentic' (1972 [2009]: 11). Under the criteria of authenticity, however, to present oneself as none other than one's social role would be to live an inauthentic existence.

A similar criticism is made by Jean-Paul Sartre who equates sincerity with bad faith, which, as we will see in Section 2.4., is equivocal to inauthenticity. As Sartre explains, 'the essential structure of sincerity does not differ from that of bad faith since the sincere man constitutes himself as what he is *in order not to be it*' (2013: 65). Thus, for Sartre, sincerity is ironically an attempt to avoid bad faith by being what one is. Namely, for Sartre, any attempt to portray one's true self can only end in failure because there is no essential self. However, as already established, authenticity rejects the idea of upholding externally imposed values. To equate oneself with one's social role is thus to be inauthentic, or as Sartre claims, to live in bad faith. Authenticity thus goes beyond sincerity in that it emphasizes that one should instead determine one's own values.

A second ethical ideal which bears a resemblance to the concept of authenticity is integrity. On a general understanding, to be a person of integrity is to possess certain commitments and to identify oneself with these. To maintain these commitments is then to remain true to oneself. According to Lynne McFall there are two forms of integrity: moral and personal (1987). The difference between these two approaches is that personal integrity is characterized by partiality and subjectivity, whereas moral integrity is impartial and universal. In order to distinguish these, McFall offers the example of a captain on a ship whose husband and two other passengers have fallen overboard and are drowning. Her thought experiment places one's husband starboard and the two other passengers portside – as such, one cannot save both parties. Personal integrity suggests, as a wife, to save one's husband; moral integrity, as the captain, expects one to save the two passengers. Moral integrity thus requires that one place external moral constraints before one's own personal convictions; in this sense it is easily distinguishable from authenticity, insofar as the authentic person would side with their own personal conviction. This idea is also exemplified by Thomas Kasulis, who explains that 'to preserve integrity, I should treat other people as autonomous agents having the privilege of being able to determine their own actions freely, including choosing the relationships into which they enter' (2002: 117).

The second approach, personal integrity, however, is not so easily distinguished. As McFall explains, 'personal integrity requires that an agent subscribe to some consistent set of principles or commitments and, in the face of temptation or challenge, uphold these principles or commitments for what the agent takes to be the right reasons' (1987: 9). This ethical idea is espoused by Bernard Williams, who claims that 'to act with integrity is to act in a way that accurately reflects your sense of who you are, to act from motives, interests, and commitments that are most deeply your own' (1981: 49). A lack of personal integrity is thus attributed to someone who, either through cowardice or ignorance, fails to maintain their commitments. A further facet of integrity is that the various parts of our personality are integrated into a unified whole. This idea is well portrayed by Harry Frankfurt who advocates the organization of our beliefs and desires into a hierarchy of importance (1971: 5–20).

There is real overlap between the ethic of authenticity and integrity, in terms of commitment, as will become evident in the succeeding chapter, and the desire for a unified self. However, the main difference between authenticity and personal integrity is that integrity is an attribute which one possesses, whereas authenticity is a state which one attains through rejection of externally imposed values which one does not consciously endorse. That is, by acting in accordance with the desires or volitions which other desires are subordinated to, and which one is committed to, one can be said to be a person of integrity. To be authentic, on the other hand, thus far construed, is to realize one's values for oneself, rather than simply acting out of desires which one may not have consciously chosen. Understood negatively, one who lacks integrity does so because they fail to uphold their commitments, whereas one is inauthentic when one is not conscious of oneself as an individual.

Autonomy, as we have already determined, was the ethical idea heralded and upheld by advocates of the Enlightenment. Kant, for example, developed the categorical imperative, that agents ought to 'act only in accordance with that maxim through which you can at the same time will that it becomes a universal law' (1993: 30). This is built upon the 'golden rule', that one ought to treat others how one wishes to be treated oneself, though it emphasizes that we have a moral duty not to negatively impinge upon the freedom of others. Autonomy does not derive ethical validity from external values upheld within society, but from an abstract principle of the agent's own rendering. The concept of autonomy is more problematic than sincerity and integrity in that it co-exists alongside authenticity and shares a number of similarities. First, both ideas are opposed to tradition-based notions of what constitutes 'right'. That is, both ideas reject that moral principles should be determined by social or cultural influences but instead grounded in the self-governing individual. Secondly, in both approaches, that which is to be considered right is determined by acting consistently and in accordance with a self-imposed principle.

Where the two ethical ideas differ is in terms of how rigidly one adheres to that which one considers right. On an autonomous ethical approach, one advocates a formal principle, such as the categorical imperative, and considers deviance from this to be opposed to right conduct. Authenticity, however, takes a broader ethical view. The crucial difference, according to Alessandro Ferrara, is that the ethic of authenticity introduces the idea that there are motives, desires and commitments that sometimes should outweigh the restrictions of rational reflection (1993: 88). That is, part of being human is experiencing a variety of moods and emotions, and although these may cause one to diverge from one's principles, what is important is that one recognizes this and reconciles these with oneself. As Ferrara elsewhere elucidates, 'all ethics of authenticity start from the assumption that in order to be a worthy moral being, we must not deny or try to suppress, but rather acknowledge the urges which deflect us from our principles, while at the same time continuing to orient our conduct to the moral point of view' (1998: 7).

Ferrara here suggests that we need to be aware of and celebrate our particularity rather than suppress it. According to Ferrara, this emphasis upon particularity is a fundamental feature of ethics of authenticity, and which ethics of autonomy do not account for. Thus, whilst autonomy emphasizes freedom to choose, it does not insist upon this choice as particular to the individual. Although authenticity is distinct from autonomy, it is nevertheless dependent upon a conception of autonomy. Namely, in order to live authentically one must be able to freely reflect upon and enact one's desires and values. Authenticity thus requires one to be free from manipulation and self-distorting influences, in order to be able to reflect and choose, and act from desires that are in some sense one's own.

The preliminary articulation of authenticity, as a distinctly modern ideal, which emphasizes the rejection of externally imposed ethical standards and the actualization of one's own ethical values, can now be expanded upon. In engagement with sincerity it was discovered that authenticity is an end in itself. That is, whilst sincerity suggests actualizing one's true self for the benefit of others, authenticity is pursued for its own sake. In contrast with integrity, it was determined that to be authentic one must be conscious of oneself as an individual. Whilst personal integrity focuses upon the maintenance of one's commitments, being authentic concerns being true to oneself. And contrary to autonomy, it was revealed that whilst authenticity involves a self-imposed principle, deviation from this does not detract from one's authenticity, but can in fact highlight it. That is, the ethic of autonomy demands strict adherence to moral values, whilst authenticity recognizes that humans are fallible and incapable of consistently acting in accordance with moral absolutes. Having expanded our preliminary definition of authenticity – in relation to the rival ethical ideals of sincerity, integrity and autonomy – we will now proceed to further develop our definition by considering the alternative views upheld by its advocates. In the following section, we will consider the sources from which contemporary advocates of authenticity derive their understanding.

2.3 The socio-ethical turn

Authenticity is perhaps most commonly associated with existentialism. As a cultural and philosophical movement, 'existentialism' has been obscured by commentators' desire to incorporate anyone who concerns themselves with modern existence.[2] Even with regard to philosophical advocates, this term has been used as a catchall to incorporate thinkers who existed prior to the establishment of the phrase, such as Kierkegaard and Nietzsche, and those who later came to reject this label, including Karl Jaspers, Martin Heidegger, Gabriel Marcel and Albert Camus. However, in this chapter we will seek to avoid the difficulties which arise through employing 'existentialism' as an umbrella term, by focusing on the primary proponent of this philosophical movement: Jean-

---

[2] Walter Kaufmann, for example, in his well-regarded *Existentialism: From Dostoyevsky to Sartre* includes excerpts from Fyodor Dostoyevsky, Franz Kafka and Rainer Maria Rilke in order to express the central tenants of existential philosophy.

Paul Sartre. Ironically, when the term 'existentialist' was initially applied to Sartre he resisted acceptance.[3] As Simone de Beauvoir explains in her autobiography, 'Sartre had refused to allow Gabriel Marcel to apply this adjective to him: "My philosophy is a philosophy of existence; I don't even know what 'Existentialism' is". I shared his irritation. [...] But our protests were in vain. In the end, we took the epithet that everyone used for us and used it for our own purposes' (1965: 45–6).[4]

However, within contemporary socio-ethical literature, existential authenticity has largely been ignored. Associated with self-creation, many theorists believe that this leads to a form of aestheticism and egoistic self-indulgence. As Alessandro Ferrara attests, 'the notion of authenticity is no longer used mainly in an existentialist sense or as a shorthand term for capturing the cipher of a moral climate characterised by a one-sided emphasis on self-realisation, intimacy, privatism and scepticism concerning all values that transcend the self' (1998: ix). A further consequence is that by focusing on the subject, it is believed the existentialists are incapable of offering a satisfactory account of moral norms. As Charles Taylor suggests, 'moral dilemmas become inconceivable on the [Sartrean] theory of radical choice' (1985: 30). That is, if one determines one's own values in solitude then there is no moral standard to validate the content of one's choices and actions. It is precisely this attitude towards existentialism that has led modern advocates of authenticity to disregard the existential account as a valid approach. Instead, they suggest looking for an alternative source of inspiration for their concept and have found such a source within the thought of Jean-Jacques Rousseau.

The claim that an ethic of authenticity is inherent within the thought of Rousseau was first posited by Lionel Trilling, according to whom, 'from Rousseau we have learned that what destroys our authenticity is society – our sentiment of being depends upon the opinion of other people. The ideal of authentic personal being stands at the very centre of Rousseau's thought' (1972 [2009]: 93). Alessandro Ferrara further explicates this claim in his monograph *Modernity and Authenticity*, where he argues that an ethic of authenticity is inherent within Rousseau's novel *Emile*. According to Ferrara, 'the significance of the novel has

---

[3] As Sartre and Beauvoir lived together for twenty years, it is difficult to determine the extent to which Beauvoir influenced Sartre – we will assume existentialism to be a consequence of their joint effort.

[4] Soon after adopting this philosophical classification, Beauvoir and Sartre launched their 'existential offensive'. Publishing plays, novels and philosophical treatises, they advocated living authentically as a remedy to the meaninglessness of contemporary European society. The 'existential offensive' included Sartre's lecture, *Existentialism Is a Humanism*, and Beauvoir's article *Existentialism and Popular Wisdom*, which was published in the journal *Les Tempts Modernes* which they jointly edited, alongside Maurice Merleau-Ponty.

to do, in my opinion, with its touching on the all-modern conflict between an *ethic of autonomy* and an *ethic of authenticity*' (1993: 103). Charles Taylor also derives his understanding of authenticity from Rousseau, whom he takes to be an early modern articulator of this ideal. Taylor's reason for supposing Rousseau to be an advocate of authenticity is because his moral outlook entails 'following a voice of nature within us' (1992: 27). Somogy Varga also mirrors this perspective, arguing that 'Rousseau considered this individual difference as the key to finding out how one should live' (2012: 21).

However, it was not only Rousseau who upheld authenticity as an ideal but rather, this notion also permeated the thought of several theorists during the romantic movement. According to Charles Taylor, Gottfried von Herder also contributed to the development of an ethic of authenticity. As Taylor elucidates, 'it was Herder [...] which added the epoch-making demand that my realization of the human essence be my own, and hence launched the idea that each individual has its own way of being human' (1975: 15). More importantly, though, Herder places a strong emphasis on social context. In his *Outlines of a Philosophy of the History of Man*, Herder advocates a collectivist theory. That is, he believed that the individual derived value in belonging to a group. As Isaiah Berlin states, 'he conceived and cast light upon the crucially important social function of "belonging" – on what it is to belong to a group, a culture, a movement, a form of life [and that] the notion of belonging is at the heart of all Herder's ideas' (1976: 194–5). Moreover, 'the individual, for him, is inescapably a member of some group; consequently all that he does must express, consciously or unconsciously, the aspirations of his group' (1975: 201). Thus, whilst he advocates a Protagorean maxim, that each individual has their own way of being, it is not subjectively conceived, but gains validity from one's social grounding.

A further theorist whom contemporary advocates of authenticity draw upon is Friedrich Hölderlin. Within his novel, *Hyperion*, Hölderlin creates an atmosphere of nostalgia for a lost sense of wholeness. That which the protagonist longs for is 'to be one with all that lives, to return in blessed self-forgetfulness into the All of Nature' (2010: 23). According to Charles Guignon, an air of authenticity is invoked because 'reunification with nature is achieved not by knowing, but by being fully immersed in the life-process in such a way that the "inmost of our inmost selves" resonates with all that is' (2004: 55). Here we can detect a rejection of the scientific rationalization of the Enlightenment, which places a premium on knowledge acquired through empirical means. Hölderlin's approach, on the other hand, is to find unity with nature and derive knowledge about the world through an understanding of oneself.

The claim that it is this desire which motivates the romantic turn inwards is also maintained by Somogy Varga, who claims 'Hölderlin's work displays another feature, which is added to the idea of authenticity during the Romantic period.... This is the attempt to recover a sense of wholeness by turning inward – a wholeness that is assumed to be lost with the emerging modern world' (2012: 22). The recognition that a sense of unity has been lost is well expressed by Novalis's 'blue flower', which became a motif for modern discontent and the futile quest to recover meaning. Within the novel *Henrich von Oftendingen*, Novalis's protagonist dreams that he is venturing through a forest when he glances upon the most beautiful blue flower he has ever perceived. However, as he reaches down to pluck the flower he is aroused from his sleep, left alone with his longing and the realization that it is unobtainable.

In what way, then, can we understand an ethic of authenticity to be inherent within romantic literature? Through Rousseau we can see the rejection of autonomy, as a too rigidly conceived ethical ideal. Herder determined that human essence was not universal, but individual, and informed by one's own social context. Hölderlin attempted to acquire unity through discovering oneself in relation to nature. What we thus find with Rousseau, Herder and Hölderlin is the attempt to discover an essential self through the process of looking inwards. The romantic approach to authenticity thus insinuates that each of us possesses an inner essence which is to be discovered through introspection. It is from this particular approach that Taylor and various other contemporary advocates of authenticity orientate their trajectory. Thus, what we find is that contemporary advocates of authenticity tend to by-pass existentialism and instead appeal to the ethical ideal inherent within the thought of Rousseau and the romantics.

Although contemporary advocates of authenticity side with a social perspective, contrary to the existential approach to authenticity, it will be argued that the difference lies in that which these two approaches problematize. Although we can certainly find early modern articulations of the ideal of authenticity, this search for an alternative source of authenticity than the existentialists leads to a historical rupture in the tradition of authenticity. This dislocation of approaches, however, can be resolved if we consider these two seemingly opposed accounts in terms of the problems they address. That is, in what follows, we will argue that existential authenticity, as developed by Sartre, was intended to engage with the problem of nothingness; moreover, social-ethical authenticity, as advocated by Taylor, was designed in reaction to the problematization of authenticity itself. Thus, although it has been demonstrated that contemporary literature on authenticity draws upon the romantic tradition for an ethical ideal, it will be argued that by engaging with the concept of authenticity that they are the existentialist's successors, whether they acknowledge it or not.

2.4 Sartre's existential authenticity

Sartre begins *Being and Nothingness*, his magnum opus, by attempting to elucidate the ontological structure of being; however, the problem which propels his enquiry is that of nothingness. Beginning with the attempt to articulate being, like Hegel before him, Sartre determines that being includes its antithesis, non-being.[5] As he recognizes and articulates, 'the permanent possibility of non-being, outside us and within, conditions our questions about being' (2007: 29). This claim is elucidated through Sartre's well-known example of waiting for Pierre within a café. Glancing around, one focuses one's attention on the appearance of Pierre, whom one does not perceive to be present. And although the café is full of people and objects, one does not focus on these, but only Pierre's absence. As Sartre puts it, 'nevertheless if I should finally discover Pierre, my intuition would be filled by a solid element, I should be suddenly arrested by his face and the whole café would organize itself around him as a discrete presence' (2007: 10). In this way, then, Sartre suggests that we experience a non-being through our perception of the absence of being.

However, it is not only in one's experiences of the external world that we encounter nothingness. According to Sartre, the concept of nothingness is also fundamental to our ontological structure. Unlike inanimate objects, whose being is predetermined, a significant dimension of human existence is that we are not any thing in particular. That is, to use a concrete example, unlike a chair, which will always be a chair even if it is broken or disassembled, human beings do not possess a fixed essence which defines them. Whilst the chair cannot but be a chair, that which defines each individual not only changes but is also determined by that individual. Sartre explains this through the distinction between *being-in-itself* (*en-soi*) and *being-for-itself* (*pour-soi*). The chair possesses *being-in-itself*, insofar as it is none other than a chair, whilst each human being, on the other hand, must determine its *being-for-itself*. That is, it is up to each individual to choose their fundamental projects, that which defines them and the *telos* of their life for themselves.

---

[5] In Hegel's account, indeterminate being, as devoid of any content, also contains its negation – nothing. See 'The Science of Logic', in *The Hegel Reader*, trans. Stephen Houlgate (London: Blackwell, 2013).

This ontological fact, that our being is itself without foundation, however, causes the individual to experience anxiety.[6] Sartre derives this concept from Heidegger, who in turn borrows it from Kierkegaard, and each differentiate anxiety from fear.[7] Fear is always induced by an object, one is afraid of a spider, for example, but with anxiety there is no-thing which gives rise to the feeling of angst. It is precisely this nothingness, in Sartre's account, that an individual does not possess *being-in-itself*, and the subsequent realization that each individual is required to determine *being-for-itself*, which causes anxiety. As Sartre explains,

> anguish is characterized by a constantly renewed obligation to remake the Self which designates the free being. As a matter of fact when we showed earlier that my possibilities were filled with anguish because it depended on me alone to sustain them in their existence, that did not mean that they derived from a Me which to itself at least, would first be given and would then pass in the temporal flux from one consciousness to another consciousness. (2007: 35)

Acceptance of this ontological fact, made manifest by anxiety, leads us to realize that we possess ontological freedom. As Sartre explains, 'it is in anguish that man gets the consciousness of his freedom, or if you prefer, anguish is the mode of being of freedom as consciousness of being; it is in anguish that freedom is, in its being, in question for itself' (2007: 29). Through anxiety then, individuals arrive at the realization that they do not possess *being-in-itself* and are faced with the understanding that it is their role to determine *being-for-itself*. A further implication of this realization is that since all of our choices are self-determined, they lack any firm foundation. It is then for this reason Sartre exclaims 'my freedom is anguished at being the foundation of values while itself without foundation' (2007: 38). We therefore experience anxiety at the realization that our choice of project is itself foundationless. As a consequence, Sartre claims, 'I emerge alone and in anguish confronting the unique and original project which constitutes my being; all the barriers, all the guard rails collapse, nihilated by the consciousness of my freedom' (2007: 39).

As a consequence of anguish, induced by the realization that an individual does not possess *being-it-itself*, Sartre claims many people live in bad faith

---

[6] Julian Young argues that Sartre employs the concept of anxiety in two opposing senses. In parts I and IV of *Being and Nothingness* Sartre claims we feel anguish because we must choose what we become, however, in parts II and III he suggests that the cause of anxiety is because we cannot choose what we become. See *The Death of God and the Meaning of Life* (New York: Routledge, 2003), 144.

[7] For an analysis of Kierkegaard's influence on Heidegger, see Jean Wahl, *Transcendence and the Concrete: A Selection of Essays,* trans. Alan D Schrift and Ian Moore (New York: Fordham University Press, 2016).

(*mauvaise foi*).⁸ That is, rather than accepting that each individual is free to determine *being-for-itself*, a large percentage of people convince themselves they already possess an essence. As Sartre puts it, 'this nihilating power nihilates anguish in so far as I flee it and nihilates itself in so far as I am anguish in order to flee it. This attitude is what we call bad faith' (2007: 44). In order to elucidate, Sartre offers the well-known example of the Parisian waiter who wholly identifies himself with his social role. The waiter's movements are a little too robotic, too well rehearsed. His actions suggest that he is none other than a waiter, and in doing so, denies his freedom and possibility to be otherwise. However, as Sartre explains, 'a waiter cannot be a waiter in the same way as an inkwell is an inkwell' (2007: 59–60). It is precisely this concern which leads to the development of his thoughts on authenticity.⁹

Sartre's proposed resolution, to the realization that our lives are fundamentally meaningless, is to overcome our contingency, to become the foundation of our own being – to become *in-itself-for-itself*. As Sartre explains, 'the ideal of a consciousness which would be the foundation of its own being-it-itself by the pure consciousness which it would have of itself. It is this idea which can be called God' (2007: 587). This project, however, is doomed to failure, for the reason that we cannot establish our own foundation. That is 'while the meaning of the desire is ultimately the project of being God, the desire is never constituted by this meaning' (2007: 587). As Jonathan Webber notes, 'it is only those people who are in bad faith who have the fundamental project to be God' (2009: 109). For this reason, Thomas Anderson has suggested that Sartre only discusses self-deception within *Being and Nothingness* and that the positive phase is not enacted until his later work *Notebook for Ethics*.¹⁰ Nevertheless, by engaging with the problem of nothingness, and explaining negative modes of existence which lead to self-deception, Sartre can be seen to point towards the alternative as a means to live authentically.

Many of the criticisms levelled against existential authenticity are a consequence of Sartre's disavowal of traditional moral theory. As Mary Warnock makes apparent, '[it is] doubtful whether it can be claimed that there is any direct

---

⁸ Jonathan Webber offers an excellent analysis of the various ways in which *mauvaise foi* is employed by Sartre. He notes that it is used to express (i) self-deception, (ii) a particular epistemic attitude towards evidence, (iii) belief in fixed natures, (iv) belief that one's own fixed nature does not include traits that one does possess. See *The Existentialism of Jean-Paul Sartre* (2009).

⁹ Catrin Gibson has recently determined that although Sartre's attempt to develop authentic love fails in *Being and Nothingness*, this can be established, not through *eros*, as Sartre attempts to convey, but through the mother–child relationship. See 'Authentic Love', *Sartre Studies International* 23, no. 1 (2017): 60–79.

¹⁰ See *Sartre's Two Ethics: From Authenticity to Integral Humanity* (Chicago: Open Court, 1993).

contribution to philosophy which should be described as Existentialist ethics' (1970: 57). This problem is perpetuated by Sartre himself, who, in the closing comments of *Being and Nothingness* rejects the idea that which he has devised is capable of establishing an ethical basis. As Sartre himself suggests, 'ontology itself can not formulate ethical precepts. It is concerned solely with what is, and we can not possibly derive imperatives from ontology's indicatives' (2007: 645). These closing lines suggest that Sartrean authenticity is incapable of supporting an ethical ideal, and a promise is made to readdress this concern. This, however, is something which he unsuccessfully attempts to develop within *Existentialism Is a Humanism*.

In this famous lecture, Sartre attempts to determine the ethical precepts of his existential approach; however, his argument ultimately infers that since our choices and actions are freely determined, our values cannot be objective (2007). This claim has quite rightly been met with heavy criticism, and it is this short-sighted suggestion which Taylor picks up on. Focusing on Sartre's example of the student, seeking help to resolve his moral predicament of joining the resistance or staying with his mother, Taylor claims that 'it is a dilemma only because the claims themselves are not created by radical choice. If they were the grievous nature of the predicament would dissolve, for that would mean that the young man could do away with the dilemma at any moment by simply declaring one of the rival claims as dead and inoperative' (1985: 30). Taylor's point is that if we adhered to Sartre's concept of radical choice, and only endorsed that which we deem to be agreeable, then the student's dilemma would not exist for it rests upon objective criteria such as his mother's happiness, or the overall good of the French nation, but if that which is of value is subjectively determined, then he has no grounds to acknowledge his mother's desire to be happy or France's need for liberation.

This characterization of Sartre, as a one-sided thinker, may seem unfair, and restricted to his early thought. One may interject that a more developed theory of recognition can be seen to take place within *What Is Literature*, *Anti-Semite and the Jew*, and *Notebook for Ethics* and that a sound ethical ideal can be constructed from his corpus, as T. Storm Heter has done.[11] However, our intention is not to portray the development of Sartrean authenticity. Rather, the purpose is to

---

[11] Heter argues that Sartre's corpus can be interpreted as an attempt to resolve this problem by developing an ethic of authenticity based upon Hegel's concept of recognition. Heter recognizes that it is precisely this which was missing in Sartre's early work, where he notes that the other effects how we view ourselves through 'the look' but rejects that the other is required for mutual recognition. Sartre equates objectification with alienation, see *Jean-Paul Sartre's Ethic of Engagement* (New York: Continuum, 2006).

explain the neglect of the existential approach by contemporary advocates of authenticity, and attempt to demonstrate that the social approach, championed by Charles Taylor, does not deviate from the existential approach, as one may be led to believe. On the contrary, it will be argued that by understanding both approaches to be concerned with a particular problem that we can see the social approach as a continuation of the same tradition of authenticity as that perpetuated by the existentialists.

In the preceding analysis, an overview of Sartre's early reflections on nothingness was offered and how this problem led him to develop existential authenticity as a response. Sartre's account, that each person does not possess *being-in-itself*, but rather we must construct our values for ourselves, is therefore contrary to the socio-ethical approach upheld by Rousseau, Herder and Hölderlin. Whilst the romantic theorists claimed that we possess an individual essence which we discover through introspection, Sartre goes one step further in rejecting any notion of essence whatsoever. Furthermore, instead of suggesting that we discover who we truly are, for Sartre one must create one's authentic self. It was also illustrated that Taylor rejects Sartre's approach for its emphasis on radical choice, which undermines any attempt to seriously address moral problems. In the following section, it will be demonstrated that Taylor characterizes the phenomenon of authenticity in accordance with this criticism of Sartre and that he attempts to circumvent this problem by appealing to an ethical ideal inherent within romantic thought. Having demonstrated Sartre's existential authenticity is a response to nothingness, we will now turn to elucidating Taylor's ethic of authenticity and to demonstrating that he problematizes the phenomenon of authenticity itself.

2.5 Taylor's ethic of authenticity

Charles Taylor begins his seminal work on authenticity, *The Ethics of Authenticity*, by noting that, although authenticity has been criticized as leading to ethical relativism and egoistic self-indulgence, it offers a valuable ideal. Taylor divides the philosophical responses into the broad categories of 'knockers and boosters' (1992: 11). The knockers are critical of any form of individualism and refer to their contemporary social setting as a 'culture of narcissism' (1992: 11). The boosters, on the other hand, are advocates of self-creation and claim that since there is no ethical framework from which to orient oneself, subjective ethics are the only option. Although Taylor does not specifically name those whom he deems to be 'boosters', from the criticism given earlier, we can safely assume that he has the existentialists, specifically Sartre, in mind. Taylor, however, does not side with one approach against the other, but agrees with both to a certain extent. Agreeing with the 'knockers', Taylor acknowledges that a subjective approach to authenticity, which leads to relativism, is an ethically undesirable one. However, he views authenticity as not only valuable but the means to also live a meaningful life within the modern age. As he himself claims, 'I do not believe that everything is as it should be in this culture. Here I tend to agree with the knockers. But unlike them, I think that authenticity should be taken seriously as a moral ideal' (1992: 22).

As a consequence of the breakdown of social hierarchies, we no longer possess a shared conception, or singular subjective notion of the good. This has led to what Taylor refers to as 'liberalism of neutrality'. As he elucidates, 'one of its basic tenets is that a liberal society must be neutral on questions of what constitutes a good life. The good life is what each individual seeks, in his or her own way' (1992: 17–18). In this respect, Taylor recognizes that authenticity offers a powerful and useful ideal. That is, insofar as a communal conception of the good cannot be re-established, it falls upon each individual to determine the good for ourselves. Thus, according to Taylor, 'not only should I not fit my life to the demands of external conformity; I can't even find the model to live by outside myself. I can find it only within.' Furthermore, as Taylor continues, 'being true to myself means being true to my own originality, and that is something only I can articulate and discover. In articulating it, I am also defining myself. I am realizing a potentiality that is properly my own' (1992: 29). It is precisely this role which authenticity fulfils and the reason why it has become so prevalent within modern occidental societies.

In articulating the sources of an ethic of authenticity, Taylor suggests that such an ideal found articulation within the thought of Jean-Jacques Rousseau. However, in his account, '[authenticity] becomes crucially important because of a development that occurs after Rousseau and that [he] associates with Herder [whom] put forward the idea that each of us has an original way of being human. Each person has his or her own "measure" is his way of putting it' (1992: 28). It is precisely this which Taylor takes to be the ethical ideal inherent within the concept of authenticity. As he continues to elucidate,

> there is a certain way of being human that is *my way*. I am called upon to live my life in this way, and not in imitation of anyone else's. But this gives a new importance to being true to myself. If I am not, I miss the point of my life, I miss what being human is for *me*. (1992: 29; 1994: 30)

Although we find this ideal at work within existential philosophy, it could be argued, in line with Taylor's earlier criticism against Sartre, that he equates existential authenticity with subjective ethics, which reduces to a form of relativism. The ethic of authenticity inherent within romantic thought, on the other hand, provides an intersubjective account insofar as it recognizes that society shapes who we are whilst simultaneously emphasizing that each individual determine this for themselves.[12]

In order to defend authenticity against the 'knocker's' criticisms, Taylor addresses the main flaw in the 'boosters' account, that of self-indulgence, and states that it is not possible to be an individual in the sense which they advocate. That is, we cannot simply abstract ourselves from our social context and engage in a form of radical choice because the conditions which provide us with our choices exist independently of us. More specifically, Taylor first explains that this is impossible because communities share a language with fixed values. That is, 'selfhood and the choice of moral goals can operate only within a shared framework of significance and meaning, without which they lapse into incoherence' (1994: 30). Secondly, it is this shared meaning which enables one to choose that which one understands to be meaningful. As Taylor explains, 'things take on importance against a background of intelligibility', which he elsewhere refers to as a 'horizon of significance' (1994: 37).

Taylor claims that we are still free to choose our identity, but from within a horizon of intelligibility. That is, we choose what is important from within a horizon of pre-established beliefs and values. Far from diminishing our possibilities, it is this horizon which makes our choices significant and enables us to define ourselves as individuals.[13] That is, one cannot be authentic unless one is distinguished from others and by choosing in accordance with this. As Taylor explains, 'defining myself means finding what is significant in my difference from others' (1992: 35–6). In order to be authentic, in Taylor's account then, we must define ourselves through properties with human significance. Thus, disagreeing with those who equate authenticity with narcissism, Taylor argues that not only does it provide a desirable, modern mode of existence but it also should be understood as an ethical ideal. As Taylor himself explains, 'by "morality" I mean a picture of what a better or higher mode of life would be, where "better" and

---

[12] Although romantic approaches to authenticity were claimed to emphasize self-discovery through introspection, Taylor does not advocate that there is an essential self, but employs 'self-discovery' as a metaphor.

[13] Taylor is here influenced by Hans Georg Gadamer's 'Fusion of Horizons', *Truth and Method*, trans. Joel Weinsheimer and Donald G. Marshall (London: Continuum, 2004), 302.

"higher" are defined not in terms of what we happen to desire or need, but offer a standard of what we ought to desire' (1992: 16).

A crucial feature of human life, according to Taylor is that it is fundamentally 'dialogical'.[14] In his own words, 'people do not acquire the language needed for self-definition on their own. The genesis of the human mind is in this sense not monological, not something each person develops on his or her own, but dialogical' (1994: 230). What this means is that individuals develop their understanding of themselves in dialogue with others, as opposed to in monologue with themselves. Thus, that which permits the possibility of articulating one's inner and outer ideas is enabled through language. Therefore, in order to conceive of oneself as an individual, one is dependent upon one's community with which one shares this language. Furthermore, although one may believe that it is possible to isolate oneself and reject the cultural practices which previously defined us, one would still be employing the same learned language, or mode of thinking which has been socially imposed. For these reasons, Taylor claims that 'the making and sustaining of our identity remains dialogical throughout our lives' (1992: 35). Thus, according to Taylor, unlike the claim made by Sartre in *Being and Nothingness*, our identity is not chosen in isolation, but rather he sides with Rousseau and Herder in claiming that this is informed by our society as a whole.

A further dimension of Taylor's account is that to form successful relationships, in which individuals define themselves in dialogue, it is necessary to recognize that we have an obligation towards our interlocutors. His concept of dialogical self is thus underpinned by a theory of recognition.[15] Although this was previously built-in to social hierarchies, their collapse led to the emergence of recognition, alongside authenticity, as a modern social condition. In his own words, 'democracy has ushered in a politics of equal recognition, which has taken various forms over the years, and which now has returned in the form of demands for the equal status of cultures and genders' (1992: 47; 1994: 27). However, in order for us to recognize others as equal, there has to be some external standard which we can appeal to. As Taylor emphasizes, 'to come together on a mutual recognition of difference [...] we have to share also some standards of value on which the identities concerned

---

[14] This concept also exists in the thought of Martin Buber, for whom man developed in dialogue with God. Placing a secular spin on this term, Taylor employs it to explain the formation of human character. See *I and Thou*, trans. Ronald Gregor Smith (Edinburgh: T.&T. Smith, 1937), Pt.1 Aphorisms 19–22.

[15] For an excellent analysis of the theory of recognition, see Cillian McBride, *Recognition* (Cambridge: Polity Press, 2013).

check out as equal' (1992: 52). Where do we derive this value from? In Taylor's account it is the same cultural framework which gives meaning to our choices which provides us with a standard for recognition. As he explains, 'recognizing difference, like self-choosing, requires a horizon of significance, in this case a shared one' (1992: 52).

Through emphasizing that our values are not determined through radical choice, but are in part informed by our cultural context, and that authenticity can offer a valuable ethic through drawing upon the validation of our horizon, Taylor is able to overcome the problems he perceived within Sartre's early approach. However, despite the fact that Taylor overcomes Sartre's account and salvages authenticity as an ethical ideal worth preserving, his own account is not without its flaws. The primary pitfall of his approach is that he does not provide a formal account of what this ideal looks like. As Eric Hall makes explicit, 'Taylor's own work on this particular issue lacks some explicatory content . . . these lacunae include a lack of explicit and developed definition and an intellectual cultivation of the means by which authenticity, as an ethical ideal is pursed in the first place' (2015: 43). That is, although Taylor develops an ethic of authenticity, he does not offer an account of what an authentic existence would look like or how one engages in the cultivation of one's authentic self.

Although there are certain aspects which require further development in Taylor's account, and which we will address in the following chapter, he can nevertheless be understood to resolve the problems which Sartre's early approach encountered. That is, since Sartre's account ultimately results in ethical relativism, as a consequence of his claim that individuals determine their values for themselves, Taylor appealed to an ethical ideal inherent within romantic thought to revive the concept of authenticity. Thus, although Taylor rejects Sartrean authenticity as ethically impaired, to the extent that he attempts to rescue the concept of authenticity from aestheticism by resolving this tension, he can be seen to continue the existential tradition of authenticity. That is, insofar as Taylor takes up the challenge left by Sartre, and endeavours to develop authenticity into a functioning ethical ideal, he can be seen to continue the trajectory set by Sartre. Thus, rather than considering the socio-ethical approach to authenticity as a rival to the existentialist approach, we can consider the former to be the continuation, or development, of the latter. Thus, by understanding each of these approaches in terms of that which they problematize, we can perceive of them as one unified tradition, as opposed to two distinct approaches.

2.5 Summary

This chapter began with a preliminary account of authenticity, where it was defined as a distinctly modern concept which emphasizes individuality and is understood in relation to inauthenticity. This account was then differentiated and further defined in relation to the alternative ethical ideals of sincerity, integrity and autonomy. What these comparisons revealed was that authenticity is an end in itself, insofar as it is pursued for its own sake; that authenticity requires being conscious of oneself as an individual and being true to oneself; and that deviation from one's self-imposed principle does not detract from one's authenticity, but in fact highlights it. Having expanded our definition, we then turned our attention to the various approaches to authenticity. Here it was suggested that existential authenticity has fallen out of philosophical fashion and modern advocates instead turn to sociopolitical thought for inspiration. However, rather than presenting the existential and social accounts of authenticity as two alternative approaches, it was suggested that we instead understand them as concerned with two different problems. Having considering the advantages and flaws of each approach, the task towards which we will now turn is to devise a formal account of authenticity which incorporates those aspects deemed desirable and which is capable of overcoming the problems which the preceding approaches encountered.

3

Dimensions of socio-existential authenticity

In the previous chapter, it was argued that Taylor's account could be understood as a continuation of the existentialist concept of authenticity, rather than at odds with it. In this chapter, our aim will be to continue this line of thought and construct a socio-existential account of authenticity, by which we mean that we will incorporate aspects from both the social and existential approaches to authenticity. In light of living within a post-metaphysical culture – that human beings lack a predetermined essence – we will draw upon the existential approach, advocating that our authentic self is created by choice, rather than discovered through introspection. However, due to the criticisms aimed against the existential approach – that it is ethically unsound – we will also incorporate aspects of the social account, which insists authenticity ought to be socially grounded. The purpose of devising a socio-existential approach will be to build upon the existing literature in order to address the modern problems of freedom and meaning. That is, our aim will be to demonstrate how authenticity can provide an ethic by which to orientate one's actions and grant meaning to an absurd existence. Rather than providing a survey of every approach which exists, the aim here will be to construct an account through engagement with existing literature. This chapter will be structured in a dialectical fashion, and our concept of socio-existential authenticity will be shown to be constructed of several dimensions which necessarily arise in response to the problems encountered within the previous dimension.

We will begin by asking what it is precisely that determines our authentic self (Section 3.1). Here it will be claimed that since there is no underlying essence we begin with the dimension of *choice*. However, since free choice can be said to undermine meaningfulness it will be further argued that we can avoid this problem through the dimension of *commitment*. We will then consider how it is possible to ensure our ideal of an authentic existence is achievable (Section 3.2). Namely, we will demonstrate that it is possible to avoid the pursuit of an inauthentic existence, or one which we cannot actualize, through the dimension of *maturity*. In the third section, we will consider the problem as to where our choices are derived from (Section 3.3). Here it will be claimed that groundless choice of a particular project can be avoided through the dimension of *becoming what one is*. In the fourth section, the problem as to that which validates our choices will be addressed (Section 3.4). We will here demonstrate that our choices can be given ethical validity through the dimension of *intersubjective consciousness* and that we can understand our limitations of choice through the dimension of *heritage*. In the final section, we will offer a preliminary account of how our socio-existential approach to authenticity is able to address the problems of freedom and meaning (Section 3.5). More specifically, it will be claimed that by living in accordance with the six dimensions (*choice, commitment, maturity, becoming what one is, intersubjective consciousness* and *heritage*) that one can avoid the restriction of freedom and live a meaningful existence.

3.1 What determines our sense of authenticity?

The primary dimension of our account, and starting point of this chapter, is existential *choice*. This notion is perhaps best expressed by Jean-Paul Sartre who argues that as a consequence of 'the human condition', humans possess absolute freedom. The key to understanding Sartre's concept of authenticity lies within his famous maxim, 'existence precedes essence' (2007: 22). What this existential axiom suggests is that contrary to theistic accounts, which advocate that human beings were designed by a divine creator to fulfil a particular end, there is no determined end to human existence. In this sense, it is also opposed to an Aristotelian approach, which advocates that human beings possess a fixed essence.[1] In order to explicate, Sartre offers the example of a paper knife which was designed with the specific function to open letters, noting that it is precisely this purpose which defines it (2007: 20–1). However, he claims that, unlike commodities, human beings do not possess a natural teleology, or purpose for which they were designed to achieve.

In Sartre's account, rather, one is nothing other than that which one makes oneself. That is, rather than possessing a fixed essence, one exists first and then defines oneself within existence. Although Sartre denies there is such a thing as

---

[1] Marjorie Grene notes that whilst Sartre's account is explicitly atheist, this also leads to a rejection of the Aristotelian position, though Sartre does not make this argument. See *Dreadful Freedom: A Critique of Existentialism* (Chicago: Chicago University Press, 1948).

human nature, he suggests there is a human condition of absolute freedom. This, however, is perceived negatively by Sartre who claims, 'man is condemned to be free' (2013: 439; 2007: 23). What this suggests is that freedom is something which one is forced to endure – a situation which we are thrown into. A consequence of this undesired freedom is that one often conceals this fact, deceiving oneself and instead existing in *bad faith*. As discussed in Section 2.4, Sartre explicates this state of existence through the example of the waiter who wholeheartedly associates himself with his role, believing this is something he is essentially.

However, since each individual is required to determine *being-for-itself*, we do not possess a predetermined essence, but must choose this for ourselves. To recap on our discussion in the previous chapter, there is no essential thing which humans are, rather, they are free to choose their essence. In the former, a thing's essence is immanent, whereas humans possess transcendent possibilities, to become other than what they are. To exist in bad faith, therefore, is to attribute oneself a fixed essence and deny one's capacity for transcendence. In the example of the waiter, he lives in bad faith because he conceals his transcendent possibilities. Thus, by understanding his being as in-itself, insofar as he believes that he is essentially a waiter – the waiter allows his social role to define him. The reason why one chooses to live in bad faith, according to Sartre, is because one experiences anxiety in confronting one's boundless freedom.[2] However, Sartre notes that anxiety ought to be understood as a positive state, insofar as the nothingness which one confronts offers awareness of one's possibilities which are yet to be actualized.

A further negative consequence of *being-for-itself* is that there is nothing outside of oneself which can be appealed to in order to inform one's actions. Sartre offers the example of his student who approaches him with the dilemma as to whether to join the resistance or stay with his mother, who has already lost her husband and two sons (2007: 30). In making such a decision, Sartre emphasizes that there is no code of ethics which one can appeal to; instead, one is responsible for one's choice. One cannot even depend on another person, for in choosing one's adviser one has already committed to a particular approach, which one hopes to elicit and have confirmed by one's interlocutor. As a result of the human condition, one must decide for oneself what one is to become. Thus, not only are humans completely free but also are completely responsible. That is, rather than possessing a fixed essence, it is up to each individual to

---

[2] Here Sartre borrows from Kierkegaard (*The Concept of Dread*: 38) and Heidegger (*Being and Time*: 228) who distinguish between fear and anxiety, noting that the former is induced by an object whilst the latter is brought about by no-thing, or nothingness.

determine their essence for themselves. By 'essence' Sartre does not mean that there is something which individuals naturally are, but instead suggests that this is determined by the projects one pursues. As Sartre himself concisely puts it, 'man is nothing other than his own project. He exists only to the extent that he realizes himself, therefore he is nothing more than the sum of his actions, nothing more than his life' (2007: 37).

This dimension of authenticity, that one's project ought to be freely chosen, can be aptly illustrated through Leo Tolstoy's novella *The Death of Ivan Illych* (2006). This short story depicts the life and demise of a high court judge, who, upon confronting his temporarlity, begins to resent his life. He recalls how he made friends according to their social standing, married because he was encouraged to do so by his peers and furnished his house, not according to his taste, but to reflect his status. It is only when he discovers that he is terminally ill that Ivan comes to recognize the inauthenticity of his existence. Although his lifestyle may seem desirable because it illustrates the ideal of social success, he acknowledges that he himself did not choose this life, but that it was the consequence of external forces. His profession, for example, was not the result of hard work and determination, but was obtained through his connections. Moreover, even if one has lived a fulfilled life, unless one has chosen one's life for oneself then it cannot be said to be an authentic existence. As Kierkegaard wonderfully puts it, 'the richest personality is nothing before it has chosen itself, as on the other hand even what one might call the poorest personality is everything when it has chosen itself; for the great thing is not to be this or that but to be oneself, and this everyone can be if one wills it' (1987: 181).

What can be derived from Sartre's account is that authentic choice requires freedom to choose one's project. However, one's choice is partially determined by other people. Through anticipation of judgement, one's decision is informed by guilt, shame or fear, induced by how we imagine others to perceive us. It is for this reason Sartre claims that 'hell is other people' and stresses that one must embrace the human condition which presents the possibility to change one's character and choose for oneself (1989: 45).[3] It is one's choice of project that then gives meaning to all of one's subsequent actions and desires. That is, one's decisions and how one perceives objects and one's situation are shaped by and orientated towards one's fundamental project. As Sartre explains, '[it is] this

---

[3] In his early work, Sartre's theory of recognition suggests that the other's gaze is objectifying. However, in his later work, particularly *The Critique of Dialectical Reason*, his position is closer to Hegel, to the extent that he develops an intersubjective account of recognition, akin the of the master/slave dialect.

projection of myself toward an original possibility, which causes the existence of values, appeals, expectations, and in general a world' (2013: 63). Thus, one's choice precedes the reasons for pursuing that project which determines one's character and gives meaning to one's life. In his own words, 'what we usually understand by "will" is a conscious decision that most of us take only after we have made ourselves what we are' (2007: 23). One consequence of Sartre's theory of freedom is that one is able to freely change the project which shapes one's behaviour.

Maurice Merleau-Ponty takes issue with this consequence of Sartre's theory of freedom and the dimension of choice itself.[4] The reason is because the act of rejecting one's project and engaging in a new project for no reason at all undermines the very concept of projects themselves. For if one can willingly change projects then it makes no sense to talk of undertaking or maintaining a project, since one cannot be committed to anything. In Merleau-Ponty's account, on the other hand, 'we must recognize a sort of sedimentation of our life: when an attitude toward the world has been confirmed often enough, it becomes privileged for us' (2012: 467). Contrary to Sartre, the notion which Merleau-Ponty advocates is that one's freedom is restricted to one's physical abilities and social context. Thus, rather than possessing absolute freedom of mind, one is only free to the extent that one's society and biology permit. These then constitute a 'field of freedom', which determines one's range of possibilities and the degree to which each possibility can be actualized (2012: 481). One's ability to form a project for Merleau-Ponty is restricted by one's material and social environment, and the degree to which these enable one to realize one's project. Thus, not only is Merleau-Ponty's account contrary to that of Sartre but also has profound implications for his notion of undertaking or maintaining a project. However, one need not necessarily accept Merleau-Ponty's notion of freedom in order to preserve a consistent theory of projects.

In order to remedy this oversight, and patch a hole in Sartre's argument, Simone de Beauvoir borrows the idea of 'sedimentation' from Merleau-Ponty.[5] However, rather than accepting Merleau-Ponty's perspective of freedom – that one does not possess absolute autonomy of mind, but that one's ability to act is determined by

---

[4] Although Sartre, Beauvoir and Merleau-Ponty jointly edited the journal *Les Temps Moderne*, Sartre published a segment of his book on communism without first consulting Merleau-Ponty. According to Jonathan Webber, 'This was the start of a series of infractions and breaches of collegial etiquette that increased the tension between them until Merleau-Ponty resigned from the journal a year later.' *Rethinking Existentialism* (Oxford: Oxford University Press, 2018), 57.

[5] Beauvoir makes evident that Merleau-Ponty's critique of Sartre is valid in a review of *The Phenomenology of Perception* by Maurice Merleau-Ponty in Simone de Beauvoir, *Philosophical Writings*, ed. Margaret A. Simons (Urbana: University of Illinois Press, 2004), 159–64.

one's material and social situation – Beauvoir adapts the idea of sedimentation to Sartre's notion of freedom. She suggests that one's project becomes 'sedimented' over time – namely, the longer one engages in a project the more closely it becomes associated with one's person, and the more difficult it is to reject. The reason why it is important for Beauvoir to maintain this theory of freedom is because it emphasizes a notion of responsibility which Merleau-Ponty's theory lacks. In responding to this criticism of Sartre's radical freedom, Beauvoir maintains the claim that authenticity requires freedom to choose one's project. In her own words, 'I am free, as my projects are not defined by pre-existing interests' (2004a: 212). What Beauvoir proposes is that through commitment to a particular project that project becomes indicative of who one is as an individual. That is, the longer one pursues a particular project, the more ingrained it becomes in one's consciousness, determining one's secondary decisions and choices.

Thus, a fundamental feature of the concept of authenticity, thus far construed, is that a project is made meaningful by *commitment* to one's ideal. This commitment to one's project, as constitutive of one's identity, can be elucidated through Beauvoir's metaphysical novel, *She Came to Stay*. Her story depicts the unconventional relationship between Françoise and Pierre, who, despite their fondness for one another, agree to an arrangement which permits the other to pursue additional romantic interests.[6] However, despite both agreeing to these terms, Françoise begins to experience anxiety at the prospect of Pierre's intimacy with Xavière. One's initial reaction to her behaviour might be to suggest that Françoise is emotionally incapable of seeing her partner with another woman. However, this is not the first time Pierre has exercised the conditions of their agreement, and Françoise herself admits to being attracted to Xavière. An alternative interpretation, which explains the reason for her reaction, is that Françoise and Pierre share a common project and set of values that Xavière undermines.

Although Françoise and Pierre believed they had obtained freedom from convention, Xavière claims that their lives are no different to the tediously regimented lives, which they believed they had escaped (2006). However, it is not simply Xavière's critique of their shared project, but Pierre's favourable reception to it which causes Françoise's anguish. As Jonathan Webber explains, 'Pierre's admiration for Xavière indicates that he has not been committed to their shared values in the same way that she has been, the way that she thought he had been. For if he had, then those values

---

[6] The biographical nature of this novel, depicting Sartre and Beauvoir's relationship with their student Olga Kosakilwewicz, is made evident by Hazel Rowley in *Tete-a-tete: Simone de Beauvoir and Jean-Paul Sartre* (New York: HarperCollins, 2005), 416, and Dierdre Blair's *Simone de Beauvoir: A Biography* (London: Cape, 1990), 718.

would now be as sedimented in his outlook as in hers' (2018: 64). Thus, although both have chosen this project of an open relationship, only Françoise is committed to it. This is problematic because in Françoise's commitment to their supposedly shared project and values, it became sediment within her, and was something with which she identified. However, Pierre brings this project into question through his lack of commitment. His rejection of these values is therefore a threat not only to their relationship but also to Françoise's very identity itself. In this section, we have portrayed the dimensions of *choice* and *commitment*, both of which arose in order to explain that which determines our authentic self.

3.2 How can we ensure our ideal is achievable?

One serious problem with the account of authenticity thus far elaborated, which Charles Guignon and Somogy Varga raise, is the concern that one's project may be unrealizable. That is, what if one reverently pursues a particular project and fails to achieve one's goal? Guignon argues that not only is this a possible outcome but also 'for many people, the quest for authenticity has turned out to be a setup for disappointment and failure' (2004: 8). In order to elucidate the concern that one may fail to become that which one has devoted one's life to becoming, Guignon focuses specifically on the modern cult of 'self-help'. He notes that many self-proclaimed 'gurus' promise the means to an authentic existence but deliver only disappointment. Self-help can be seen as synonymous with authenticity insofar as they both aim towards the same end of realizing one's 'true self'.

However, the supposed emancipatory ideals which self-help guides espouse advocate the author's own ideological bias which is often incompatible with those seeking help. The consequence, as Guignon explains, is that 'many of those who start out thinking their lives are empty or directionless end up either lost in the mind-set of a particular program or feeling they are "never good enough" no matter what they do' (2008: 9). In this case, the consequence of self-help programmes is that they result in the opposite of that which they are intended to achieve. In this instance, one who pursues an authentic existence is destined to fail because one does not actively choose one's life for oneself, but follows a pre-established set of norms. Thus, whilst superficially similar, self-help and authenticity are two distinct notions. The former provides an ideological formula, a paint-by-numbers approach to self-fulfilment. Authenticity, on the other hand, does not offer any such framework which one must adhere to, but requires that one determine this by oneself.

Although one may object that authenticity and self-help are two very different approaches, Somogy Varga develops Guignon's line of thought further, making a connection between the pursuit of an authentic existence and the rise of diagnosed cases of depression. Varga claims that 'depression occurs more frequently in individuals who pursue unobtainable goals and have difficulties in capitulating when it comes to status struggle' (2012: 155). This itself is not controversial and seems relatively intuitive. However, Varga makes the argument that the concept of authenticity, which was once a response to mass society, has paradoxically become a prerequisite for capitalism. That is, 'individuals are called upon to "invent themselves" in a way that facilitates flexible production' (2012: 150). It is this particular 'performative' model of authenticity which Varga links with the epidemic rise of depression. His claim, then, is that the attempt to fulfil the institutional demands of authenticity creates the social precondition that leads to the exhaustion of the self. Under the performative model of authenticity, Varga claims 'the constant activity of performing authenticity may at least explain some of the preconditions under which a rapid rise in the frequency of depression and sales of pharmaceutical anti-depressants becomes intelligible' (2012: 154).[7]

An apt response to this apparent problem is proposed by Alessandro Ferrara, who suggests that one can determine what is beyond one's capacity through 'maturity'. For Ferrara, maturity is a form of *phronesis* which emphasizes knowledge of oneself in the world. Unlike the Kantian concept which emphasizes intellectual independence and responsibility, Ferrara defines maturity as 'realism in conceiving one's ideals and as a capacity to emotionally accept one's limitations' (1998: 103). Immaturity, on the other hand, Ferrara tells us, is a consequence of '*indulgence in wishful thinking*' (1998: 100). To be mature, in Ferrara's account, is therefore to align one's ideal self with one's capacities. It is this concept which prevents one from constructing an unrealizable project which will ultimately fail. Applying Ferrara's argument to Varga's concern, the performance of authenticity will not lead to exhaustion or depression because maturity requires reflection and knowledge of self, which will prevent one from undertaking an unachievable project. Thus, whilst Guignon and Varga both illustrate a difficulty in obtaining authenticity, the dimension of *maturity* enables one to overcome this problem. Through application of Ferrara's concept of maturity, one can aptly illustrate that this is not a problem with the concept of authenticity per se, but the individual's inability to reflect upon who they truly

---

[7] The paradox which both Guignon and Varga allude to, that authenticity which was initially a means of resisting mass society has been commodified to a necessary feature of capitalism, will be addressed in Chapter 7.

are. Thus, a further dimension of authenticity is that in order for one's choice to be authentic it must be the result of *mature* decision.

A concrete example of this can be explicated through the life of the Japanese novelist, Mishima Yukio, who had enlisted to join the military as a youth, though being deemed physically unfit for service. Although he radically improved his health in his later years through weightlifting, karate and kendo, his immature desire to fight for the glory of the Japanese Empire consumed him.[8] After the surrender of the Imperial Japanese military in 1945, Mishima continued to possess romantic yearnings and assembled a militia of disillusioned youths. His small force then marched on the National Defence Force's headquarters and attempted a coup d'état which culminated in Mishima performing *seppukku*, or ritual suicide. However, one would not be willing to claim that Mishima's life was an authentic one because he acted out of nostalgia for a past which was no longer present and attempted to fashion himself into something which was beyond his capacity. To avoid endorsing such a project, it was argued that one ought to be mature enough to comprehend the limits of one's abilities. Nietzsche cleverly summarizes the futility of an immature decision through the following epigram: 'whoever does not know the approach to find the way to his ideal lives more frivolously than one who does not have an ideal' (1991: §133). Thus, as illustrated, although one may have made a free choice and was committed to one's project, it was still possible to fail to live up to one's ideal, and that to do so could lead to negative psychological implications. Thus, through the dimension of *maturity* we are able to avoid the pursuit of a project which we are able to actualize.

3.3 Where do our choices derive from?

A more fundamental issue with which authenticity must contend is the problem of decisionism, as posed by Charles Guignon.[9] What this entails is that there are no grounds to justify or validate our decisions. Moreover, that any decision to

---

[8] This is evident through Mishima's non-fictional writings. In his commentary on *Hagakure*, an eighteenth-century samurai handbook, Mishima glorifies the ascetic mind-set of the samurai, and their orientation towards death. *Mishima on Hagakure: The Samurai Ethic and Modern Japan* (London: Penguin, 1979). Likewise, in his autobiography he idealizes himself as a warrior through his practice of martial arts which he portrays as a balance to rectify the 'corruption of words' *Sun and Steel* (New York: Kodansha, 2003).

[9] This criticism of decisionism was originally charged against Heidegger by Karl Löwith who argues that Heidegger's discussion of resoluteness commits him to an indefensible position in which resolute *Dasein* is said to choose who it will be without recourse to any reasons or evaluative standards. Karl Löwith, *Martin Heidegger and European Nihilism*, ed. R. Wolin (New York: Columbia University Press, 1995), pp. 33–68, 159–66, 211–25, 4.

embark upon a particular project is entirely arbitrary. Ultimately, this problem reduces to the claim that there are no real grounds to one's choice. In his own words, Guignon states there are 'innumerable ways we might constitute ourselves in imparting a narrative shape to our lives and there are neither inner nor outer criteria that tell us whether our life story is truly worth living' (2004: 142). Thus, it would appear that one consequence of becoming the author of one's own life is that there are no real reasons for one's preferences, and as such, any choice is fundamentally groundless. The consequence of one's decision lacking a foundation is that any attempt to justify it necessarily results in an eternal regress. In self-fashioning one does exactly that – partaking in a narrative of one's own devising. As Guignon explains, 'if *any* story can be mine, then no story is *really* mine. When we recognise the multiplicity of stories we can tell and the ultimate arbitrariness of every choice of storyline, we can begin to sense the utter groundlessness of any attempt at self-formation' (2004: 143). Thus, in order to avoid a reduction of one's decision to none other than personal preference, it is necessary to modify the account of authenticity so that there is a ground to one's choice.

One means of surmounting this problem is to define the drive to obtain authenticity as Nietzsche does, as 'becoming what one is' (2007: II 9). At first thought, this injunction appears to incite the reader to discover an inner essence to be made manifest. This, however, is not Nietzsche's intention. This is evident in the claim that 'we, however, want to become who we are, human beings who are new, unique, incomparable, who give themselves laws, who *create* themselves!' (1991: §335). Thus, rather than self-discovery, Nietzsche's maxim seems to suggest self-fashioning. This, however, appears to result in a paradox, since in order to become what one is, one first has to create oneself. In creating oneself, one is thus determining what one is, rather than becoming what one already is. As Alexander Nehamas notes, it is problematic 'how that self can be what one is before it comes into being itself, before it is itself something that is' (1983: 393). How then is one to understand this dictum? In *Ecce Homo* – which should be seen as 'Nietzsche's own interpretation of his development, his works, and his significance' (Kaufmann 2017: 201) – it is claimed that one becomes what one is unconsciously, through an overarching, organizing idea. In his own words:

> To become what one is, one must not have the slightest notion of what one is. . . . The whole surface of consciousness – consciousness is a surface – must be kept clear of all great imperatives. . . . Meanwhile the organizing 'idea' that is destined to rule keeps growing deep down – it begins to command; slowly it leads us back from side roads and wrong roads; it prepares single qualities and fitnesses that will one day prove to be indispensable as a means towards the whole – one by

one, it trains all subservient capacities before giving any hint of the dominant task, 'goal', 'aim', or 'meaning'. (2007: II 9)

Nietzsche is not suggesting an essential self, which is discovered, but one which is formed and emerges unconsciously. This, however, seems to contradict the dimension of choice which was introduced in the first section. For if one becomes something unconsciously then it would appear that one does not have the freedom to choose. Again, one can appeal to Nietzsche, specifically to the idea of the 'greatest weight' as discussed in Section 1.4. The question which this thought experiment poses is: If one were to be forced to eternally relive one's life, would one be willing to affirm it?[10] For Nietzsche, it is the ability to say 'yes' to the eternal recurrence of the same, to love one's fate, which denotes that one has lived a genuine existence. However, although the greatest weight inhibits one's choice, one could conjecture that it does not coerce one into accepting one's fate. If one's response to the eternal recurrence of the same were 'no', then one is free to pursue an alternative project.

Although Nietzsche asks his reader to affirm one's decisions, one's decisions are constitutive of who one is as an individual, even when these do not conform to one's contemporary outlook. As Nietzsche himself suggests, 'something you formerly loved as a truth or a probability now strikes you as an error; you cast it off and believe your reason has made a victory. But maybe that error was as necessary for you then, when you were still another person – you are always another person-as all your present "truth"' (1991: §307). Thus, becoming what one is, which Nietzsche advocates, is presented as a form of self-narrative, incorporating every aspect of oneself. On his account, then, what one *is* results from an act of creation, and what gives this act validity is that one is willing to affirm it eternally. In short, what gives one's choice foundation is that one wants to be what one becomes. In responding to Guignon's challenge, the basis for one's choice is not without foundation, but given grounds in one's ability to eternally affirm that choice as constitutive of who one is as an individual.

This dimension of authenticity, that one's choice can be given grounds as a consequence of becoming what one is, can be aptly illustrated through Oscar Wilde's only novel *The Picture of Dorian Gray*. At the outset of the novel, the protagonist, Dorian, is portrayed as an innocent, naïve and impressionable

---

[10] For the argument concerning the eternal reoccurrence as a thought experiment, as opposed to a cosmological hypothesis about the nature of the universe, see Aaron Ridley, 'Nietzsche's Greatest Weight', *Journal of Nietzsche Studies*, no. 14 (Autumn 1997): 19-25.

young man. And although he sits for Basil Hallwards's portrait, it is to Lord Henry that he becomes a subject. As a result of Dorian's susceptibility, Henry convinces him that youth and beauty are the only things worth possessing. By instilling a fear of finitude within Dorian, Henry then introduces him to a hedonistic lifestyle. Lord Henry continues to exercise his influence over Dorian, to the extent that Dorian recognizes the impact he has had upon his words and actions, informing Henry, 'that is one of your aphorisms. I am putting it into practice as I do everything you say' (1991a: 47). Despite Dorian's indulgence in a decadent lifestyle, towards the end of the novel he comes to realize that his life has been one of moral decay. However, rather than accepting that which he has become as his inner essence, he chooses not to affirm his concurrent lifestyle. On the contrary, he takes responsibility for his life by destroying the painting and in doing so, reveals his true image.[11]

In confronting the problem of decisionism, that there was no real ground to one's choice, it thus seemed that this may simply be the result of none other than personal preference. The reason why choice appeared arbitrary was because any attempt to justify one's decision was supported by another choice and so on, ad infinitum. In order to avoid this problem, it was suggested that one's choice can be grounded through 'becoming what one is', that is, to accept one's actions by willing them. By willing one's actions one thus shows that one wants to become what one will become. Since it was this choice which made one an individual, this criticism posed a major threat to the concept of authenticity. However, through the dimension of *becoming what one is* we are able to circumvent the claim that one's choice is groundless. It is therefore this ensemble of willed actions and one's project which constitute not only what is unique to an individual but also that which provides a foundation for their choice. Individuals may not have any choice over that which they unconsciously become, but one has the choice to affirm or reject one's project.

3.4 What validates our choices?

One of the primary criticisms of the existentialist account is that their pursuit of an authentic self is a subjective and purely narcissistic endeavour. It is perceived as a pretext to 'be what you want' and 'do what you like', emphasizing freedom

---

[11] For further elaboration of the connotations of authenticity in *The Picture of Dorian Gray*, see Shuttleworth, 'An Existential Interpretation of the Picture of Dorian Gray: A Heideggerian Perspective', (2019).

from objective judgement. This has also led commentators to question whether the existentialist account of authenticity has any ethical application. On the one hand, critics like Mary Warnock claim '[it is] doubtful whether it can be claimed that there is any direct contribution to philosophy which should be described as Existentialist ethics' (1970: 57). On the other hand, there are those who see authenticity as an existential ethical ideal. Marjorie Grene, for example, claims 'what the existentialist admires is not the happiness of a man's life, the goodness of his disposition, or the rightness of his acts but the authenticity of his existence. This is, I think, the unique contribution of existentialism to ethical theory' (1952: 266). Although the account under construction is not an existentialist one per se, the task here will be to illustrate that it provides us with an ethical ideal, and one which is capable of circumventing any criticisms of immorality.

The necessity to establish an ethic of authenticity is because if it truly lacks an ethical dimension, one could end up establishing an ethically and morally undesirable project. Thus, in order to overcome this dilemma, it must be shown that authenticity does not permit the attainment of negative ethical standards. The problem, however, is perpetuated by the existential advocates themselves. Martin Heidegger, who concerned himself primarily with ontology, denounced any moral implications within his thought, instead suggesting that '[ethics] begin to flourish only when ordinary thinking comes to an end' (1993: 219). Sartre, in following Heidegger, likewise suggested that his thought was ethically neutral and that 'ontology itself cannot formulate ethical precepts. It is concerned solely with what is, and we cannot possibly derive imperatives from ontology's indicatives' (2013: 645). Rather than a normative account, Heidegger and Sartre both suggest that they are instead simply presenting a formal account of authenticity. This, however, is an ethically naïve approach since there can be no such thing as a philosophically non-ethical or neutral claim as regards human existence. The very language with which Sartre attempts to articulate his formal account of authenticity is itself morally infused. Bad faith, for example, contains an ethical judgement insofar as it posits this particular mode of existence as undesirable. Moreover, in claiming his philosophy is non-ethical he is establishing an ethical claim.

This criticism can also be extended to Heidegger, for whom authenticity is portrayed as not only desirable but also the correct mode of existence. In his account there are two forms of existence: authentic (*Eigentlichkeit*) and inauthentic (*Uneigentlichkeit*). In Heidegger's analysis, *Dasein* exists for the most part inauthentically.[12] This is a result of values which are externally imposed by

---

[12] Distinct from consciousness, Heidegger claims that *Dasein* (literally being-there) is neither subjective nor objective but being-in-the-world. He further defines it by stating *Dasein* is 'that entity

that which Heidegger terms *das Man* or '*the One*'. Suggestive of a form of social conformity, Heidegger notes that 'we take pleasure and enjoy ourselves as *das Man* take pleasure; we read, see, and judge about literature and art as *das Man* see and judge' (2010: §127). In everyday existence, *Dasein*'s actions are influenced by the idle talk of *das Man*. A consequence is that one's death is presented as something to be feared rather than confronted.[13] However, Heidegger notes that death is one's own-most possibility, insofar as it is non-relational and not to be outstripped. As something which *Dasein* must experience by itself, Heidegger claims that it enables one to discover one's authentic existence. It is only through a call of conscience that one gains awareness of one's own-most, authentic self.

Authenticity is thus a relative term, insofar as it is only encountered in relation to inauthenticity. In Heidegger's account, then, an inauthentic existence is one in which one's own-most possibility is concealed. In order to live a truly authentic life, one must therefore oppose 'the dictatorship of *das Man*' which conceals *Dasein*'s own mode of being. By suggesting that one's values are determined by others, which one must reject in order to obtain authenticity, Heidegger seems to reject the horizon from within which one is fostered. However, as will be argued later, all value judgements are a product of one's community. Furthermore, he appears to offer a prescriptive account of being, which would suggest that inauthentic existence is something to be overcome, which is itself an ethical claim.[14]

A more lucid articulation of this argument is made by Watsuji Tetsurō, who offers not only a critique of Heidegger's concept of authenticity but also individualistic accounts of ethics in general.[15] Watsuji begins with a critique of the perspective that Western culture, in virtue of being predominantly individual, is superior to the communal structure of Asian societies. However, rather than arguing in favour of a communal approach, as one might expect, Watsuji claims both perspectives are fundamentally flawed. The negative

---

which in its Being has this very Being as an issue'. *Being and Time*, trans. John Macquarrie and John Robinson (Oxford: Blackwell, 2005), 68.

[13] For an analysis of the phenomenology of death, see Shuttleworth, 'The Role of Death within the Phenomenologies of Hegel and Heidegger' (2013).

[14] Despite Heidegger's self-professed ethical neutrality, there have been several attempts to interpret and import an ethic into his thought. These include, but are not limited to, Joanna Hodge's *Heidegger and Ethics* (1995), Lawrence J. Hatab's *Ethics and Finitude: Heideggerian Contributions to Moral Philosophy* (2000), Frederick J. Olafson's *Heidegger and the Ground of Ethics: A Study of Mitsein* (2008), David Webb's *Heidegger, Ethics, and the Practice of Ontology* (2011), and Michael Lewis, *Heidegger and the Place of Ethics* (2013).

[15] Although Watsuji received a letter of introduction to Heidegger he never redeemed it. He was, however, living in Germany when *Being and Time* was published and worked through the German text, with his criticisms leading to the publication of his first major philosophical text, *Climate and Culture*.

structure of human existence (*ningen sonzai* 人間存在), according to Watsuji, is that to be an individual one must rebel against the whole, whilst to adhere to the whole one must relinquish one's independence as an individual. In light of this, Watsuji's suggestion condemns both approaches, instead positing the alternative of *double negation*, by which he means the negation of both one's individuality and community. His reason for doing so is because 'both individuals and the whole subsist not in themselves, but only in the relationship of each with the other' (1996: 101). That is, to be an individual, or to solely identify with one's society, is to negate the betweenness which makes one human (人間). What Watsuji is presenting is therefore an intersubjective account of ethics.

Whilst Heidegger's approach to authenticity was achieved through distancing oneself from *das Man,* for Watsuji the negation of one's community is a one-sided approach to existence. As Yasuo Yuasa explains, '*Dasein* is grasped with an emphasis on its individuality and without sufficiently considering the social relationship between the self and others' (1987: 169). In Watsuji's own words, 'what Heidegger calls *authenticity* is, in reality, inauthenticity. And when this in-authenticity becomes further negated through this nondual relation of self and other, that is to say, when the "self" becomes annihilated, only then is authenticity realised' (1996: 225). Watsuji's 'concept of authenticity'[16] thus suggests that one can only know one's true self in relation to one's community, and the only means to achieve this is to affirm neither aspect but reject both. The ontological foundation of this claim is derived from the Buddhist concept of nothingness. To obtain authenticity (*honraisei* 本来性) for Watsuji is to know 'one's true countenance before the birth of one's own parents' (1996: 187).[17] This, however, is a rather abstract concept and one which is all too foreign to a Western audience. What Watsuji is attempting to do is to posit a Buddhist concept of authenticity which claims that there is something essential which one is and that realization of this leads to an authentic existence. However, one must question if Watsuji is correct to suggest an essentialist approach, and whether his concept of authenticity is a viable one.

An essentialist approach to authenticity, which we earlier associated with Rousseau and the romantics (2.3), was rejected on the grounds that we now live within a post-metaphysical culture; however, it is problematic for more practical reasons. One issue which Varga flags is that such a 'model of authenticity relies on

---

[16] For the arguments surrounding Watsuji's 'concept of authenticity', see Shuttleworth, 'Watsuji's Concept of Authenticity' (2019).
[17] This phrase is derived from the famous Zen *koan* 'without thinking good or evil, in this moment, what is your Original Face?' *The Gateless Gate.*

the assumption of an inner-directed mechanism whereby we have "privileged" perceptual access to our inner states' (2012: 62). Within this 'inner sense' model, one's mental states, which Ferrara refers to as 'a kind of psychological DNA', are understood as stable entities that await introspective discovery through self-reflection (1998: 53). However, Varga notes that 'the idea is flawed because one cannot simply detect an *independently obtaining* state of mind' (2012: 64). That is, it is impossible to discover one's essential self through reflection because who we are is constituted by conflicting wishes and desires. As Varga further elucidates, 'the fact that a particular wish (desire, etc.) is stronger than others does not warrant regarding it as more expressive of ourselves than any of the other less resilient ones' (2012: 68). Thus, one is not able to determine one's 'true self' through privileged access to one's propositional attitudes because what one discovers is not a permanent state. Although an essentialist account fails to locate a fixed inner essence, the intersubjective vision which Watsuji suggests can be upheld in absence of such.

This is precisely the position which is advocated by Charles Taylor through his concepts of dialogical-selves and horizon of significance. To recap on the account articulated in Section 2.5, for Taylor, we do not develop on our own but only through our interactions with others. As he explains, 'my discovering my own identity doesn't mean that I work it out in isolation, but that I negotiate it through dialogue, partly overt, partly internal, with others. My own identity crucially depends on my dialogical relations with others' (1989: 36). However, these need not be physical dialogues, but also include imagined conversations. One might imagine what advice one's late grandfather would give regarding a course of action, or be remorseful of one's behaviour having imagined one's mother's reaction. What is important in Taylor's account, as Ruth Abbey explains, is that 'the idea of the dialogical self points to [. . .] a psychological blurring of boundaries between self and other' (2000: 68). Thus, on Taylor's approach, our identity is not chosen in isolation, but is informed by our society as a whole.

In conjunction with his concept of dialogue, Taylor emphasizes that since we do not develop in monologue, but are shaped by our interactions with others, things gain importance or significance against a horizon of significance.[18] In his own words, 'my identity is defined by the commitments and identifications which provide the frame or horizon within which I can try to determine from case to case what is good, or valuable, or what ought to be done, or what I endorse

---

[18] Taylor is here influenced by Hans Georg Gadamer's 'Fusion of Horizons', *Truth and Method,* trans. Joel Weinsheimer and Donald G. Marshall (London: Continuum, 2004), 302.

or oppose. In other words, it is the horizon within which I am capable of taking a stand' (1989: 26). However, to claim that our society limits our choices does not adequately illustrate the extent of our limitations, our capacities for self-realization and historical determination.

There are simply some possibilities which are not available to modern individuals. A modern Homeric hero, such as Achilles, vowing to destroy an opposing nation for the glory of his city would not be conceived of as a hero. Although we can think of narrow-minded nationalists who would romanticize such an ideal, the general consensus would be that the person in question is nothing but a cold-blooded murderer. Likewise, we cannot conceive of a medieval saint, such as Joan of Arc, in twenty-first-century Europe. Were one to proclaim to possess a direct link to God and be an instrument of divine action, it is doubtful whether even the church itself would believe the person in question; rather, we would imagine that they would be referred to a psychiatric ward. However, one might object that these are pre-modern notions of the good, and as such, this is the reason why they are not genuine possibilities for a modern individual. The hero was a desirable character in ancient Greece because they sustained the autonomy of their *polis* and way of life of its citizens. The saint was likewise upheld as an archetype to emulate because they epitomized the values of the church, which were predominant within medieval Europe. There is, however, a more concise explanation.

To revisit the example of Mishima Yukio attempting to cultivate himself into a modern-day samurai, we can appeal to a criticism which John Horton levels against the protagonist of Jim Jarmusch's film, *Ghost Dog*. The motion-picture depicts a modern assassin who lives according to *bushido*, or the 'way of the samurai'. However, Horton's claim is that 'the social context for such a life is entirely absent. He cannot adopt the identity of a samurai because such a way of life is not a genuinely meaningful option in late-twentieth-century, urban America. At best, he can adopt a few ersatz approximations of some features of such a life' (2010: 181). Thus, in both examples of Mishima and *Ghost Dog*, the reason why their lives are conceived of as disingenuous is because, despite being freely chosen and committed, their choices were not genuine, mature possibilities which are afforded by their social context. As Horton exemplifies, 'it is the meanings afforded by our language, culture and history that determine the social possibilities that are available to us. Only some ways of living and understanding ourselves make sense in the societies in which we live' (2005: 180).

To exemplify this claim, that our choices are historically limited, we can think of modern social trends, such as bohemians, hippies and punk-rockers.

In these examples, we would likewise agree that to attempt to cultivate oneself in accordance with the fashion or values of one of these trends would be inauthentic. One reason, as expressed by David Boyle, is that people attempt to 'buy in' to these trends. As Boyle himself makes explicit,

> every generation since has dressed differently from the last – even if they didn't dress differently from each other. They believed in self-actualization, and struggled against becoming subsumed in the nine-to-five workaday world. But it is an ironic paradox that gets sharper with every new generation: they are increasingly lured by marketing into the consumer world in order to afford to buy themselves the badges and outfits of revolt – but the further they get drawn in, and the more they spend, the more they find themselves part of the very world they were trying to break free from. (2004: 114)

A more specific reason why such trends have become commodified, and why it is no longer authentic to fashion oneself in such a way, is because the conditions that once made these options historically meaningful and authentic have changed. That is, it was possible to be an authentic punk in the 1970s, for example, but not now. To expand on this, the reason why these projects can no longer be considered authentic is because in each case they were reactions to social oppression at a specific time.[19] Since the conditions which made these projects meaningful no longer exist, to attempt to fashion oneself in accordance with an outdated social trend is but nostalgia for a past one never experienced. Although this could be explained through the dimensions of maturity and intersubjective consciousness – that one has not realistically conceived of the possibilities present within one's social context – this does not sufficiently address the issue, and as such, a historical dimension is required.

However, the question arises as to why we can omit such possibilities as those which no longer exist, yet permit those which do not yet exist? Let us imagine Sartre's student has decided his country needs him more than his mother and has formed a project to become a resistance fighter, in what way can this be considered authentic? To follow from the examples of bohemians, hippies and punks, it can be inferred that this is a reaction to social injustice. To expand on this, social movements are ephemeral because there are certain factors which make them possible, such as corruption, and loss of autonomy and identity. These consequences lead to the realization that authenticity is not a state which one permanently attains, a level which we arrive at, akin to the concept of Buddhist

---

[19] Mass society in the case of the bohemians, senseless consumption and violence for the hippies, and the 'establishment' for the punks.

Enlightenment. Rather, we may have been living an authentic existence, but due to political circumstances, or personal relationships, one is no longer able, or willing, to actualize that state of existence. Authenticity is therefore not a static, fixed mode of existence but requires constant attention and readjustment. This point is aptly illustrated by Beauvoir in her novel *The Mandarins*, where her characters Robert and Henri demonstrate their support for communism in response to the horrors of Nazism. However, they are faced with difficulties, and their positions then shift after the discovery of Russian gulags.[20]

Both of these aspects, of socio-historical conditions and the temporality of authenticity, can be expressed by Martin Heidegger's concept of 'heritage'. What this entails is that we derive the content of our lives from our personal and social heritage.[21] As Heidegger explains, 'the resoluteness with which *Dasein* comes back to itself, discloses current factual possibilities of authentic existing, and discloses them as that heritage which that resoluteness as *thrown*, takes over' (2010: §383). In other words, *Dasein* 'historicizes', that is takes on certain aspects of traditions that it has received and reconfigures them in order to found a new mode of Being. Heidegger calls this process 'repetition' and a 'handing over', which constitutes the 'fate' and 'destiny' of *Dasein* (2005: §386). Thus, those genuine possibilities which can be authentically manifested are made available by our own contemporary surroundings. From what has been claimed earlier, we thus ought to supplement Heidegger concept of 'heritage' with the injunction that when social conditions facilitate a loss of agency or threaten to destroy a particular way of life, the possibilities for counter-movements emerge and determine the conditions which permit whether a project is authentic or inauthentic.

3.5 Meaning

Now that we have illustrated how authenticity can be understood as an ethical ideal, attention will be turned to demonstrating a consequence of the six dimensions of our socio-existential approach, which enables one to respond to the problem of meaning. To recapitulate the problem, in Chapter 1 it was stated that there were

---

[20] It has been argued that Beauvoir is here representing the ideological feud and eventual unravelling of the friendship between Sartre (Robert) and Camus (Henri). See Ruth Kitchen's 'From Shame Towards an Ethics of Ambiguity', *Sartre Studies International* 19, no. 1 (2013): 55–70.

[21] Contrary to traditionalism or conservativism, which emphasize the commitment to maintain traditional cultural beliefs and values, and which oppose change, we will employ the concept of heritage in a much more restricted sense. The manner in which we will use 'heritage' is simply to refer to the limitations imposed upon us by our historical context.

three major developments which led to the historical formation of the modern world view. These were (i) the rise of modern science, which Weber describes as disenchantment, (ii) the emergence of Protestantism, which focused on the inner self and emphasized *contemptus mundi*, and (iii) the Enlightenment's emphasis on rationality as the teleological end of human civilization. As a combined result of these, there occurred a levelling of the 'great chain of being', which had previously determined the function and place of things and how people ought to act. The consequence of this loss was one of disorientation and displacement, with humanity no longer occupying a fixed place within the universe. The purpose which humans had previously believed to be their natural end had thus been lost, and for those who understood the logical implications of these vicissitudes, life appeared to be meaningless. It is precisely this problem, of freedom and meaning, which this book will engage with – namely, to overcome the nihilistic implications of the loss of natural teleology and the compartmentalization of the modern individual's personal identity. In what way then, is our socio-existential approach to authenticity able to respond to this predicament?

In order to explain how one can live a meaningful life, it will be helpful to provide a concrete account of what an authentic existence looks like. Let us imagine one whose project is to become an academic. According to the first dimension, one must have chosen this career path for themselves, rather than being pressured into doing so, for example, because one's parents were academics and one was encouraged to pursue this profession. Secondly, one must also be committed to this vocation. In order to elucidate, consider two people who desire a career in academia. The first attends university, pursues postgraduate studies and begins a PhD. The second reads *Nausea* and decides spur of moment that they wish to become an academic. Using this analogy to illuminate Beauvoir's point, to relinquish one's project of becoming an academic would be a much more difficult choice to make for the person who has obtained the necessary qualifications than for the person who has not already committed their life to realizing their project. Thirdly, in order to ensure one's project is realistic, one must have maturely analysed one's physical and mental capacities. If one does not possess the mental stamina to conduct research, or is unable to communicate one's ideas coherently, then to pursue a career in academia which requires these abilities will not be a project which one can fulfil.

Fourthly, what provides a foundation for one's choice is that one must not only be able to accept that one has become an academic but also be willing to eternally affirm one's vocation. That is, one must not only be naturally inclined towards academia but also enact these abilities through teaching and research.

Fifthly, one's project cannot be simply subjective. One does not just become an academic for the social status of being a 'doctor', or for the accomplishment of having published a book. This cannot be a subjective affair because the concept of 'doctor' only gains significance from the fact that other people recognize it as an achievement; moreover, in publishing, one has an intellectual impact upon those who read it. Furthermore, one's area of expertise is derived from within an existing field which one contributes to. Finally, we must recognize that current modes of existence are inauthentic because they are untimely and also that authenticity is not a fixed state, but can be lost through the change in social and personal situations. That is, one may have fulfilled the previous criteria and lived as an authentic academic, however, the outbreak of war may require one to leave one's position and instead contribute towards the war effort.

In what way can this account of authenticity enable the modern individual to live a meaningful life? One aspect which has been hinted towards, but not fully elucidated, is the cohesive nature of one's project which brings unity to one's lesser projects. As already noted, one's project is tied up with one's identity. That is, in forming a project one also determines what one is. To continue with the example of the would-be academic, in terms of commitment, the completion of a PhD, publication of research papers, a lecturing position and teaching, all add to the sedimentation and entwinement of one's identity to academia. Likewise, if they were to immaturely pursue their studies to doctoral level, but fail their viva voce, and thus their PhD, not only will they lose the coherence which their project gave to their life, but they will also experience an existential crisis through the loss of how they identified themselves. These dimensions then constitute one's identity, but more than this, they give it cohesion. This cohesion is exemplified by Nietzsche's concept of becoming what one is, that one's beliefs and values are unconsciously ordered into one meaningful whole. This then engages with the problem of the compartmentalization of the individual, organizing one's lesser projects into a unified identity. Furthermore, this concept of authenticity addresses the loss of natural teleology by affirming one's unified self as that which one has not only become, but freely chosen. In this way, one's existence is given subjective meaning, and as such impedes the onset of nihilism.

3.6 Summary

The aim of this chapter was to provide a formal account of authenticity, explicate its ethical implications, and illustrate how this enables one to live a meaningful life. These aims were achieved through engagement with contemporary literature and with the problems which it poses. Here it was determined that there are six dimensions to our concept of authenticity. The first dimension is *choice*, which entails that one must freely, of one's own accord, choose one's project for oneself (as opposed to socially imposed projects) as exemplified by *The Death of Ivan Ilych*. The second dimension is *commitment*, that one's choice/project is meaningful because one is committed to that project. If one is not committed, then one's choice seems arbitrary and cannot be said to be authentic, as was exemplified through Beauvoir's novel, *She Came to Stay*. The third dimension is *maturity*, which requires that one be aware of one's physical and social restrictions. One's choice may be one's own, and to which one is committed, but unless it is a realistic project which one is capable of fulfilling, then one cannot live an authentic existence, as illustrated through the life of Mishima Yukio. The fourth dimension is *becoming what one is* and emphasized that one must be willing to affirm what one is, and which was given expression through the novel, *The Picture of Dorian Gray*.

The fifth dimension, *intersubjective consciousness*, addressed the charge against the existentialists that their accounts were narcissistic and led to ethically undesirable projects. It was here illustrated that our concept of authenticity was able to circumvent these claims, insofar as individuals develop through dialogue and their choices are given meaning through a shared horizon of intelligibility. It was also shown that one not only chooses from within one's horizon but also contributes towards it. To be conscious of our dialogical development then prevents one from advocating a solipsistic, subjective ethic of the self and making narcissistic decisions. The sixth dimension, *heritage*, enables one to recognize that projects become authentic/inauthentic in accordance with social and personal situations. Through adhering to these dimensions, it was then suggested that one obtains a sense of *meaning*, which illustrated how authenticity provides a cohesive account of personal identity which is capable of overcoming the loss of natural teleology by giving meaning to the individual's existence. Through these six dimensions, we have constructed not only a formal account of authenticity but one which offers an ethical ideal and which responds to the problem of meaning as well. Having achieved the aim outlined at the beginning on this chapter, the next step will be to consider alternative contemporary responses to the problems of modernity, and it is to this task to which we will now turn.

Part Two

Challenges for authenticity

4

Can the Enlightenment project be completed?

The first alternative approach we will consider, which also problematizes modernity in terms of freedom and meaning, is offered by Jürgen Habermas. Heavily influenced by Max Weber, Habermas also argues that the Enlightenment project of rationalization led to decreased freedom and increased meaninglessness. In Habermas's understanding, economic and administrative systems not only were increased through rationalization but also came to impinge upon, or 'colonize', the public and private spheres of the lifeworld. However, unlike Weber, who believed that modern individuals had been subject to mechanized petrification, which was induced by bureaucratic procedures, Habermas holds a more optimistic perspective of modernity. Although the Enlightenment failed to deliver upon its promise of emancipation, Habermas believes that it is nevertheless possible to complete the Enlightenment project. Moreover, he believes that completing the project would resolve the problems of cultural impoverishment and reverse what he has termed the 'colonization of the lifeworld'. In order to achieve this, Habermas's response is to unconceal the form of rationality which underpins communicative practices. What this entails is that the increase in communicative rationality, with the aim of developing free intersubjective interaction, would lead to a properly balanced rationalization of the lifeworld, which would in turn reverse the 'colonization' caused by the systems sphere. In this chapter, however, we will argue that Habermas's approach is unsatisfactory for the reason that it relies upon an unrealistic dichotomy of system and lifeworld, and that he relegates ethics to morality, which leads to a performative contradiction at the heart of his work.

To demonstrate that Habermas does not provide a satisfactory resolution to the loss of meaning and the restriction of freedom, we will begin by outlining his perspective of modernity (Section 4.1). Here it will be illustrated that his understanding of modernity problematizes freedom and meaning in contemporary societies in terms of 'cultural impoverishment' and 'colonization' of the lifeworld. The positive aspect which we will take from our analysis of Habermas is that resistance to the colonization thesis provides the continued possibility of living an authentic existence. In the following section we will address Habermas's resolution to the perceived problem (Section 4.2). Here it will be demonstrated that, believing modernity possesses unfulfilled potential, Habermas suggests we can resolve the problems of freedom and meaning through the realization of communicative action. However, it will be argued that his approach appears to downplay particularity, which is important for the concept of authenticity, insofar as it enables us to live a meaningful existence. Furthermore, his dualism of lifeworld and system will be criticized on the grounds that it proposes an unrealistic restriction of power to systems. We will then turn to the ethical–moral implications of his theory of communicative action (Section 4.3). Here we will argue that his account is subject to a performative contradiction. More specifically, although he prioritizes morality (justice) over ethics (good), his account of morality in fact depends upon a prior conception of the good.

4.1 The project of modernity

In his acceptance speech for the Theodor W. Adorno Award, Jürgen Habermas outlines his philosophical trajectory, and in doing so provides a concise account of the way in which he understands the concept of modernity. Although this term has been employed throughout European history to designate a 'renewed relationship to classical antiquity', Habermas notes that it took on an entirely different meaning in the eighteenth century. As he explains, 'Romanticism produced a radicalised consciousness of modernity that detached itself from all previous historical connection and understood itself solely in abstract opposition to tradition and history as a whole' (1996: 39). The 'project of modernity' which the Enlightenment initiated was one which sought the development of rational science and through which its advocates hoped to provide a foundation for morality, law and art. Furthermore, the common belief which spurred their advancements was not simply to control nature, but to arrive at a deep understanding of the individual and their place within society. However, the Enlightenment project failed to achieve its end, dispelling any optimistic hopes of progress which its advocates may have possessed. According to Habermas, this negative outcome then leaves us with two options. As he rhetorically questions, 'should we continue to hold fast to the intentions of the Enlightenment, however fractured they may be, or should we rather relinquish the entire project of modernity?' (1996: 45–6). Habermas's response to this crisis is to endorse the former, and although he ultimately argues for the continuation of the Enlightenment project, he also recognizes that certain aspects are fundamentally flawed. In order to complete the project, Habermas claims that there are two features which it is essential to address: (i) the process of social modernization needs to be turned in directions which do not place an emphasis on technological and economic gain alone, and (ii) the lifeworld must be allowed to develop its own institutions, uninhibited by economic and administrative systems.

In order to explicate what is meant by this, it will be useful to compare Habermas's analysis with Weber's cultural diagnosis, to which he is largely indebted.[1] Although Habermas agrees with Weber that modern European culture is the culmination of a world-historic rationalization process, his explanation departs significantly. In Weber's account, disenchantment was the logical consequence of the process of rationalization. For Weber, rationalization entails the development of social organizations through economic and bureaucratic systems. More specifically, he understood this development to take the form of an increase in the complexity of productivity and efficiency in economic and organizational (administrative) systems, the development in the level of self-reflection and the ability to assume an increasing number of interactive roles within the family and society. However, contrary to Weber, Habermas claims that these strands were subject to an imbalanced development, which has led to the 'ambiguity' of modernity (1987a).

In Habermas's account, modern societies are comprised of two central components: lifeworld and system.[2] Lifeworld refers to the public and private spheres of social life, which include civil society, politics, education, mass media, culture and family. As Habermas tells us, 'the cultural tradition shared by a community is constitutive of the lifeworld which the individual members find already interpreted' (1984: 82). In this way, the lifeworld is akin to Taylor's horizon of intelligibility, insofar as it is the repository of shared meaning. However, for Habermas the lifeworld reproduces society by preserving culture through 'taken-for-granted background assumptions and naïvely mastered skills'

---

[1] For an excellent analysis of Weber's influence on Habermas, and to which I am greatly indebted in this chapter, see Breen's *Under Weber's Shadow: Modernity, Subjectivity and Politics in the Work of Habermas, Arendt and MacIntyre* (Farnham: Ashgate, 2012).
[2] Habermas borrows the term 'lifeworld' from the founder of phenomenology, Edmund Husserl which is first set forth in *The Crisis of European Sciences and Transcendental Phenomenology*.

(1984: 335). Through these shared assumptions it also enables agents to reach a consensus and act. For this reason, Habermas claims communicative reason is that upon which the lifeworld functions. Systems, on the other hand, are composed of spheres which are governed by money and power and manifested in the economic sphere and bureaucratic administration. Money and power are what Habermas terms the 'steering media' of the capitalist economy and state administration (1984: 335). Within systems, agents are conditioned to act in an instrumental way which pursues and achieves material ends, as opposed to acting towards their own ends in a community with others. In much the same way as the primary role of the lifeworld was social reproduction, the purpose of systems is the material reproduction of society. That is, the economy creates and distributes goods, whilst state administration provides services which ensure the day-to-day functioning of society.

Where Habermas's and Weber's accounts diverge is in their understanding of rationalization. Although Weber argues that modern European society has come to be determined by instrumentalization, Habermas claims that Weber's account is significantly one-sided. As he himself states, 'there is a rationalisation of everyday practice that is accessible only from the perspective of action orientated to reaching understanding – a rationalisation of the lifeworld that Weber neglected as compared with the rationalisation of action systems like the economy and the state' (1984: 340). Habermas's argument is that instrumentality, the theory of rationality which Weber focuses on, is that which is proper to systems. However, according to Habermas, Weber fails to acknowledge the potential to develop communicative rationality within the lifeworld. Habermas is not opposed to rationalization per se; however, his explanation for the failure of the Enlightenment project is that these two strands were subject to an imbalanced development. There were two consequences of this one-sided rationalization: cultural impoverishment, which is connected to the loss of meaning, and colonization of the lifeworld, which addresses the loss of freedom.[3]

The first problem, which addresses the loss of meaning, is cultural impoverishment. Noting that there has been a distinct decline in communal traditions within modern culture, Habermas traces this back to the loss of universal validity on account of a differentiation of life spheres. Without a

---

[3] Although Habermas claims that cultural impoverishment and the colonization of the lifeworld are two mutual developments (2:327) this is challenged by Maeve Cooke, who claims that 'Habermas regards the loss of meaning both as a pathological development that runs prior to the lifeworld and as a social pathology that is caused by the colonisation of the lifeworld'. *Language and Pragmatics: Study of Habermas*', Pragmatics (Cambridge, MA: MIT Press, 1997): 191 n59.

unifying form of validity, the value spheres of science, morality/law and art have become fragmented. As he himself puts it, 'the dying out of vital traditions, goes back to a differentiation of science, morality, and art, which means not only an increasing autonomy of sectors dealt with by experts, but also a splitting off from tradition' (1987a: 327). These independent spheres then began to be monopolized by experts who determine the validity claims of each of these spheres. The rise of professionalism is problematic for Habermas because, in determining their own values, professionals alienate these spheres from the communicative structure of everyday life. As Habermas makes explicit, 'one of the features of Western rationalisation is the creation in Europe of expert cultures that deal with cultural traditions reflectively and in so doing isolate the cognitive, aesthetic-expressive, and moral-practical components from one another' (1990: 107). This deprives ordinary people of a unified cultural tradition, as it can no longer be preserved and reproduced through everyday culture. The consequence is that 'ordinary subjects experience fragmented consciousness, with the inability to interrelate the various roles and aspects of their lives', and subsequently a loss of meaning (1987a: 352). Although Weber also makes this claim, referring to experts as 'specialists without spirit', he understood cultural impoverishment to be a consequence of the 'independent development of cultural value-spheres' (2005: 124). Habermas, on the other hand, claims that the cause of cultural impoverishment was the 'elitist splitting-off of expert cultures from contexts of communicative action' (1987a: 330).

The second problem, which refers to the loss of freedom, and which sustains Habermas's interest, is the 'colonisation of the lifeworld' (1987a: 330). In his dualist understanding of society, the development of system spheres is informed by and depends upon developments within the lifeworld. A concrete example of this would be the theoretical advances in universities which lead to increased scientific and economic knowledge, which, when applied to systems spheres, leads to organizational and business models defined by increased efficiency. However, despite the fact that systems are dependent upon the lifeworld, in Habermas's account there has been a role reversal with systems dictating and limiting the functions of the lifeworld. As he metaphorically explains, 'when stripped of their ideological veils, the imperative of autonomous subsystems [. . .] make their way into the lifeworld from the outside – like colonial masters coming into a tribal society – and force a process of assimilation upon it' (1987a: 355).

To continue with the example of academic institutions, rather than determining the conduct of systems, universities are being subjected to and governed by economic goals and administrative procedures which impinge upon academic integrity and freedom.[4] This is made explicit by Timo Jütten, who claims that 'universities are forced to compete in markets for students and research funding, because the imperatives of the economic subsystem leave them no other choice but to assimilate their behaviour to market imperatives' (2013: 598). This point is also articulated by Noam Chomsky, who, concerned with tuition hikes and the increase of administrators in relation to academics, discusses how the imposition of a business model which measures success output in extremely narrow, commercial terms has decreased the quality of academia. In his own words, 'increasing class-size or employing cheap temporary labor, say graduate students instead of full-time faculty, may look good on a university budget, but there are significant costs. They're transferred and not measured. They're transferred to students and to the society generally as the quality of education, the quality of instruction is lowered' (2011). In a later articulation of the same issue, Chomsky claims the consequence is that 'the university imposes costs on students and on faculty who are not only untenured but are maintained on a path that guarantees that they will have no security. All of this is perfectly natural within corporate business models. It's harmful to education, but education is not their goal' (2014).

Although Habermas claims that communicative reason enables the functioning of lifeworld, the consequence of colonization is the replacement of this by instrumental reason. This encroachment of systems imperatives thus results in a loss of freedom, as administrative and economic restrictions limit the individual's ability to act towards their own end. As Habermas makes explicit, 'as the private sphere is undermined and eroded by the economic system, so is the public sphere by the administration system' (1987a: 480). In this way, the colonization thesis can be seen to resemble Weber's 'iron cage', insofar as it also makes the claim that economic pursuit has become a defining feature of modern existence.[5]

Therefore, in Habermas's analysis, the account which Weber proposes, whilst extremely beneficial, does not sufficiently explain the modern condition. Upon determining that the communicative infrastructure of modernity is undermined by 'systematically induced reification and cultural impoverishment', Habermas

---

[4] This is made explicit by academics who have become marginalized within their own profession by the external pressures and measures applied by middle-management. Joshua Knobe, for example, claims that 'the very people who seem clearly to be controlling the direction of their fields have been made to feel peripheral to those fields', 'Interview on Experimental Philosophy' with Joshua Knobe in *Warwick Review Journal* 4, no. 1 (2016): 14–28.

[5] As Weber claims, 'In Baxter's view the care for everyday goods should only lie on the shoulders of the "saint like a light cloak, which can be thrown aside at any moment". But fate decreed that the cloak should become an iron cage.' *The Protestant Ethic and the Spirit of Capitalism* (2005).

follows in the Frankfurt School tradition of critical theory, attempting to work Weber's diagnosis into his interpretive framework (1987a: 480).[6] The purpose of incorporating Weber's insights, and the end which Habermas seeks to achieve, is to explain why technical progress, capitalist growth and rational administration are served by science, whilst the individual's understanding of oneself and the world has been neglected. Specifically, Habermas wishes to explain two negative features of the modern world: (i) why public and private spheres are not protected by institutions against the reifying effects of administrative and economic systems, and (ii) why modern culture has been impoverished by the effects of cultural differentiation and the rise of cultural experts.

In order to answer these questions, Habermas appropriates Weber's diagnosis from a Marxist perspective.[7] His reason for doing so is because whilst Weber offers an analysis of the loss of meaning, this does not address the problem of social inequality. Marxism, on the other hand, offers the means to address social issues, but the mutation of capitalism has rendered Marxism's original solution obsolete.[8] A consequence of cultural impoverishment is that the Marxist critique of ideology is no longer valid. The reason is because the criticism of ideology suggests that we have been subjected to a false consciousness. However, in Habermas's account this cannot provide a convincing critique because our culture has become fragmented. As Habermas himself explains, 'in place of a false consciousness there appears today a fragmented consciousness' (1987a: 355). That is, with the increase of expertise, certain dimensions are no longer accessible to the majority of individuals. As Stephen K. White elucidates, 'what Habermas appears to be arguing here is that, as the insulation of expert cultures grows, so does the incapacity of the average individual to make effective use of the cognitive arsenal of cultural modernity' (1988: 117). Habermas thus claims that within communicatively structured domains the effects of a new type of reification arises in a way which is no longer related to social class. Traditional Marxist theories are therefore unable to make any criticism or contribution to this debate. Thus, in order to address social inequality, which is no longer connected to social class, Habermas offers a modified account of Marxism.

Following from György Lukács, who argued that a consequence of rationalization was 'reification', Habermas offers a 'second attempt to appropriate

---

[6] In doing so, he follows the Frankfurt tradition, which has engaged with Weber since *Dialectic of Enlightenment.*
[7] For an analysis of Habermas' relationship to Marx, see Agnes Heller's 'Habermas and Marxism', in *Habermas: Critical Debates,* eds. Thomas B. Thomas and David Held (London: Macmillan, 1982).
[8] Moreover, in *The Philosophical Discourse of Modernity* Habermas argues that Marxism fails to ground its critique in an intersubjective conception of subject and reason.

Weber in the spirit of Western Marxism' (1988: 302). Reification refers to the objectification of individuals, with the consequence that people understand their powers and abilities, and those of others, as commodities to be bought and sold. Habermas, however, whilst accepting Lukács's diagnosis, disagrees with his formulation of reification,[9] instead reinterpreting it as the 'pathological de-formation of the communicative infrastructure of the lifeworld' (1987a: 375). It is this particular problem, that the communicative capacities of the lifeworld have been deformed, which Habermas focuses his attention on. In this way, Habermas understands reification as a consequence of the colonization of the lifeworld, that is, of instrumental reason replacing communicative reason. Thus, rather than treating people with mutual respect, and as individuals with their own ends, they are treated as means to an end.

Although Habermas agreed with Weber's cultural diagnosis regarding the contradictory development of rationality, as already discussed, he criticized Weber's account of rationality as 'one-sided' (1987a: 340). According to Habermas, the process of rationalization inherent within the Enlightenment project, rather, ought to be understood as a dual process. First, as the increase in the complexity of productivity and efficiency of economic and administrative systems. Secondly, as the development in the level of self-reflection and the ability to assume an increasing number of interactive roles within the lifeworld spheres of family and civil society. Weber's account, however, focused exclusively on the economic and administrative development at the expense of communicative rationality of the lifeworld. According to Habermas, this is not an accurate analysis and the development of these two aspects was imbalanced. Namely, whilst systems have become increasingly more complex, the potential of the lifeworld has been left unfulfilled. Moreover, systems outstripped and began to colonize the lifeworld, by which he means the 'penetration of forms of economic and administrative rationality into areas of action that resist being converted over to the media of money and power because they are specialised in cultural transmission, social integration, and child-rearing, and remain dependent on mutual understanding as a mechanism of coordinating action' (1987a: 375). Thus, for Habermas, the loss of freedom is to be restored through the rationalization of the lifeworld and resistance to systemic colonization of the lifeworld, which he believed could be resolved through appropriating Marx through Weber.

---

[9] Although György Lukács advocated a phenomenologically based concept of reification, Habermas rejected this, claiming that 'phenomena of reification lose the dubious state of facts that can be inferred from economic statements about value relations [and] instead make up an object domain for empirical enquiry. They become the object of a research program.'

Within this enquiry we have taken the two themes of freedom and meaning to be our central concern and those to which our concept of authenticity is a response. Within his diagnosis of modernity, Habermas has also been shown to be concerned with these two issues. Through his engagement with Weberian disenchantment, Habermas raises the concern that modern life has become fundamentally meaningless. His incorporation and preoccupation with the Marxist inspired phenomenon of reification brings him into confrontation with the problem of freedom. As J. M. Bernstein accurately notes, 'from traditional Marxism critical theory inherits its concern for the problem of freedom, while from Weber's appropriation of Nietzsche critical theory inherits its concern for the problem of nihilism and the question of meaning' (1995: 28). The concept of freedom which he develops, however, varies from that which authenticity emerged in response to. Habermas focuses upon the effects of reification upon the subject, whereas authenticity was a response to ontological freedom. The consequence of his Marxist understanding of freedom is that he simultaneously addresses the socio-economic concern of resisting systemic incursion in the lifeworld. Habermas's colonization thesis, that the lifeworld has become oppressed by systemic logics and imperatives, provides an important avenue of enquiry, and one which has not been addressed by our socio-existential concept of authenticity.

Habermas raises a real problem, as made explicit by Jütten's aforementioned claim regarding the pathological encroachment of systems imperatives upon academic institutions, and this is something which needs to be addressed. Namely, if our lives are governed by external demands for efficiency and capital, then we do not possess freedom to pursue our own ends. In this way, Habermas's colonization thesis has practical implications for living a meaningful life, for if our freedom is restricted by system imperatives, then one cannot achieve self-realization, or live a life that has been determined to be individually meaningful. Thus, resistance to colonization provides the grounds for the continued possibility of living authentically. In light of this, we ought to expand the scope of our concern to engage with the implications of this upon our concept of authenticity. Although it has been noted that it is this aspect of Habermas's work which is most important to our enquiry, this conceptual expansion will be more fully developed within Chapter 7, where we can allocate adequate space to this undertaking without detracting from the enquiry at hand.

Although we can learn from Habermas's perspective of modernity, by extending our area of enquiry to engage with the colonization thesis, the space which his understanding of modernity presents is much too confined. Although he also acknowledges the failure of the Enlightenment as the cause of the problems of freedom and meaning, Habermas's vision is restricted to two possible outcomes. The first is to abandon the project, which would require one to ethically return to some form of Aristotelianism or accept a position of ethical relativity, and the second is to attempt to continue the Enlightenment, which he sees inherent with Kantian project. This dichotomy, however, is too restrictive, suggesting that these are the only possibilities. Offering a middle ground between these two choices, the theory of authenticity neither deludes one into believing that a new teleological conception of the good can be derived nor is overly optimistic in believing in the Kantian project. That is, unlike Kant, who believed the rational end of human civilization necessarily entails increased autonomy, authenticity does not elucidate any such higher end. Rather, as discussed in Section 2.2, theories of authenticity are premised on the recognition that the Kantian project is an unrealistic goal. However, instead of descending into solipsism, authenticity suggests natural teleology need not be necessary, but that values can be determined by individuals and shared by a community. Our approach to authenticity thus offers a more realistic approach than Habermas insofar as it accepts our existential condition and attempts to engage with it, rather than overcome it by attempting to establish an ideal concept of human civilization in either traditional Aristotelian terms or modern Kantian terms.

Having explained the way in which Habermas problematizes freedom and meaning with regard to modernity, and how this differs from how we orientate our trajectory, we will now turn our attention to his proposed resolution. In the following section, we will discuss Habermas's suggestion that the Enlightenment project can be completed through an increase of communicative rationality. In order to demonstrate this, we will construct Habermas's resolution in three parts: his account of the subject, his social theory and his account of democracy. In order to advance our argument, that Habermas's response to modernity is itself insufficient, we will criticize him on two grounds. First, it will be claimed that his theory of autonomy offers an unrealistic account of human beings and offers a much too rigid perspective which neglects those aspects which make us human. Secondly, we will argue that his dualism of system and lifeworld offers a restricted view of the possibilities of emancipatory thinking. That is, it will be illustrated that Habermas believes power can be restricted to systems, though it will be argued that this is not a realistic account, and that power in fact permeates all aspects of human society.

4.2 Completing the project

In *The Philosophical Discourse of Modernity*, Habermas claims that by abandoning the Enlightenment project of modernity the potential for emancipation not only remains unfulfilled but that this very possibility has been relinquished as well. Furthermore, he argues that the project itself contained an immanent critique of modernity, and that this was the only means to critically engage with the Enlightenment. Thus, as a consequence, those who reject the claim that human civilization has a rational end are unable to offer a rational critique, since they have abandoned the means to do so. Habermas's reason for attempting to revise the Enlightenment with the tools of the Enlightenment then is because he sees those attempting to form counter-discourses as mistaken (1987b). Furthermore, he stresses that 'the philosophical discourse of modernity, as initiated by Kant, already drew up a counter reckoning for subjectivity as the principle of modernity' (1987b: 295). What Habermas means here is that the means to avoid descending into a dead-end subjectivist standpoint remains latent within Kantian philosophy. In order to illustrate this, Habermas re-examines the philosophical paths taken by those attempting to reconstruct European culture in light of the intellectual fallout of the Enlightenment.

In his analysis of the philosophical trajectories of Hegel, Marx, Heidegger and Derrida, Habermas notes they each had alternative paths which they did not choose to travel. The purpose of his analysis is to recall the counter-discourse inherent in modernity itself. However, he notes that although Hegel, Marx, Heidegger and Derrida's counter-discourse provides the potential for communicative reason, they each adopted a subject-centred understanding of reason. It is for precisely this reason their attempts at critique have failed, that is, because it is impossible to critique reason from a subjective standpoint. Thus, in Habermas's account, although the means to surpass the monological philosophy of the subject was present in various responses to the Enlightenment, this was never actually realized. For Habermas, then, 'the paradigm of the knowledge of objects has to be replaced by the paradigm of mutual understanding between subjects capable of speech and action' (1987b: 295–6). Insofar as Habermas perceives postmodernism to be the logical end of subject-centred reason, he claims that it forces us to retrace the path of the philosophical discourse back to its starting point. Thus, in re-examining the directions taken by those who have determined the course of Western philosophy, Habermas locates the theory of communicative reason as a path not travelled and which is capable of resolving the predicaments which modernity has given rise to.

Therefore, rather than the Cartesian self-knowing subject, which has led to our current predicament, Habermas proposes communicative rationality. As he himself claims, 'we need a *theoretically constituted perspective* to be able to treat communicative action as the medium through which the lifeworld as a whole is reproduced' (1987b: 299). It is this very perspective of communication which he proposes as the means of reproducing (and reasserting) the lifeworld. Thus, whilst the logical conclusion of postmodernism is to reject that which the Enlightenment strived for, Habermas notes that 'instead of overturning modernity, [mutual understanding] takes up again the counter discourse inherent within modernity and leads it away from the battle lines between Hegel and Nietzsche' (1987b: 310). His aim, then, is to demonstrate the increase of communicative rationality in the lifeworld, which Weber failed to account for due to his subjectivist understanding of reason and action and his one-sided understanding of rationalization. For Habermas, it is precisely the concept of linguistically generated intersubjectivity which is capable of overcoming the problems of subjectivism. The ideal of communicative action is based on individual self-determination, by which Habermas means the autonomous collective agreement on general rules of co-existence, and which he equates with 'morality'. This is contrasted with self-realization, which is defined as the self's capacity to determine conceptions of the good and to combine these into a coherent narrative, or 'ethic'. Since communicative rationality is dependent on self-determination, Habermas prioritizes this over self-realization. What this ultimately results in is the belief that moral norms are self-determined, rather than derived from a natural or essential ethical good, though this will be addressed in the succeeding section.

According to Habermas, rationality is a capacity inherent within language, especially argumentation. In his theory of communicative action, Habermas claims that a distinctly human existence is formed through the attempt to reach understanding through speech as opposed to subjective consciousness or introspection. This is Habermas's theory of communicative action, which is governed by mutual understanding. For these reasons, Habermas believed that the defining moment of modernity was 'the bourgeois public sphere ... of private people coming together as a public' (1989: 27). That is, the public use of peoples' own communicative reason, which was used to challenge the power of the sovereign. This was important because social intercourse was now devoid of social status – guided by the principle that enlightenment would be achieved through the public use, and practice, of reason. As Keith Breen concisely puts it, 'the bourgeois public sphere revealed that it is the ability to communicate with other human beings and to subject one's opinion to their judgement that defines mature personhood' (2012: 33).

Within *The Theory of Communicative Action*, Habermas turns towards language to offer an alternative to the subject-centred philosophies of consciousness. As language is shared and something which individuals mutually understand, Habermas sees communication as the basis of an intersubjective perspective. However, rather than providing an epistemological theory of how language relates to objects in the world, Habermas offers a pragmatic theory. What this means is that he attempts to articulate the function of language, as opposed to the content which language expresses. The pragmatic function, which Habermas determines to be intrinsic to language, is the ability of language to achieve mutual understanding through the attainment of intersubjective consensus. By taking a pragmatic approach Habermas is effectively prioritizing the function of language over its descriptive use. Thus, the primary function of speech is not to simply express the existence of phenomenon, but to coordinate action between individual agents. As Gordon Finlayson explains, 'the pragmatic meaning of an utterance depends on its validity. The meaning of actions, utterances, and propositions are essentially public or shared, and that this is because meaning depends on reasons and reasons are essentially public or shared' (2005: 35).

In Habermas's theory, in order to make ourselves understood and engage in meaningful speech it is necessary that we are truthful, and that our verbal utterances are both right and true. In order to reach understanding we must therefore satisfy these three validity claims. These are (i) the statement made is true (ii) the speech act is right, in respect to the normative context and (iii) one is truthful or sincere in one's intention. These three forms of validity respectfully relate to the objective, intersubjective (social) and subjective worlds. The first validity claim, truth, appeals to objective criteria insofar as it is grounded in universal reason. When one appeals to truth, one does so with awareness that there are good reasons for one's claim to be believed and which one's interlocutor is capable of recognizing. The second validity claim, rightness, is upheld by moral–practical principles, which can be justified by an underlying norm. For example, to claim that it is wrong to murder is supported by social norms which all members of one's society ought to recognize. The third validity claim, truthfulness, appeals to a subjective standpoint. This refers to individual experience and relies upon one being honest in one's intentions. As Finlayson concisely puts it, 'validity claims function as a warranty that the speaker could adduce supporting reasons to convince their interlocutor. When someone understands and complies with a verbal request they move from communication to action. Thus actions are coordinated by validity claims' (2005: 40–1). Habermas's theory of communication thus helps to reorder the validity spheres of the lifeworld.[10] Through his analysis of language, Habermas locates the rational basis of the coordination of action in speech. In order to validate and justify his approach of communicative action, he considers three alternative forms of action.

The first alternative form of action is teleological, which refers to the end, or purpose, towards which one's actions are directed. Within this form, Habermas tells us 'the central concept is that of a *decision* among alternative courses of action, with the view to realisation of an end, guided by maxims, and based on an interpretation of the situation' (1984: 135). Insofar as it is goal driven, Habermas claims that teleological action is an attempt to arrive at truth, and as such, it derives validity from the objective world. The second form, normatively regulated action, is performed by members within a society who orientate their actions to common values. Thus, unlike teleological action, normatively regulated action 'does not have the cognitive sense of expecting a predicted event, but the normative sense that members are *entitled* to expect certain behaviour' (1984: 135). In this way it appeals to both truth and rightness, deriving validity from the objective and intersubjective realms. The third account, dramaturgical action, refers to one who discloses their subjectivity in order to present a particular impression of themselves to others. As Habermas himself puts it, 'a performance enables the actor to present himself to his audience in a certain way' (1984: 139). Here, Habermas can be seen to have the existentialists in mind and philosophical approaches which advocate self-creation. In making explicit their subjective world to an intersubjective audience, Habermas claims that dramaturgical action appeals to the validly claims of truth and truthfulness. This critique may be extended to the likes of Sartre, who, in his early work, does not recognize what Habermas refers to as intersubjectivity or rightness. However, it is not applicable to our socio-existential approach to authenticity, for the reason that our approach incorporates Taylor's horizon of significance, which includes social norms.

However, in communicative action the actor themselves seek consensus, measuring it against truth, rightness and truthfulness, and as such appeal to the objective, intersubjective and subjective worlds. As Habermas explains, 'the actors seek to reach an understanding about the action situation and their plans of

---

[10] That said, Habermas has been criticized on account of his theory of values in several respects. First, whether there are actually three distinct value spheres, and secondly, in virtue of understanding one another does this entail that members of a society will adhere to the same social and moral rules?

action in order to coordinate their actions by way of agreement' (1984: 136). The linguistic medium enables the actor to understand their relation to the world. As Habermas claims, 'the concept of communicative action presupposes language as the medium for a kind of reaching understanding, in the course of which participants, through relating to a world, reciprocally raise validity-claims that can be accepted or contested' (1984: 147). Communicative action thus relates to the objective world, insofar as one can arrive at a universal truth through reason. It engages with the intersubjective realm in that one's interlocutor can challenge or reject one's claim based on the normative context of one's society based on dialogue. Finally, it satisfies subjective standards insofar as one is truthful in one's intention in attempting to arrive at mutual understanding.

To further elucidate and demarcate the limits of communicative action, Habermas compares it with instrumental and strategic action. He notes that although instrumental and strategic action are both orientated towards success, the latter is social, whilst the former is not. Although communicative action is also social, like strategic action, it is orientated towards reaching understanding. As Habermas himself puts it, 'in communicative action participants are not primarily orientated to their own individual success; they pursue their individual goals under the condition that they can harmonise their plans of action on the basis of common situation definitions' (1984: 161). By reaching understanding, Habermas means 'a process of reaching agreement among speaking and acting subjects'. Moreover, he believes that 'reaching understanding is the inherent *telos* of human speech' (1984: 162). In order to arrive at understanding, the speaker's proposition is tested against the validity claims to determine whether that which the speaker states is true, if it is sincerely inferred and if it is normatively appropriate.

Whenever we enter into serious dialogue, we do so with the intention of reaching agreement, as autonomous and equal partners. Communicative action is thus orientated to the attainment and reproduction of mutual understanding through the means of conversation, political debate and decision-making processes. Unlike commands, or coercive measures, communication is open to challenge. Habermas offers the example of a professor asking a student for a glass of water (1984: 306). The three forms of validity in this request are the truth of availability, the professor's sincerity in asking for it and the normative appropriateness of his request. The student can reject the professor's request on normative grounds, because it is not a duty which one is expected to fulfil in one's role as a student. Thus, it is through communicative action and arriving at mutual understanding, via the three forms of validity that Habermas thinks an increase in the rationality of the lifeworld comes about.

Is Habermas's approach, however, a realistic one, or is it excessively rationalist? That is, can individuals reason as effectively as his theory demands? Given the conditions required for communicative action, this seems problematic, as Steven Lukes makes explicit, 'ideally rational people in an ideal speech situation cannot but reach a rational consensus' (1989: 140). We thus ought to question whether we are as rational as Habermas requires.[11] As Agnes Heller stresses, 'the lack of the sensuous experiences of hope and despair, of venture and humiliation, is discernible in the structure of his theory: the creature-like aspects of human beings are missing' (1982: 21). Heller's claim is that the agents of Habermas's account do not offer accurate representations of human beings, but cold calculative rational machines.[12] This criticism is reminiscent of that made by Ferrara in his distinction between authenticity and autonomy (Section 2.2). To reiterate, according to Ferrara, ethics of autonomy are far too rigid, and as such, unable to account for our emotional side which is a defining feature of who we are. More specifically, autonomy misses out on particularity and we need an ethic of authenticity to make up for that lack. For Ferrara, an ethic of authenticity is needed to account for this, and, as such, from the perspective of authenticity, Habermas's communicative action does not provide a sufficient account of rational agents.

Moreover, we might question the legitimacy of Habermas's dual-structured social sphere. The claim that there can be a realm that is primarily defined by communicative action and mutual understanding, and a realm that is primarily defined by instrumental/strategic action and power/money, is something which we will reject.[13] This argument is made by Nancy Fraser, who argues that it is unrealistic to 'analytically separate strategic action from the context of shared norms and meanings' (1989: 118–20). Fraser's reason is because the division of lifeworld from system and the neat reduction of communication to lifeworld and power to systems are untenable. Thomas McCarthy also makes a similar criticism, claiming that the dualism of system and lifeworld is questionable. The problem for McCarthy is that the 'role of social groups in concrete struggles

---

[11] Byron Rienstra and Derek Hook appeal to recent studies in social-psychology to argue that the existence of psychological biases impact upon rational decision-making. 'Weakening Habermas: The Undoing of Communicative Rationality', *Politikon* 33, no. 3 (2006): 313–39.

[12] A similar criticism is made by Kierkegaard of Hegel that the construction of his philosophical system was unrealistic because it was unable to account for individual idiosyncrasies. As Karl Jaspers summarizes, '[Hegel is], as a *man, like someone who builds a castle, but lives next door in a shanty. Such a fantastical being does not himself live within* what he thinks.' *Reason and Existenz*, trans. William Earle (London: 1956), 26.

[13] A further line of criticism concerns the distinction between communicative and strategic action. For this argument, see James Johnson, 'Arguing for Deliberation: Some Skeptical Considerations', in *Deliberative Democracy*, ed. Jon Elster (Cambridge: Cambridge University Press, 1998).

against the pathologies of system integration is relegated to a sphere supposedly free of power relations' (1985: 27–53). This line of argument is further advanced by Axel Honneth, who argues that Habermas's distinct division of the lifeworld and system spheres conveniently separate communication from power, and in doing so produces the 'complementary fiction' of a 'norm-free' domain of power and a 'power-free' domain of communication. In Honneth's own words, Habermas's division leads to '(1) the existence of norm-free organisations of action and (2) the existence of power-free spheres of communication' (1991: 298). Honneth opposes the notion of 'norm-free' strategic action by arguing that 'the organisational structures of management and administration can be generally clarified only as institutional embodiments of both purposive-rational and political-practical principles' (1991: 298). Thus, rather than conceiving of two distinct spheres, with instrumental power and economic exchange restricted to systems, we ought to instead consider these to also be part of the lifeworld.

Siding with Fraser, McCarthy and Honneth, it is agreed that Habermas's division of system and lifeworld is unrealistic. Our own explanation for rejecting this division, however, is because it offers a rather restricted view of the possibilities for emancipatory thinking. That is, Habermas's dualism suggests that power resides in systems and the lifeworld is free from this. A further reason for rejecting Habermas's division between system and lifeworld, however, is a matter of the relationship between power and inauthenticity. In the following chapter, we will present the exercise of power over subjects as an expression of inauthenticity and one which seeps into all aspects of society, not simply administrative and economic spheres. In this respect, we will side with Foucault's concept of power, which dominates and produces subjects, as opposed to Habermas's concept which only operates within the system sphere. This claim, however, will be more fully elucidated in Chapter 5.

Habermas continues his project of critical social theory in *Between Facts and Norms* where he develops an account of deliberative democracy. Here it is claimed 'only those statutes may claim legitimacy that can meet with the assent of all citizens in a discursive process of legislation that in turn has been legally constituted' (1996: 192). He begins with a 'two-track' structure of politics which contains formal and informal elements. The formal political sphere is constituted of institutional arenas of communication and discourse which are designed to make decisions. These include parliaments, cabinets, elected assemblies and political parties. Here the designated representatives make decisions, pass laws and formulate and implement policies. The informal political sphere, on the other hand, is not institutionalized or designed to make decisions, but rather is 'chaotic' and 'anarchic'. Furthermore, members of voluntary organizations, political associations and the media participate in discourse in order to reach understanding and form opinions on matters of shared concern. According to Habermas, when decision-making institutions of the formal political sphere are receptive to the input from the informal political sphere this leads to a healthy democratic institution. That is, when civil society and public opinion have an active input and influence the formation of polices and laws, then laws tend to be rational and contribute to an equitable society.

Turning his attention to the role of public discourse, Habermas argues that democratic control over systems can help contain instrumental reason. Civil society generates communicative power through decision-making bodies. Administrative power exists in the state and government bureaucracy. A healthy democratic society is capable of translating communicative power into administrative power. Communicative power thus only becomes manifest through administrative bodies which employ strategic and instrumental reasoning. Habermas's claim is that modern democracy thus requires administrative power to make democratic deliberation possible, even though it is structurally incompatible with communicative power. How then does he resolve this logical tension? He explains that this problem is surmountable through laws, which transform communicative power into administrative power. As he explains, 'laws can regulate the transformation of communicative into administrative power inasmuch as they come about according to a democratic procedure, ground a comprehensive legal protection guaranteed by impartial courts, and shield from the implementing administration the sorts of reasons that support legislative and judicial decision making' (1996: 192). In this way, communicative power steers administrative power, and in doing so, it contains instrumental reason within the systems sphere. Thus, it can be seen how Habermas proposes to resolve the problem of system encroachment upon and the subsequent colonization of the lifeworld. As William Scheuerman argues, he offers 'a *defensive* model of deliberative democracy in which democratic institutions exercise at least an attenuated check on market and administrative processes' (1999: 156).

These considerations then lead Habermas to an intermediary standpoint between liberal democracy and republican democracy. The former emphasizes individual freedom that is protected by human rights. Freedom here is conceived of in terms of negative liberty, in that one is considered free when one is able to accept or decline. Liberal democracy is thus neutral with regard to that which constitutes the good, leaving this entirely to the discretion of the individual.

Republicanism, on the other hand, privileges collective, public autonomy at the expense of the individual. Thus, rather than the ability to accept or decline an opportunity, autonomy is conceived in terms of collective actualization. Habermas's 'two track' theory then leads to the amalgamation of these two concepts. The aspects which he derives from liberal democracy are human rights and cultural tolerance.[14] However, in accordance with republicanism, he claims that rights are only acquired through socialization. As he makes explicit, political freedom is 'the freedom that springs simultaneously from the subjectivity of the individual and the sovereignty of the people' (1996: 468).

In his extension of communicative rationality to the political realm, Habermas continues to bracket instrumental reason, attempting to restrict it to the systems sphere. Here, his claim is that instrumental reasoning can be contained by democratic control. Moreover, since communicative power steers administrative power, this restricts instrumental reason to systems. However, Habermas's position is untenable because instrumental reasoning cannot simply be restricted to systems. The reason is because means–end thinking is necessary in social life, and we engage in such thinking in everyday decision-making. This is exemplified when we make simple decisions, such as whether to order our usual cappuccino, or try something new in a café, to more important decisions, such as whether to pursue postgraduate studies, or to join the labour market. Habermas's theory requires that the spheres of system and lifeworld are separated because communicative rationality must act towards the *telos* of reaching mutual understanding through communication, regardless of the sphere. As Darrow Schecter emphasizes, 'communication would inevitably turn into oppressive steering if the life-world were entrusted with organizing the mediation of humanity and external nature' (2010: 212). Furthermore, communication is, by its very nature, unable to fully address the problem of instrumentality because if it were to do so then it would mutate into a form of power. As Schecter continues to elucidate, 'communication may break, inflect upon and rechannel power, but it may not become power. It follows that if communication becomes power, it is by definition lost, and political control of the economy would indeed bring about this structural transformation in his estimation' (2010: 212).

In the first section of this chapter we demonstrated that Habermas concerned himself with the problems of freedom and meaning and that a fundamental aim of his project was to address the one-sided development of rationality. Here it

---

[14] Here he can be seen to reverse his position in *The Structural Transformation of the Public Sphere* where he attempted to dissolve plurality, for which he received heavy criticism.

was argued that Habermas's resolution, of communicative action, relies upon an unrealistic account of rational agents, missing out on particularity, which is contained within an ethic of authenticity. Moreover, although Habermas attempts to preserve freedom by resisting the colonization of the lifeworld, his dualism of system and lifeworld offers a rather restricted view of the possibilities of emancipatory thinking. In the following section, we will discuss Habermas's resolution of discourse ethics as an alternative to authenticity. Here it will be argued that although Habermas is concerned with the problem of meaning, that he makes a philosophical mistake by relegating ethics to morality. One consequence of his priority of morality over ethics, for our theory, is that authenticity is placed within a secondary position, and this undermines its importance. However, it will be argued that by relegating ethics, Habermas relegates the most central concern.

4.3 Ethics or morality?

The concept of authenticity which has been advocated within this book is an ethical ideal. That is, the attainment of authenticity is upheld as a goal to be actively pursued. In this way, authenticity offers a vision of the good; that is, it makes a normative claim about what it means to live a good life. Habermas, on the other hand, responds to the loss of freedom and meaning, induced by the colonization thesis, by developing a theory of moral discourse. Although he does offer an ethical ideal, of self-realization, our criticism will be premised on his relegation of ethics to morality. In order to defend our concept of authenticity, we will now turn our attention to analysing the development of Habermas's moral discourse theory. Here it will be argued that Habermas's prioritization of morality, of right over the good, results in a performative contradiction. Namely, that moral norms rely upon a prior conception of the good, and as such, Habermas's theory cannot be sustained. Although we have thus far argued that Habermas's response to disenchantment is insufficient, he does offer a limited account of how the individual derives personal meaning and it is to elucidating the moral and ethical implications of his thought to which our enquiry now turns.

In *Moral Consciousness and Communicative Action*, Habermas draws out the moral and ethical implications of his theory of communicative action. Unlike many modern moral theories which are developed in abstract, Habermas's account is developed in order to address the aforementioned social issues of meaning and freedom. In this way, Habermas begins by assuming that a moral standpoint exists. In order to justify this assumption, he attempts to demonstrate that a principle exists which is capable of distinguishing between moral and non-moral actions. Derived from and contained within his theory of communication, as outlined in the preceding section, he offers a criterion for generalizing maxims of action which he terms the 'discourse principle' (D). According to this principle, 'only those norms may claim to be valid that could meet with the consent of all affected in their role as participants in a practical discourse' (1990: 197). The discourse principle is an intuitive claim, which suggests that in order for a norm to be valid it necessarily requires consensus. However, this principle cannot determine which norms are valid by itself; rather, it functions in a negative manner, determining which norms are not valid. In order to test whether a norm is valid, one must consider whether it could be accepted through discourse with those whom a particular action will affect. In this way, the principle of discourse is not a particularly strong claim but enables one to reveal whether a proposed action can be considered moral.

In order to develop a more substantial moral theory, Habermas supplements his discourse principle with the additional principle of universalization (U). This entails that for any norm under consideration '*all* affected can accept the consequences and the side effects its *general* observance can be anticipated to have for the satisfaction of *everyone's* interests' (1990: 65). This bridging principle contains an ethic of discourse, insofar as it presupposes that we can justify our choice of norms. The principle of universalization is a much stronger claim than discourse principle (D) in that it functions both negatively and positively. In expanding to include all affected, it is able to not only determine which norms are invalid, but also, if a norm can be said to be accepted by all affected then it ought to be constituted as valid. In his account then, in order for a norm to be considered valid it has to fulfil the Kantian condition of universalization. Namely, 'the moral principle is so conceived to exclude as invalid any norm that could not meet with the qualified assent of all who are or might be affected by it' (1990: 65). As it stands, Habermas has simply assumed that a moral standpoint exists, and as such, he is required to justify his concept of discourse ethics. He attempts to achieve this in terms of the discourse principle (D), which communicative action presupposes. However, he must show that the moral principle of universalization (U) can be grounded upon the presuppositions of argumentation through a transcendental-pragmatic argument. In order to achieve this, he turns to grounding it in the norms which emerge through moral discourse. As he himself claims, 'the universal principle functions like a knife that makes razor-sharp cuts between evaluative statements and strictly normative ones, between the good and the just' (1990: 104). What this entails is that the principle of universality differentiates moral norms from ethical evaluations, and it is the former which is more important to Habermas.

In order to further elucidate what is meant by discourse ethics, it will be helpful to compare it with Kantian morality, to which it bears a resemblance. Both approaches are deontological in that they propose rules which enable one to determine one's moral course of action. Kant's categorical imperative commands one to 'act only according to that maxim whereby you can at the same time will that it should become a universal law' (1993: 30). Habermas's principle of discourse proposes something very similar, namely, to act only in a way which can be considered universal by all persons affected. One major difference is that Kant's deontological principle is only concerned with the principle upon which one acts. That is, for Kant, as long as one adheres to one's self-imposed principle, regardless of the outcome, one can be said to have acted justly. Habermas, on the other hand, introduces the condition of consequence. This is implied in the principle of universalization (U) through its imperative to think through the 'consequences and side effects' (1990: 63). Thus, even if one acts according to the agreed upon principle, unless the end of one's action is in line with this, then one cannot be said to have acted justly. A further significant difference is the process by which one arrives at the principle. Kant's principle can be said to be monological in the sense that the individual themselves determine what is just 'in the loneliness of his soul' (1990: 203). By thinking through the maxim of whether one's action can become a universal law, one determines for oneself that which constitutes a moral principle. Habermas, on the other hand, replaces the Kantian categorical imperative with an intersubjective account, insofar as it is determined through discourse with others. Rather than a solitary individual determining moral implications through a thought experiment, for Habermas, this principle must be derived through intersubjective communication with others. By his own admission, he states that the structure of his theory is to 'reformulate Kantian ethics by grounding moral norms in communication' (1990: 203).

In *Justification and Application*, Habermas makes the distinction between ethics (*Sittlichkeit*) and morality (*Moralität*). Up until this point, Habermas used 'ethics' and 'morality' interchangeably in his theory of discourse ethics. However, he later comes to distinguish between these two terms, employing 'ethics' to demarcate conceptions of the good, which he discusses in terms of self-realization, or consciously led life, and 'morality' to discuss questions of right and justice, in terms of self-determination or autonomy. This is made explicit in his short essay 'Individuation through Socialization', where he notes that there are two components to his account of the development of the individual subject: 'autonomy' and 'a consciously led life'. As Habermas himself clearly states, 'from the point of view of the individuals affected by it, the process of societal individualization has two distinct aspects: both autonomy and a consciously-led life are progressively required of them culturally and institutionally' (1992a: 183). In order to explicate autonomy, he applies the term 'self-determination' and refers to a consciously led life as 'self-realization'. This latter notion, of self-realization, is conceptually akin to authenticity, insofar as it emphasizes the subject's own individual mode of existence. As Maeve Cooke makes explicit, '[by self-realization] he means the progressive differentiation of individuals from other individuals by virtue of their uniqueness and originality' (1992: 272). These two notions are further differentiated in terms of freedom, where self-determination is understood as moral, whilst self-realization is classed as ethical. One consequence of this late demarcation is that the concept of 'discourse ethics' is misleading as it is in fact a form of morality, insofar as it engages with questions of justice, rather than ethics, or questions of the good as he distinguishes them. Thus, although Habermas does not make the linguistic distinction in *Moral Consciousness and Communicative Action*, he understands theories of justice, which he later connects to morality, and questions of good, which he attributes to ethics, to be two separate concerns.

His concept of ethics is restricted to questions of the good, that is 'what is good for the individual/community?' and for this reason, ethical values are only applicable to specific social groups or particular individuals. Ethical values are therefore fostered within cultural frameworks, and as such, Habermas claims that ethics/questions of the good only possess relative validity. Values determine goods, collective identities and self-understanding. Morality, on the other hand, determines what is right/wrong, what is just and how one ought to act. Whilst ethics determines what is good for a particular individual or community, morality is supposed to determine what is right for everyone, regardless of tradition. Thus, whilst he classifies ethics as relative, he claims that morality is universal, insofar as it is not limited to a particular cultural framework. A further difference is that whilst ethical questions of 'the good' are based on values, Habermas claims that morality establishes norms. These are 'behavioural rules, anchored in the communicative structure of the lifeworld, based on very general and universally shared interests' (Finlayson 2005: 97). The purpose of morality, according to Habermas, is to establish valid norms, which he suggests discourse ethics – or, more accurately put, discourse morality – is capable of achieving.

Thus, rather than opposing theories of duty, centred on the principle of justice, with theories of the good, which emphasize the common weal, Habermas follows Hegel, to the extent that he criticizes such one-sidedness (1990: 201). Although Habermas distinguishes between ethics and morality, he does not pose them as two competing theories, but rather as two components of self-understanding. However, he does prioritize morality, or questions of justice, over ethics, or questions of the good. His reasons for relegating ethics to morality are threefold. First, within post-conventional society, identities are not rooted in any particular tradition, as with traditional ethical theories, but that we regard ourselves as equal persons with equal rights that are universal, and as such, moral theories are best suited to our current cultural context. Secondly, as a consequence, moral norms are not derived from ethical theory, but reside within the communicative structure of the lifeworld. Thirdly, as such, agents cannot resolve fundamental conflicts within the lifeworld through theories of the good or ethical discourse, but instead must engage in moral discourse. The consequence is that unlike conventional ethics, which determined what was moral, Habermas reverses this relationship, instead suggesting that morality informs ethics. In his own words, 'the means to the solution of this problem is the very same perspective structure of a fully decentred understanding of the world that created the problem in the first place' (1990: 161). Thus, in Habermas's account, norms are more important than the good, and determine values, insofar as they operate within the bounds of moral permissibility.

Habermas concurs with Taylor in noting that the positing of 'right' over 'the good' is a fundamental dispute between communitarians and liberals.[15] However, he attempts to bridge these two approaches, offering an intermediary standpoint through his discourse ethics. Like Kantian-inspired liberalism, discourse ethics advocates a deontological understanding of freedom, morality and law. It simultaneously draws upon the intersubjective understanding of individuation from socialization, which is indicative of Hegelian derived theories of communitarianism. The stance which Habermas himself takes on this dispute is one of 'right' over 'the good'. One consequence of this position, which Habermas notes, is that discourse ethics is vulnerable to objections of contextuality and tradition. In his own words, ethical discussions, in contrast to moral arguments, are always already embedded in the traditional context of a hitherto accepted, identity-constituting form of life (1992a: 105). Furthermore, his priority of morality over ethics reduces self-realization, which focuses on

---

[15] See Charles Taylor's 'The Liberal-Communitarian Debate', in *Liberalism and the Moral Life*, ed. N. Rosenblum (Cambridge, MA: Harvard University Press, 1989).

meaning, to a secondary position, below self-determination, which emphasizes the pursuit of autonomy. This, however, challenges the priority of our concept of authenticity, which, as an ethical ideal, is to be conceived of as a form of the good. Although Habermas is not opposed to authenticity per se, and advocates something similar through his concept of self-realization, his concept of a consciously led life is secondary to autonomy. Thus, not only does it provide an alternative to our concept of authenticity, as advanced in Chapter 4, but it also challenges its importance by relegating authenticity to a secondary position.

Although we criticized Habermas on account of his theory of communicative action failing to account for particularity, he does address this concern by including an ethical dimension. Moral norms can be converted into laws, and as such, have a social function. Ethics, on the other hand, is a predominantly private matter, insofar as the choice of ethical life is left to the discretion of the subject.[16] By offering a subjective account of meaning, as something which the individual is required to cultivate once they have achieved autonomy, he focuses on the development of freedom, and as such, the problem of freedom. By leaving the question of good up to the individual, Habermas's account can be seen to present an account of authenticity similar to that of the existentialists. However, whilst the question of meaning is primordial to the existentialists, this is a secondary consideration for Habermas, as will be demonstrated later. That is, he gives the individual free rein to determine their lives for themselves. In order to avoid the same problems as the existentialists, of lacking a moral framework within which to achieve self-realization, Habermas's theory of communicative reason would have to be successful. However, we have questioned the validity of his approach by claiming that his division of lifeworld and system is unsustainable. Furthermore, in order to maintain the priority of ethics, and thus authenticity, it will be demonstrated that Habermas's concept of morality (questions of right) depends upon ethics (questions of the good), and as such, his discourse ethics is subject to a performative contraction, and ultimately collapses upon itself.

This sharp dichotomy between ethics and morality can be challenged on the grounds that morality, which Habermas grants priority to, is ultimately dependent upon ethics. Such an argument is developed by Charles Taylor in *Sources of the Self*, where he claims that morality depends upon a certain conception of the good. Here Taylor presents an analysis of morality, where he notes that in attempting to define morality in terms of justice, moral theories give 'hyper-goods' priority. By

---

[16] Habermas also claims that there is such a thing as 'ethical discourse', which presumes dialogue between people as regards values and goods.

hyper-goods he means 'goods which not only are incomparably more important than others but provide the standpoint from which these must be weighed, judged, decided about' (1989: 53). He then continues to question whether morality not only emphasizes certain hyper-goods but also depends upon a constitutive good which demarcates hyper-goods as such. This is evident in modern moral theories such as Kantian deontology and utilitarianism: Kant conceives of a rational formula for moral action, and utilitarianism rationally calculates the greatest good for the greatest number. However, neither approach can explain why particular goods constitute the greatest good. That is, they are unable to articulate the substantive qualitative distinctions about what constitutes a moral good and how differing goods can be of differing value.

Taylor's argument is, thus, that it is only by articulating this good that one is able to provide an explanation as to why one ought to act morally in the first place. Theories which place questions of justice beyond questions of the good, as Taylor explains, 'leave us with nothing to say to someone who asks why he should be moral or strive to the "maturity" of a "post-conventional" ethic' (1989b: 87). This point is further expounded by William Rehg who makes explicit that 'only by articulating this good can one answer the question, Why be moral? And it is precisely because modern moral theory is inarticulate about its moral sources that it cannot answer this question – with the result that moral action appears as just one choice or good among others' (1997: 118). Taylor's position is therefore that moral norms and hyper-goods exist within an evaluative framework which determines the priority of such norms and hyper-goods, as opposed to the reverse. To put this in Habermasian terms, Taylor prioritizes the ethical over the moral – that norms are given validity by a constitutive good.

Although Taylor does not directly address Habermas's discourse ethics, we can nevertheless extend his argument to Habermas's account by rephrasing the question, 'Why be moral?' to 'Why should we rationally accept the discourse principle?'[17] As Rehg explains,

> if accepting a discourse-ethical procedure depends on the prior acceptance of some hyper-good or constitutive conception of the good of human life, then it

---

[17] Maeve Cooke offers an alternative approach to supplement Habermas's account of discourse ethics with Taylor's concept of the good. As she explains, by 'drawing on his account of moral validity, we could say that, under conditions of Western modernity, only those conceptions of the good that satisfy the minimal conditions of universalizability as formulated in D are deemed acceptable reference points for individual autonomy. This would eliminate, for instance, conceptions of the good that are inherently supremacist, racist, patriarchal and so on, while permitting ones that are aestheticist, utilitarian, religious, liberal, and many more.' 'Habermas, Feminism and the Question of Autonomy', in *Habermas: A Critical Reader*, ed. Peter Dews (Oxford: Blackwell, 1999), 200.

would seem that discourse ethics depends on prematurely settling a competition among conceptions of the good. In that case, discourse ethics either presupposes as settled precisely the kind of issue it claims one cannot settle in universally binding terms, or it presupposes as indisputable precisely the kind of thin conception of the common good which it claims should be the result of moral discourse. (1997: 118)

Thus, if Habermas's discourse ethics does tacitly select one hyper-good among various competing hyper-goods, then it is incapable of providing a rational foundation for rational consensus when debates between hyper-goods do arise. Illustrating this will demonstrate that ethics cannot be relegated to morality, as Habermas supposed, but rather ethics is foundational, and moral norms derive from ethics. More importantly for our enquiry, this will reassert the importance of authenticity as an ethical ideal, over moral theory.

The argument that Habermas's discourse ethics presupposes some form of the good is further supported by Keith Breen who argues that 'Habermas' Kantian division between ethical "values" and moral "norms" does not hold, since the basis of his discourse theory of morality is in the last instance an understanding of identity formation, that is, a substantive *ethical* vision' (2012: 58). Breen's claim is that the social and intersubjective identity to the self which Habermas relies upon is ultimately informed by an underlying good. Moreover, autonomy relies upon a concept of the individual as a social being. Cultural impoverishment refers to damaged subjectivity and intersubjectivity which emanates from affirmative ethical intimations of the good life. As Breen further argues, 'as this positive image of lifeworld reproduction has as much to do with ethical self-realisation as with self-determination, we are entitled to doubt the prime role accorded to morality and, thus, to question Habermas' separation of moral norms from ethical values as a feasible response to Weberian subjectivism' (2012: 71). Thus, since Habermas's theory of communicative action presupposes a form of the good, his notion of morality is dependent upon ethics, and as such, his approach is subject to a performative contradiction. That is, his own theory is in tension with itself.

Having thus established that Habermas's account is ultimately informed by an ethical vision, his approach cannot be said to provide a satisfactory response to the problem of freedom and meaning. Moreover, his relegation of ethics to morality undermined the importance of authenticity, but this concern cannot be sustained because moral norms are themselves dependent upon ethics. The concept of a good, as developed by Taylor, emphasizes that there are in-built qualitative distinctions, that there are modes of life which are higher than others.

Certain goods are independent of our desires, inclinations and choices, and that these goods provide standards by which choices, and desires, are judged. That is, morality cannot precede ethics, for Taylor, because foundational public questions, such as 'who we are' are ethical questions. Habermas, however, fails to acknowledge that his theory of morality is dependent upon an ethical basis. The consequence is that his theory not only lacks a sound foundation but also cannot provide a more satisfactory response to the problems of freedom and meaning than our concept of authenticity.

4.4 Summary

Within this chapter, we began by addressing Habermas's approach to modernity, which he problematizes in terms of freedom and meaning. Having determined that its failure was a consequence of the imbalanced development of the lifeworld, which he understood to thrive on communicative reason, Habermas then proposed the theory of communicative action to remedy this. However, despite his admirable aim to address the one-sided rationalization of society, we criticized Habermas's claim by stating that there are two separate spheres: of lifeworld, which contain communicative rationality; and systems, which contain instrumental rationality. The positive outcome of our consideration, however, was the realization that resistance to systems imperatives within the lifeworld provides us with the continued possibility to live an authentic existence. We then continued to explore the extension of his theory to questions of ethics/morality, where he addresses questions of the good. However, although Habermas advocates a concept of self-realization, or authenticity, in his account he gives priority to self-determination, or autonomy. This prioritization not only relegated questions of the good to a secondary position but also undermined our concept of authenticity, as it is an ethical ideal. We then argued that Habermas's prioritization of morality over ethics was shown to rest upon a prior conception of ethics, and as a consequence his account was subject to a performative contradiction and, as such, could not be deemed a sufficient response to the problems of freedom and meaning. Having explicated Habermas's account of modernity, and the way in which he can be said to address the problems of freedom and meaning, we will now turn to considering an alternative response to the problem of modernity, that advocated by Michel Foucault.

5

Is the 'self' a fiction?

A second and very different response to the problems of modernity can be found within the thought of Michel Foucault. Whilst Habermas sought to return to the Enlightenment project, with the intention of completing it, Foucault seeks to overcome the Enlightenment project, rather than repair a fragmented framework. The Habermasian perspective was that communicative rationality possessed unfulfilled potential; for Foucault, on the other hand, discourses of power have penetrated every aspect of modern life and made individuality impossible. Unlike Habermas, Foucault accepts the consequences of the Enlightenment's failure to establish a rational end to human action. The consequence for Foucault is that the promise of increased freedom was not delivered, but that the sense of individuality which supposedly emerged was a myth. Although we believe ourselves to possess the potential of self-determination, Foucault claims that we are subjected to discourses of power which produce truth and determine how we conceive of ourselves. However, rather than resigning in vain to a pessimistic fate, it will be suggested that Foucault's approach is to seek out a method of self-creation which has not been subjected to discourse. In order to achieve this aim, he turns to pre-modernity where he discovers the ethic of care which was championed by the Stoics and which he believes provides the means to combat the subjection of modern subjects. However, although Foucault focuses on self-creation, he does not say anything substantial about meaning but instead offers an empty aesthetic.

This chapter will begin with an analysis of Foucault's account of modernity (Section 5.1). Here we will explicate his claim that the Enlightenment, which promised increased freedom, in fact led to subjection, with institutions creating subjects through discourses of power. Although a response to this problem can be found within Foucault's later work, we will question the continuity of his oeuvre (Section 5.2). In this section we will illustrate that the concept of power devised in his early work prevents any form of resolution, and that he must modify this to provide a constructive account. It will also be claimed that thinking in terms of power relations enables us to develop a more refined understanding of authenticity, which will become useful later in our book. Having resolved the tension in Foucault's account, we will then proceed to discuss his response to subjection (Section 5.3). Here we will turn to his ethical analysis of pre-modernity and his argument that we ought to appropriate the Stoic-inspired 'care of the self'. With an adequate understanding of Foucault's resolution, we will then argue that in comparison with socio-existential authenticity, Foucauldian care is an inferior ethic (Section 5.4). Although Foucault quite explicitly engages with the problem of freedom, he does not satisfactorily address this issue. In order to determine whether he provides an adequate response to the problem of meaning we will question whether his idea of turning one's life into a work of art can fulfil this role.

5.1 The subjection of individuality

Like Habermas, Foucault has an ambivalent attitude towards modernity. Rather than upholding it as progressive or arguing that it was instrumental in the cultural decomposition of society, his approach was to reject this simple distinction of, for or against, noting that acceptance of this 'would trap us into playing the arbitrary and boring part of either the irrationalist or the rationalist' (2001a: 328). Thus, where Foucault differs from Habermas is in his rejection of this dichotomy of advocate or detractor. This is evident in his claim that 'the "Enlightenment," which discovered the liberties, also invented the disciplines' (1991a: 222). Thus, like Weber, Foucault understands that the Enlightenment simultaneously advanced and limited individual freedom. His attitude towards modernity is perhaps best expressed in his homage to Kant 'What is Enlightenment'. In this short essay, Foucault understands Kant's achievement to be the critical analysis of his own contemporary social setting. However, rather than a historical period, Foucault refers to modernity as an attitude. Furthermore, he believes 'modernity is not a phenomena of sensitivity to the fleeting presents; it is the will to "heroize" the present' (1991b: 40). It is precisely this attitude of acceptance that introduces not only a permanent critique of our historical era but also the ability to 'free ourselves from the intellectual blackmail of "being for or against the Enlightenment"' (1991b: 45). Only by accepting modernity as it is, rather than attempting to overcome it, can one recognize and criticize history. According to Foucault, 'a philosophical life in which the critique of what we are is at one and the same time the historical analysis of the limits that are imposed on us and an experience with the possibility of going beyond them' (1991b: 50). Thus, only by accepting these can one recognize that the Enlightenment has not yet brought about 'man's emergence from self-incurred immaturity', as Kant prescribed.[1]

What has transpired, Foucault alleges, is that various institutions have come to dominate the individual, to the extent that one is a subject only insofar as one is 'subjected' to the discourses of power which these institutions produce. For example, whilst one who enlists in the military is defined by their punctuality, obedience to commands and reserved behaviour, these are not essential characteristics of the person in question, but norms which have been instilled by a military institution. According to Foucault, this is the effect which all institutions produce and is achieved through discipline and surveillance, which he associates with the rise of modern science. Power not only creates the rules which one must abide by but also creates those whom it dominates through obedience, submission and subjection. Categorization of social groups is presented as beneficial for the development of scientific study and the promotion of knowledge. However, it has adverse effects upon the general public, insofar as it enables them to be more easily controlled. Thus, it is through instruments of disciplinary power, within Foucault's account, that the individual is produced.

He exemplifies his theory of subjection through the roles of prisons in *Discipline and Punish* and asylums in *Madness and Civilisation*. What he here determines is that these institutions are oppressive because they label and exclude those whom they contain. In the case of prisons, the intended purpose is to reform offenders to prevent them from reoffending, but what they actually do is to isolate 'delinquents'. This is also the case with asylums, which are supposed to cure patients, but which in reality incarcerate 'lunatics'. By isolating 'delinquents' and 'lunatics' from society, these institutions turn them into negative role models, as warnings for others (1991a: 231–2). On Foucault's account then, the purpose of prisons and asylums is not to reform and 'normalize' those inside, but to normalize the general public. This normalization of the public is achieved by isolating and excluding the 'delinquent' and 'lunatic'. However, it is not only institutions which incarcerate social deviants that have this effect. Foucault explicates the effect that science also has had upon sex in *The History of Sexuality*. Here he notes that sexual acts which are non-marital became labelled

---

[1] Although Foucault and Habermas both derive inspiration from Kant, their approaches vary significantly. Whilst Habermas sought to continue what Kant started, Foucault writes off the project of modernity as untenable.

as perverse. Whilst a man who had engaged in sodomy had previously been seen as having to succumb to sin, in modernity he was no longer a sinner, but categorized as a 'homosexual'. As Foucault explains, 'the sodomite had been a temporary aberration; the homosexual was now a species' (1980: 42). This form of social conditioning is therefore applied to not only those who do not conform to the norm but also the general public, who regulate their behaviour, in order to avoid being labelled a social misfit.

This is made explicit in *Discipline and Punish*, where Foucault launches a genealogical enquiry into the origin of punishment. In this seminal work, he argues that the mechanism of discipline, which originated in prisons, has been made manifest in institutions such as education, health care and the military. Infiltrating various social institutions, punishment was utilized as a political tactic to modify and control behaviour. However, rather than physical punishment, which is used to control one's body, this technology of power controls one's soul. The consequence is that the 'modern soul' is born out of methods of punishment, supervision and constraint. Opposing the narrative that public execution was abolished due to the Enlightenment's humane disposition, Foucault claims that it was because the crowds could no longer be physically controlled. As an alternative to torture, discipline thus emerged as a new technology of power. Although power is usually associated with negative connotations, Foucault claims that it is productive, by which he means that individuals are the product of power relations. As Alan D. Schrift explains, 'the modern individual is no longer called upon as a subject to obey the law, but is produced instead as an individual who is required to conform to the *norm*' (2013: 145).

According to Foucault, modern society is structured in the same way as Jeremy Bentham's ideal prison, the Panopticon (1991a: 200). What Bentham envisaged was the construction of a correctional facility in which the incarcerated can be simultaneously seen, without being able to see their observer. As a result of believing they are being constantly observed, this encourages the prisoner to conduct self-surveillance and moderate their own behaviour. In Foucault's analysis, this same psychological disposition is instilled within subjects, who are made aware that they are constantly being observed and judged by others. The consequence is that individuals willingly conform to social norms without the need for externally imposed sanctions. This state is established, according to Foucault, through instruments of power.

In *Discipline and Punish*, Foucault claims that in the modern world, people have become nothing but 'docile bodies', by which he means they are easily manipulated and coercible. In his own words, 'a body is docile that may be subjected, used, transformed and improved' (1991a: 136). In the eighteenth century, it was discovered that a 'military air' did not need to be inborn, but that one could be trained to become a soldier. This belief however was not restricted to the military but applied to social institutions in general. It is precisely this function which is fulfilled by politics within Foucault's account. As he explains, 'politics, as the technique of internal peace and order, sought to implement the mechanism of the perfect army, of the disciplined mass, of the docile, useful troop' (1991a: 168). It is this very technique of discipline which 'subjects' individuals by making them into docile bodies. As Foucault puts it, 'discipline "makes" individuals; it is the specific technique of a power that regulates individuals both as objects and instruments of its exercise' (1991a: 170). In order to explicate the means by which individuals are 'made', Foucault offers three instruments of disciplinary power.

The first instrument which forms 'docile bodies' is hierarchical observation. This operates in the same manner as Bentham's Panopticon, insofar as it makes individuals aware that they are being observed, causing them to be aware of and regulate their own behaviour. As Foucault explains, 'the essence of discipline presupposes a mechanism that coerces by means of observation' (1991a: 170). This is not necessarily achieved through surveillance, though this has become a concern for modern individuals. What Foucault is primarily concerned with, rather, is space and the construction of architecture. Much as military camps are designed, so, too, have modern institutions and spaces been constructed. As Foucault himself explains, 'for a long time this model of the camp, or at least its underlying principle, was found in urban development, in the construction of working class housing estates, hospitals, asylums, prisons, schools: the spatial "resting" of hierarchal surveillance' (1991a: 171). The way in which architecture is manipulated to control individual behaviour is further illuminated by Walter Benjamin, who notes that Baron Haussmann's post-revolution reconstruction of Paris widened the streets to prevent protestors from once again barricading them.[2] Architecture thus assists in the application of this instrument of discipline, as Foucault subtly says, 'stones can make people docile' (1991a: 170).

The second instrument of disciplinary power in Foucault's account is normalizing judgement. Within every institution, norms are established which individuals must maintain, with failure to do so resulting in punishment. Thus, institutions devise 'a kind of judicial privilege with its own laws, its own

---

[2] *The Arcades Project,* trans. Howard Eiland and Kevin McLaughlin (Harvard: Harvard University Press, 2002). A more recent example of this is evident through 'hostile architecture', which includes anti-homeless spikes and park benches in London and other cities.

specific offences, its particular forms of judgement' (1991a: 178). Institutions therefore exploit judicial vacuums by establishing their own rules and employ penal mechanisms to sustain these. These include micro-penalties of times – deducting wages for lateness, and threat of dismissal over absenteeism; activity – enforcing zeal and punishing negligence; behaviour – conditioning one to be more obedient and to adopt a certain mode of conduct; speech – forbidding insolence and frowning upon idle chatter; body – regulating one's attitude, gestures and level of cleanliness; and sexuality – condemning indecency and impurity.

In these ways 'they defined and then repressed a mass of behaviour that the relative indifference of the great systems of punishment had allowed to escape' (1991a: 178). The pre-modern systems of punishment that Foucault refers to include capital punishment and public shaming. However, whilst these were able to physically control subjects, they were unable to effectively regulate their behaviour. The modern instruments of disciplinary power, on the other hand, such as normalizing judgement regulates the individual's behaviour in accordance with a particular institution's aims. As a consequence, 'the perpetual penalty that traverses all points and supervises every instant in the disciplinary institution compares, differentiates, hierarchizes, homogenizes, excludes. In short it *normalizes*' (1991a: 183).

A third instrument of disciplinary power, which is a combination of the former two, is that of examination. As Foucault explains, 'it is a normalising gaze, a surveillance that makes it possible to qualify, to classify, and to punish. It establishes over individuals a visibility through which one differentiates them, judges them' (1991a: 183). Examination links the formation of knowledge to the exercise of power. Unlike traditional power, which is seen, disciplinary power is exercised through invisibility – the subjects are seen and it is this which assures the hold of power which is exercised over them. 'The examination is the technique by which power, instead of emitting the signs of its potency, instead of imposing its mark on its subjects, holds them in a mechanism of objectification' (1991a: 138). Means of examination include registers for enlistment and deserters in the military, study of treatments in hospitals and the aptitude analysis of students in schools. Each of these leads to the 'formalization' of the individual within power relations. What this means is that examination makes each individual a case, an object for a branch of knowledge and a hold for a branch of power. In this way, reality is produced by power, the standards expected of individuals, and to which they are made to perform, become truth. Reality is therefore produced and manipulated by these disciplines of power.

Thus, what Foucault seems to be inferring is a rejection of the phenomenological perspective, which emphasizes a privileged subject, instead Foucault argues that the subject does not exist, but is a product of the power imposed upon them by various institutions which govern their lives. In his own words, 'there is no sovereign, founding subject, a universal form of subject to be found everywhere [. . .] the subject is constituted through practices of subjection' (1988: 50–1). By understanding individuals as none other than socially construed, Foucault strips the individual of their ability to exist in any genuine sense. This perspective is also held by Deleuze, who notes that 'Foucault does not use the word subject as a person or as a form of identity, but the words "subjectivation" as a process and "Self" as a relation' (Schrift 1995: 127). Foucault's account thus entails that the subject is but a social construction, determined by the various discourses of power which are exercised upon it. Having outlined Foucault's account of modernity, that subjects are created by institutions through domination and discourse, we will now turn our attention to his response to this problem. However, before we do, it is first important to address the logical implications of Foucault's diagnosis of modernity.

5.2 From power to subjection

One major consequence of this theory, which Foucault himself does not address, is that if there is no individual subject, then one cannot exist in any genuine sense. That is, by rejecting the self, he also rejects the possibility of subjects being able to live a life which has been given purpose. This argument is developed by Luc Boltanski and Eve Chiapello, who in criticizing postmodern thinkers, note that they not only reject the 'self' as incapable of providing a satisfactory ground for freedom but also simultaneously dismiss the possibility for living an authentic existence. In their own words, Boltanski and Chiapello note the consequence of the postmodern perspective is 'both to acknowledge the demand for authenticity as valid and to create a world where this question is no longer to be posed' (2005: 452). Habermas also makes a similar criticism, that for Foucault 'socialized individuals can only be perceived as exemplars, as standardized products, of some discourse formation – as individual copies that are mechanically punched out' (1987b: 293). This has profound implications on our enquiry, for if his analysis of modernity is correct, then the problem of meaning becomes invalidated because subjects have no say over the direction of their lives. Is this, however, the case?

These criticisms suggest that Foucault does not problematize meaning, but instead rejects any sense of the self-constituting 'subject'. However, Foucault himself later suggests that his early work outlines the problem which he intends to address, namely the subjection of the individual, and that his later work is intended to resolve this. Prior to discussing Foucault's response, however, it is first important to address the question of continuity. That is, we will attempt to determine if Foucault's oeuvre presents a linear development from power to the subject and whether he consciously outlines the problem of power with the intention of resolving it. In his early work, *History of Madness* (1961), it seems as though Foucault is primarily concerned with domination, then he focuses on power in *Discipline and Punish* (1975), and finally subjectivity in *History of Sexuality* (1976–84). Although it appears as though these are all independently focused enquiries, Foucault himself retrospectively reconstructs the aims and objectives of his publications.[3] This is made explicit in an interview where he claims 'when I think back now, I ask myself what else was it that I was talking about in *Madness and Civilization* ... but power?' (2001b: 117). However, rather than being primarily concerned with power, Foucault claims that the underlying theme of his academic output has been the subject. In his own mind, he locates continuity in the overarching aim 'to create a history of the different modes by which, in our culture, human beings are made subjects' (2001b: 326).

Should we, however, trust Foucault that this is indeed what he has been doing and that he has not simply constructed this narrative to grant continuity to an otherwise disconnected research output? Foucault's claim to continuity is supported by Amy Allen, who argues that his later work presents an 'extension rather than a radical departure from his earlier work on disciplinary power and subjection' (2013: 347). This is further reinforced by Colin Koopman, who also claims that there is no decisive break in Foucault's genealogical thought on modernity. As Koopman states, 'Foucault's writings on ethics in antiquity pick up right where his prior writings on power and knowledge in modernity left off' (2013: 527). In order to make this apparent, Koopman claims that this can be illustrated in two ways: first, we can understand Foucault to be constructing a genealogical enquiry into the emergence of modern ethical problems through the problematization of classical ethics; secondly, we can understand his later

---

[3] A similar move is made by Nietzsche, who retrospectively wrote prefaces to each of his books, in an attempt to articulate the manner in which the text in question anticipated concepts or ideas which would be explicated in succeeding publications. This practice was also employed within his autobiographical *Ecce Homo*, where he reinterprets his entire oeuvre to illustrate how each of his books was ultimately concerned with the same problem.

work on classical ethics as an ethical response to the problems diagnosed in his work on modern morality. Thus, on Koopman's reading, 'Foucault's genealogies taken together move from ancient self-care through self-knowledge and self-decipherment down to modern self-surveillance and finally self-discipline' (2013: 527–8). By offering a genealogical development of how the modern subject came to be subjected, Foucault's later work can then be seen as developing this perspective so that it may be overcome.

We have argued that there is continuity between Foucault's publications, and that he sees the subjection of individuals as a problem to be resolved, and one which he attempts to address in his later work. How does he overcome the problem of subjection? An explanation for this is provided by Steven Lukes who claims that the account of power which Foucault depicts within his diagnosis of modernity is best described as 'ultra-radical'. Lukes's reason for demarcating Foucault's concept of power as such is because it is presented as seeping into every aspect of individual existence, reducing subjectivity to delusion. As Lukes attests, 'there is no escaping domination, that it is 'everywhere' and there is no freedom from it or reasoning independent of it' (2005: 12). This account is then at odds with that against which concepts of authenticity contend.

Heidegger's concept of inauthenticity, for example, presents a view of domination within which subjects are subjected in terms of social conformity. As Heidegger puts it, 'we take pleasure and enjoy ourselves as *das Man* take pleasure, we read, see and judge about literature and art as *das Man* see and judge' (2010: 164). However, upon discovering one's existential condition, on the aforementioned Heideggarian approach, one is able to reject this externally imposed image and determine one's life for oneself. On the Foucauldian approach, on the other hand, the consequence of one's identity being constituted by none other than discourses of power can only lead to awareness of the futility of one's existence and the realization that there is no sense of transcendence beyond this condition. However, in order for Foucault to proceed and address the subjection of the self, it is necessary for the subject to be an object for itself. That is, one must be able to objectify oneself in order to cultivate oneself. As Colin Koopman explains, 'practices of self-transformation take place at the point of intersection between our being a subject for ourselves and our being an object to ourselves' (2013: 530).

Thus, on this current view of power, it is impossible for Foucauldian subjects to engage in any form of self-transformative practice which would free them from subjection. The reason is because, as produced by discourses of power, they lack the necessary freedom to choose for themselves. Upon realization that they are the result of discourses of power, they can simply recognize that every decision is not their own but a further extension of the power exercised upon them. Although this is the approach which Foucault presents within his early work, one explanation as to why he himself turns from this and instead focuses on ancient Greek ethics is because he recognized that his previous view of power was an untenable position. This approach is advocated by Steven Lukes who claims, 'Foucault came to disown this ultra-radical view, which would, in any case, both render resistance to domination unintelligible and undermine Foucault's own critical standpoint and political positions' (2005: 123). Thus, in order to address the problem of freedom, Foucault's concept of power has shifted from an ultra-radical account to a softer account which enables the individual to challenge institutional domination.

A more congenial concept of power, and one which Foucault can be understood to advocate, in order to permit an ethic of care, is proposed by Lukes. Building upon existing literature, which claims that power can be held by either decision-makers or those who set the agenda for decisions, Lukes suggests that power ought to be conceived of as 'ideology'.[4] Rather than an overtly applied force, his claim is that subjects can be manipulated through the construction of false consciousness. That is, we ought to conceive of the manifestation of power as the ability to coerce subjects into advocating beliefs and desires which are opposed to their own self-interest. For example, we can conceive of a working-class voter who opts to elect a conservative political party because they believe that society is best run by members of the upper class, or a woman who not only accepts but also advocates patriarchy, believing that women are indeed naturally inferior to men. In each of these examples, we can claim that the beliefs and actions of the individuals in question are a consequence of ideological power exercised upon them.

On the ultra-radical view, which was present in Foucault's earlier work, the concept of power produced the subject, and as such, it could not be challenged. On Lukes's account, on the other hand, ideological power does not produce the subject but a false consciousness which alienates the subject from self-interest. In this latter concept of power, upon discovering that the standards

---

[4] Within Lukes's analysis there are three faces, or dimensions, of power, these are (i) decision-making power, (ii) non-decision-making power and (iii) ideological power. In the first face, Lukes discusses the classical pluralist approach to power, that it is a behavioural attitude. Here whoever prevails within a decision-making process is considered to be powerful, that is when a parent wins an argument against a child, they gain the upper hand. The second face is based on the realization that it is possible to shape the argument by setting the agenda. This offers a further dimension of power because if one is capable of determining the limits of debate then one can prevent oneself from being challenged.

and norms which one values are detrimental to one's well-being, it is in the subject's interest to challenge these. In order for Foucault to present a response to the excessive exercise of power, he must also advocate an ideological concept of power. This concept can also be used to explain inauthenticity. By thinking in terms of power relations, we have also been provided with a platform to better understand that which constitutes inauthentic existence. That is, rather than simply understanding inauthentic existence as that which is contrary to an authentic existence, we can claim that it is inauthentic because it portrays a false consciousness. This, however, is not the right place to develop this line of argument, but rather will be reserved until and returned to in Chapter 7. Having established the concept of power which Foucault employs, and illustrated how he may proceed to posit a response to the concept of subjection, we will now turn to explicating his account, where it will be possible to determine the manner in which he addresses the problems of modernity.

5.3 Technologies of the self

Within his later work, Foucault turns his attention to providing a genealogical analysis of pre-modern ethics. In *The History of Sexuality*, he focuses on explicating the practices characteristic of Hellenic and Imperial Roman ethics. Although the Delphic oracle's maxim 'know thyself' is often taken to epitomize Hellenic ethics, Foucault suggests an alternative ethic existed and which was more important. In his account, it is rather care for oneself (*curia sui/epimeleia heautou*) that is the ultimate ethical aim of classical philosophy. He does not, however, dismiss 'knowing-oneself', but suggests that it was supplementary and a means to 'caring for oneself' (1990: 64). In the modern era, the emergence of individuality was believed to be in reaction to the decrease of freedom; according to Foucault, in ancient Greece,

> it was not a strengthening of public authority that accounted for the development of that rigorous ethics, but rather a weakening of the political and social framework within which the lives of individuals used to unfold. Being less firmly attached to the city, more isolated, from one another, and more reliant on themselves, they sought in philosophy rules of conduct that were more personal. (1990: 41)

Although Foucault emphasizes the importance of self-care over self-knowledge, he claims that 'know thyself' came to obscure 'care for oneself' in modern philosophical discourse, and it is for this reason that we associate it with classical thought. He provides two explanations for this role reversal. First, the transformation of the moral principles of Western society distorted the practice of caring for oneself in the modern era, and there occurred a shift from care of the self to knowledge of the self. In Christian morality, knowing oneself becomes a means of self-renunciation, and it is this tradition which underpins modern philosophical thought. Furthermore, in the secular tradition, external laws provide the basis for morality. So rather than looking inwards, individuals look outside of themselves for moral absolutes. Secondly, in theoretical philosophy 'knowledge-of-self' became the first step in the theory of knowledge. This is exemplified through the likes of Descartes, whose epistemological aim was to determine that which he could be certain of and whose starting point was subjectivity. As a consequence of these two social transformations, Foucault claims that an inversion of 'know thyself' and 'care for oneself' occurred. By taking this line of argument, Foucault can be seen to be attacking the philosophy of consciousness, like Habermas.

According to Foucault, the concept 'care of self' first emerged within the Platonic dialogue *Alcibiades* (2000b: 95). Here Alcibiades is portrayed as desiring to advance his political career. However, Socrates makes the argument that in order to be a successful politician it is necessary to care for others. Furthermore, in order to care for others, one must first be able to care for oneself. The concept of care is also expounded in the *Apology*, where Socrates makes the claim that he has been sent by the gods to remind his fellow man that rather than their riches and honour, they ought to concern themselves with themselves and their souls (and rather than punishment he ought to be rewarded for his service to society). The means by which Socrates conducts this practice is through question and answer, enabling one to determine what one is (the object of one's care) and what one needs (how to be cared for). This is made explicit through Socrates's role as a midwife, to help those who are pregnant with thought to conceive of truth. By his method of question and answer, one can thus determine whether one possesses expertise, or true knowledge of something. Thus, according to Foucault, within the Platonic dialogues, 'care' has a pedagogical role; in other words, it is a form of education (2000b: 97). In the Platonic tradition, caring for oneself enables one to know oneself. Furthermore, 'knowing oneself becomes the object of the quest of concern for self' (2000d: 231). For fifth-century Greeks, within the Platonic tradition, dialogue was the means of discovering truth in the soul.

Although Foucault locates this practice within Socratic dialectic, he notes that it reached maturity with the Epicurean and Stoic schools which gained prominence in the Roman Empire. In his own words, 'the first two centuries of the imperial epoch can be seen as the summit of a curve: a kind of golden age in the cultivation of the self' (1990: 45). It was the Epicureans, however, who first put a spin on the dialectic practice initiated by Plato. Rather than preparing one for political life, for Epicurus, care of the self becomes an end in itself. Turning to Epicurus' ethical approach, which is preserved within his *Letter to Menoeceus*, Foucault illustrates that Epicurus took self-development seriously. This is evident in his famous quadripartite cure: do not fear the gods, do not worry about death, what is good is easy to get, and what is terrible is easy to endure. Mentally, this maxim enables one to instil an optimistic disposition. Physically, it allows one to gain satisfaction in elementary needs as opposed to luxury. Epicureans also practised physical exercises in abstinence, despite being commonly mistaken for philosophers of indulgence. What Epicurus actually taught was that one could acquire a greater appreciation by reducing the quantity of that which one indulges in.

It is with the Stoics, however, that Foucault believed this practice reached its peak. Unlike the Epicureans who deprived themselves in order to enrich their appreciation, the Stoics did so in order 'to convince oneself that the worst misfortune will not deprive one of the things one absolutely needs, and therefore will always be able to tolerate what one is capable of enduring at times' (1990: 60). This practice is termed *praemeditatio mororum* and is utilized through three primary *techne*. The first is disclosure of self, which is achieved through the exercise of letter writing. This is exemplified by Seneca's letters, through which he gives council to Lucilius, and simultaneously asks him for advice in return. It thus ought to be understood as a form of 'soul service' through social relations. The second *techne* is examination of self, which is demonstrated through Marcus Aurelius's description of everyday life. This is important because what this disclosed was oneself – what one thought, and what one felt – but more than this, these examinations provide an account of what was done and what should have been done. Thus the second form, of examination, is achieved through self-reflection. As Foucault explains, 'to come back inside oneself and examine the "riches" that one has deposited there; one must have within oneself a kind of book that one rereads from time to time' (1990: 101). Thus, unlike the modern concept of examination, which is an instrument of power, the ancient form of examination is utilized by the subject as a form of self-cultivation.

The third technology, *áskēsis*, or remembering, is the most important for Foucault. Unlike modern moral theories, such as deontology and utilitarianism, he tells us, '*moral conceptions in Greek and Greco-Roman antiquity were much more orientated towards practices of the self and the question of áskēsis than towards codifications of conducts and the strict definition of what is permitted and what is forbidden*' (1992: 30). As Foucault further elucidates, '*áskēsis* means not renunciation but the progressive consideration of self, or mastery over oneself, obtained not through the renunciation of reality but through the acquisition and assimilation of truth' (1992: 238). Whilst Plato located truth in oneself, and which was derived through dialogue, the Stoics obtained truth from the master, whom they listened to. The master imparted truth which one appropriated, 'a truth imparted by a teaching, a reading, or a piece of advice; and one assimilates it so thoroughly that it becomes a part of oneself, an abiding, always-active, inner principle of action' (2000b: 100–101).

There are two poles of *askēsis*, and it is these which are commonly associated with Stoicism. First, meditation, which takes the form of a thought experiment, to reveal what one must accept. One is asked to imagine the worst that can happen and that it is already present and occurring. The purpose of this practice is not to endure pain, but to convince oneself that which one is contemplating is not real misfortune.[5] Secondly, self-training, which is employed to '*establish and test the independence of the individual with regard to the external world*' (2000d: 240). This took the form of *sexual abstinence and physical privation.* Plutarch gives the example of acquiring an appetite through physical exercise, sitting at a table laden with delicacies, but rather than indulging oneself, to present the food to one's servants and instead content oneself with an elementary substitute (1990: 59).

Epictetus offers a middle ground between these two poles – suggesting one watches and verifies one's own representations and thoughts like a night watchman who does not permit anyone to enter the town at night, or a moneychanger who weighs and verifies the legitimacy of currency (2000d: 240). Seneca likewise proposes an 'administrative review, where it is a matter of evaluating a performed activity in order to reactivate its principles and ensure their correct application in the future' (2000d: 61). However, Epictetus's school was regarded not merely as a place of education but also as a medical clinic. 'One can see that this control of representations is not aimed at uncovering, beneath appearances, a hidden truth that would be that of the subject itself; rather, it finds in these representations, as they present themselves, the occasion for recalling to mind a certain number of true principles' (2000b: 104). For this

---

[5] For the Stoics, real misfortune would be constituted by such a condition as one has been bereft of the means to procure food or shelter.

reason, Foucault claims 'it is in Epictetus no doubt that one finds the highest philosophical development of this theme' (1990: 47).

Beginning with *Alcibiades*, the care of oneself was advocated as a means to care for others within a political role. Socrates teaches Alcibiades that it is necessary to care for the city in order to be a good politician, and in order to care for the city one must care for oneself. However, with Epicurus, care for oneself becomes an end in itself. The Stoics then perfected this through the development of *áskēsis*. Thus, whilst Plato emphasized *techne* of life which has care for the city as its end, for Seneca, *techne* of self is upheld, which advocates care for oneself as the end. In Foucault's own words, 'a Greek citizen of the fifth or fourth century would have felt that his *techne* for life was to take care of the city, of his companions. But for Seneca, for instance, the problem is to take care of himself' (1990: 260).

In providing a genealogical account of care, what does Foucault hope to achieve? Considering the focus of his early work, and the criticisms it faced, it can be read as a response to the oppressive discourses of power, as an ethical approach to life. In Hegel's account, Stoicism is a forced turn inwards in reaction to the oppressive power of the Roman Empire. As he himself claims, 'as a universal form of the World Spirit, Stoicism could only appear on the scene in a time of universal fear and bondage' (2008b: 100). Foucault, likewise, can be seen to propose the Stoic-inspired ethic of care in response to the oppressive discourses of power, to which one is subjected. Is this, however, an adequate response? The consequence of decreased public freedom in the Roman Empire, for Hegel, is inwardness and subjectivity, 'rendering the soul absolutely indifferent to everything which the real world had to offer' (20: 318). By cutting rational thought off from the phenomenal world the Stoics gained a sense of independence because their thought was not dependent upon the world. However, because their mind has no content of its own but must take its content from the phenomenal world, their thought cannot be truly independent. One consequence of this, according to Hegel, is that the freedom of thought which the Stoics propose is purely formal. How does Foucault propose to circumvent this concern and present an approach which is capable of addressing the problem of subjection?

Influenced by the Stoics, it seems that Foucault's ethical approach is to re-implement this classical concept of care. However, when asked in an interview whether the Greeks provide an attractive alternative, Foucault replied, 'I am not looking for an alternative; you can't find the resolution of a problem in the solution of another problem raised at another moment by other people' (2000a: 256). As Koopman makes explicit, 'Foucault is not telling us that we ought to transform ourselves, but is rather telling us that the work of ethics today stands in need of a structuring tendency towards transformativity' (2013: 530). Foucault further claims that 'there is no exemplary value in a period that is not our own period.... It is not anything to get back to' (1977: 259). Thus, Foucault makes it explicit that he is advocating neither nouveau-Stoicism nor a return to a Stoic way of life. This is further elucidated by Amy Allen who argues that 'Foucault is not suggesting a simple return to the precepts of Greek or Stoic ethics as a cure for what ails us..... Ancient Greek and Stoic ethics seems a promising resource precisely because it is not bound up with juridical and disciplinary forms of subjection and normalization' (2013: 348).

It thus seems that Foucault's intention is to discover a way of being which has not been subjected to discourse and which offers the means to autonomy under the conditions of modernity. Separated from Stoicism, Foucault understands 'care' to entail 'those reflective and voluntary practices by which men not only set themselves rules of conduct, but seek to transform themselves, to change themselves in their singular being, and to make of their life into an *oeuvre* that carries certain aesthetic values and meets certain stylistic criteria' (1992: 10–11). It is thus through an aesthetic approach which we can understand Foucault's endorsement of 'care' as providing a response to the problem of freedom caused by the subjection of the individual. Modelling his approach on Nietzsche's claim that one ought to 'give style to one's character' (1991: §290), Foucault elaborates, 'art has become something that is related to objects and not to individuals or to life. [. . .] But couldn't everyone's life become a work of art?' (2000c: 261). Foucauldian care thus involves utilizing Stoic based practices, as opposed to Stoicism proper, and in this sense he also follows from Nietzsche.[6]

From this, we have determined that Foucauldian 'care' offers a means to overcome the restriction of freedom imposed upon us by rational institutions. We will now turn to evaluating the success of his theory to do so. To further elucidate his theory, Foucault contrasts his own position with the concept of authenticity espoused by Sartre. As Foucault explains, 'through the moral notion of authenticity, [Sartre] turns back to the idea that we have to be ourselves – to be truly our true self' (2000c: 262). Foucault suggests that the only practical resolution is to link Sartre's insight to creativity, instead of authenticity. This is made explicit in his understanding of Baudelaire, for whom modern man 'is not the man who goes off to discover himself, his secrets and his hidden truth; he is

---

[6] See Michael Ure, 'Nietzsche's Free Spirit Trilogy and Stoic Therapy', *Journal of Nietzsche Studies,* no. 38 (Fall 2009): 60–84.

the man who tries to invent himself' (2000b: 312). Contrary to his understanding of Sartre, Foucault claims, 'we should not have to refer the creative activity of somebody to the kind of relation he has to himself, but should relate the kind of relation one has to oneself to a creative activity' (2000c: 262). That is, rather than creative activity determining oneself, Foucault suggests that one's relation to oneself determines one's creative activity. This, however, seems to make the same normative claim as the existential concept of authenticity, namely to reject socially imposed standards and create oneself. How does this differ to the account of authenticity which we have constructed?

Within our socio-existential approach, it was claimed that our possibilities are provided by our social context. In the Foucauldian account, however, if we are to reject externally imposed power, from where do we derive our values? Foucault himself states that for the subject who attempts to develop technologies of self that one does so through 'patterns that one finds in the culture and which are proposed, suggested and imposed on one by one's culture, one's society and own's social group' (2000a: 11). Although this comes close to Taylor's horizon of significance, which emphasizes dialogical development of the self, Foucault's approach is nevertheless a subjective endeavour. The reason is because it merely internalizes and shapes that which is external to it, and as such, there is no self beyond this.

In the essay 'Moral Identity and Private Autonomy', Richard Rorty discusses and defends Foucault's position which is associated with the possibility of 'being oneself'. More specifically, he interprets Foucault's approach to be analogous with individual uniqueness, that is, to be oneself is to be unique or original in such a way that one is distinct from others. In Rorty's own words, 'what is more important is one's *rapport à soi*, one's private search for autonomy, one's refusal to be exhaustively describable in words which apply to anyone other than oneself' (1991: 193). However, as Rahel Jaeggi points out, 'what makes Rorty's [and subsequently Foucault's] description of individuality thin, among other things, is his neglect of the fact that individuality develops only in relation to, or in engaging with, something and that for this reason individuals can realize themselves only in relating to the world' (2014: 211). Thus, the attempt to be oneself by being unique is problematic because it requires one to only associate with others negatively, to see other subjects as objects which we must distance ourselves from in order to be unique.

A further concern is that Foucault's account of care cannot provide an account of ethical commitment. What one is to become is nothing other than personal choice. It is 'a choice about existence made by the individual. People decide for themselves whether or not to care for themselves' (2000a: 361). However, since there is no ethical framework outside of oneself to appeal to, one's choice appears entirely arbitrary. This very critique is made by Julian Young, who quite rightly notes that 'groundless choice cannot provide a basis of *commitment*. No one dies for ungrounded choices' (2007: 186). Thus despite distinguishing his account from that of Sartre, Foucault appears to make the same mistake, as discussed earlier; namely, that there is no authority which he can appeal to in order to ground his ethical ideal. Furthermore, with nothing to ethically ground self-creation, there is nothing to prevent one from cultivating a morally undesirable ideal.

Foucault's ethic of care thus lacks several of the dimensions which make our concept of authenticity an ethically sound theory, and as such it appears as an inferior ideal. Thus, whilst our theory of authenticity, which was determined in Chapter 3, avoids the problem of authority by establishing itself as an intersubjective ethic, Foucault's account is unable to extricate itself from this issue. And although he claims that we derive our choices from society, these appear entirely arbitrary. As a purely subjective endeavour, Foucault's form of self-creation is not grounded in an ethical authority which is capable of overcoming this problem. Foucault's account, rather, focuses on the loss of freedom and the means by which to take back our lives, to put our own stamp upon our existence, as opposed to being subjected by institutions. What he offers, therefore, is an empty aesthetic which simply provides the subject with the means to express their individuality.

5.4 Foucault's Nietzsche

Despite being unable to provide a foundation for choice, and offering a thin ethical account, Foucault nevertheless offers a response to the loss of freedom. Can he, however, be said to simultaneously respond to the problem of meaning? One way in which he could be considered to address this problem is if his ethical injunction, to turn one's life into a work of art, could be said to unify the various aspects of the individual. In order to determine whether this is possible, we will consider his account in relation to Nietzsche's. Our reason for doing so is because there are two competing interpretations of Nietzsche's position. On the one hand, the existential interpretation, heralded by Walter Kaufmann, which our account of authenticity is premised on, emphasizes the acquisition of unity in response to the cultural death of God.[7] The postmodern account, on the other

---

[7] Kauffman places a great emphasis on the importance of nihilism within Nietzsche's thought and it is this position which advocates of existentialism adhere to. See *Nietzsche: Philosopher, Psychologist, Antichrist* (Princeton: Princeton University Press, 1968) in particular, chapter 3. Karl Jaspers, on

hand, rejects the notion of fixed substance and de-centres the subject, which dismisses the possibility of unity. Thus, whilst both interpretations accept that unity is not pre-given, the existentialist response is to engage in self-creation under a unifying will, whereas the postmodernist approach out-rightly rejects unity as a goal.

Within *The Genealogy of Morals*, Nietzsche makes a claim which divides existentialist and postmodernist interpreters. Here he states that 'there is no "being" behind doing, effecting, becoming; "the doer" is merely a fiction added to the deed – the deed is everything' (2000a: §1.13). Whilst postmodernists take this to infer that Nietzsche is suggesting a rejection, or de-centring, of subjectivity, the existentialists interpret this to suggest that one simply is what one achieves. That is, for the existentialist, the individual is constituted by a bundle of competing wills, which are constantly vying to overcome one another, and which are to be tamed by one unifying will. As Sartre puts it, 'man is nothing else than his project. He exists only to the extent that he realizes himself, therefore he is nothing more than the sum of his actions, nothing more than his life' (2007: 37). Thus, depending on whether Foucault adheres to a postmodern or existentialist interpretation of Nietzsche, it can be determined whether his approach possesses the capacity to address the problem of meaning. Within this section, we will initially argue that Foucault's early work conforms to a postmodern interpretation, and as such, rejects unity. However, it will also be demonstrated that his turn from radical power in his later work leads him to endorse the unity of existence through his injunction to turn one's life into a work of art.

In order to determine Nietzsche's influence upon Foucault, attention will be turned to the concepts of power and ethics. These are the major themes within Foucault's oeuvre and both of which are indebted to Nietzsche. With regards to the former, Schrift claims, 'Foucault took from Nietzsche a number of insights concerning how to think about power and power relations' (1995: 39). Nietzsche expresses the application of power through 'the herd', by which he means clans, communities, tribes, people, states, churches. Within each of these groups the individual 'accepts whatever is shouted into its ears by someone who issues

---

the other hand, argued that Nietzschean thought is self-contradictory and that any position which appears to be advocated will also be accompanied by its opposite, which closely resembles the postmodern approach. See *Nietzsche: An Introduction to the Understanding of His Philosophical Activity,* trans. Charles F. Wallraff and Frederick J. Schmitz (Baltimore: Johns Hopkins University Press, 1965). For an analysis of the debates between Kauffman and Jaspers, see David Pickus, 'Wishes of the Heart: Walter Kaufmann, Karl Jaspers, and Disposition in Nietzsche Scholarship', *The Journal of Nietzsche Studies*, no. 33 (Spring 2007): 5–24.

commands – parents, teachers, laws, class prejudices, public opinions' (2000a: §199). The herd are therefore those who are coerced and manipulated by others in positions of authority. Thus far, Nietzsche and Foucault's concepts of power seem synonymous. However, whilst Foucault looked at the institutions of asylums and prisons, and the application of power within society in general, Nietzsche fixes his gaze upon Christian morality.

What he determines is that Christianity is a herd-animal morality insofar as it is controlled and conditioned by the ascetic priest. In Nietzsche's account, 'by prescribing "love of the neighbour," the ascetic priest prescribes fundamentally an excitement of the strongest, most life-affirming drive, even if in the most cautious doses – namely, of the *will to power*' (2000a: III §18). However, although the priests acknowledge that there is suffering in the world, rather than accepting it for what it is, their approach is to preach that it is not in vain, but a means of redemption. Thus, although they furnish a life-affirming attitude towards suffering, they do so through negative means. The consequence of this is 'the general muting of the feeling of life, mechanical activity, the petty pleasure, above all "love of one's neighbour," herd organisation, the awakening of the communal feeling of power through which the individual's discontent with himself is drowned in his pleasure in the prosperity of the community' (2000a: III §19). Thus, although Christianity effects a strong force, it is ultimately a negative one for Nietzsche. Through its doctrinal desire for redemption, Christianity rejects the physical world which it replaces with a transcendent hope for heaven. In this sense, it is fundamentally life denying in Nietzsche's account. Furthermore, in dismissing the world, Christianity rejects unity, resulting in nihilism, or what Nietzsche on occasion refers to as 'European Buddhism' (2000a: §202).

Nietzschean will to power is, therefore, composed of a dual structure, insofar as it can either be healthy or be decadent. Power is affirmative when exercised as a creative force which brings unity. For Nietzsche, Johann Wolfgang von Goethe is exemplary of this: 'what he aspired to was *totality*; he strove against the separation of reason, sensuality, feeling, will; he disciplined himself to a whole, he *created* himself' (1971: §49). In *The Birth of Tragedy*, Nietzsche also hails Dionysus as providing unity to life through the acceptance and embrace of tragedy. Although Nietzsche also attributes the will to power to Socrates for challenging the Athenian youth, and devotion to his ideal, he sees him as a nihilistic force insofar as his optimism led to the rejection of tragedy and subsequent fracturing of unity. This negative, nihilistic form of power is also exercised by the likes of Arthur Schopenhauer, who despite accepting the tragedy of existence, reacts with pessimism, advocating a form of passive nihilism. Although Schopenhauer accepts the modern condition, rather than an affirmative approach, his is one of pessimism and resignation. Whilst Schopenhauer is the philosopher of decadence, Nietzsche dubs Richard Wagner the artist of decadence, for 'he flatters every nihilistic instinct and disguises it in music; he flatters everything Christian, every religious expression of decadence' (2000: §7).

This dichotomy of power is also present in Foucault's account, within which power is both productive and repressive. That is, although it creates docile bodies through discipline, it also produces them, determining what they are. Thus, despite focusing on two distinct aspects, their concepts of power seem to be the same. However, there is one fundamental difference between their accounts; whilst Nietzsche insisted that the individual's will determines that which is powerful, Foucault claimed that it is instead social institutions. This led him to claim that 'the problem is not changing people's consciousness – or what's in their heads – but the political, economic, institutional regime of the production of truth' (1977: 133). Thus, upon this understanding, individuals are the results of discourses of power. In this sense there are no autonomous agents, since our mode of thought and limits of behaviour are determined by institutions which govern us. In light of this, Foucault's account suggests that there are no individuals, only 'subjects' in the sense that they are 'subjected' by ideologically motivated discourses of power, which dominate our society.

The postmodern rejection of subjectivity, however, makes unity impossible and exacerbates the problem of nihilism, whilst the existentialists attempted to exorcise this predicament. Thus, although both sides agree with Nietzsche's claim that there is no substantial individual, they each present alternative sides of the will to power. Whilst it is the aim of the positive conception to create and unify, the existentialists represent this in their attempt to re-imbue human life with meaning. The postmodern understanding, on the other hand, which rejects unity, is none other than the decadent, nihilistic, negative concept of power. Insofar as the Overman is exemplary of the former, and the Last Man, the latter, Ken Gemes cleverly claims, 'Postmodernists are nearer Nietzsche's idea of the Last Man than his idea of the Overman' (2001: 337–60). That is, whilst the postmodernists reject unity, the attainment of which Nietzsche associates the Overman, and instead advocate the fragmentation of identity, which Nietzsche takes to be indicative of the Last Man, the postmodernists can be understood to be closer to the Last Man than Nietzsche's ideal of the Overman.

Is this, however, an accurate description of the position which Foucault himself advocates? His understanding of subjectivity is evident in his interpretation of Nietzsche's death of God as not so much a beckoning for the Overman, but as the end of man. As he, himself puts it, 'rather than the death of God – or, rather, in the wake of that death and in a profound correlation with it – what Nietzsche's thought heralds is the end of his murderer' (2011: 385). This particular passage seems to allude to a de-centring of subjectivity, as the end of man as a subject. Thus, whilst the existentialists respond to the cultural death of God in terms of self-creation, it seems that Foucault's approach is to reject subjectivity, rather than striving for unity. In general, postmodern thinkers take Nietzsche to reject any sense of substantial self. They draw their interpretation from the untimely meditation *On the Use and Abuse of History for Life*, and in this respect, Foucault is no different.

In 'Nietzsche, Genealogy, History', Foucault focuses on the aforementioned essay and makes the argument that Nietzsche employs genealogy to disrupt the notion of a unified self. In his own words, 'the search for descent is not the erecting of foundations: on the contrary, it disturbs what was previously considered immobile; it fragments what was thought unified; it shows the heterogeneity of what was imagined consistent with itself' (1991c: 82). Not only does Foucault believe that this is what Nietzsche intended to achieve through genealogy, but he also makes explicit that it is for this very end that he employs it within his own thought. 'History becomes "effective" to the degree that it introduces discontinuity into our very being – as it divides our emotions, dramatizes our instincts, multiplies our body and sets it against itself. "Effective" history deprives the self of the reassuring stability of life and nature. . . . It will uproot its traditional foundation and relentlessly disrupt its pretended continuity' (1991c: 88). From these two analyses of Foucault's interpretation of Nietzsche, it seems to suggest that Foucault shares his understanding with the postmodernists.

Modern life is considered meaningless because the individual was fragmented, thus in order to address this problem, a response must be capable of unifying the individual. Foucault's account, however, has been shown to be incapable of providing a response which unifies the individual in totality. Thus, as a result of endorsing a postmodern interpretation of Nietzsche, Foucault's perspective is incapable of unifying the individual substantially and therefore of addressing the problem of meaning. That is, through de-centring the subject, Foucault denies there is an individual to be unified. However, rather than completely writing off Foucault's account, we ought to recall that this rejection of subjectivity, that the subject is produced by discourses of power, belongs to his early work, and which is altered in his later thinking. Thus, perhaps by turning to his later work we can find a more congenial account.

In the previous section, it was demonstrated that Foucault alters his account of power. As a consequence of reconfiguring the manner in which he conceives of power relations, he was enabled to avoid radical subjection and engage in care of the self. A further aspect of the technologies of self involved in his ethics of care is that Foucault entreats us to turn our lives into a work of art. Our socio-existential approach to authenticity has been shown to provide purpose through forming one's characteristics and traits into a unified whole. Perhaps Foucault's injunction, to turn one's life into a work of art, could likewise lead to a unified existence and meaningful life? Through this practice of care, Foucault can be understood to be suggesting that the individual can become a work of art, bringing together those aspects which one conceives to be constitutive of the self. Hence Foucault's imperative, 'to make of their life into an *oeuvre* that carries certain aesthetic values and meets certain stylistic criteria' (1992: 10–11). Through forming such an oeuvre, one's existence can thus be retrospectively interpreted as leading to and culminating in an end project. In this way, we can thus understand Foucault to advocate a form of unity in his later thinking.

Although we initially concluded that Foucault rejected unity in his early work, this was determined to be tied up with his radical conception of power. However, it was also shown that as with his approach to freedom, a further consequence of denouncing this radical conception of power, is that his understanding of unity is altered alongside his account of subjectivity. What transpired was that his ethical approach, to turn one's life into a work of art, was shown to offer a sense of unity. However, as discussed in the preceding section, on Foucault's account there can be no grounds to one's choice. A consequence is that if the reason for one's choice cannot be validated, then one's choice is fundamentally meaningless. Moreover, if one's choice cannot be justified, then to cultivate oneself into a work of art retains no merit beyond narcissistic self-indulgence. Thus, despite being shown to advocate a form of unity, and offering a potential response to the meaninglessness of modernity, Foucault's ethic falls short in its ability to adequately respond to the problems of freedom and meaning.

5.5 Summary

We began this chapter with Foucault's analysis of modernity. Here it was shown that individuals are subjected by institutions through discourses of power. The effect of rationalization upon individuals, which the Enlightenment had championed, was that they came to be subjected by discourses of power. After considering the implications of this theory, that individuals could not exist in any genuine sense, we then questioned the continuity of Foucault's oeuvre. Having determined that Foucault presents the subjection thesis as a problem to be overcome, it was illustrated that this was not possible in accordance with his radical conception of power. It was then suggested, following Lukes, that Foucault's concept of power, which he engages with in his later work, refers to 'ideology' and that we could develop our own account by thinking of inauthenticity in terms of power relations. Attention was then turned to Foucault's proposed response, which he derived from the Stoic concept of care.

Focusing upon technologies of the self, it was shown that Foucault's intention was to utilize these techniques as they had not been subjected to discourse. Although this was shown to address the problem of freedom, it was argued that one's choice still remained entirely arbitrary. We then turned our attention to whether Foucault addressed the problem of meaning, and it was inferred that his ethical injunction, to turn one's life into a work of art, could offer a sense of unity, and potentially meaning. To determine if this was possible, we considered Foucault's relation to Nietzsche and questioned whether he adhered to a postmodern interpretation, which rejects any sense of unity. Although Foucault advocates such a position within his early work, it was shown that he moves away from this interpretation when he proposes turning oneself into a work of art. However, despite being able to offer a response to the problem of meaning, as a consequence of one's choice being ultimately groundless, that which one cultivates oneself into was shown to be devoid of meaning. Although our concept of authenticity has been upheld, there remains one further challenge to our approach, and it is to this which our enquiry will now turn.

6

Are all modern ethics emotive?

The third approach to be considered, which also problematizes modernity in terms of freedom and meaning, is that advanced by Alasdair MacIntyre. Habermas's modernist response was to resolve the problem of meaning through returning to, and completing, the Enlightenment project. Foucault's postmodern approach was to turn inward, in classical Stoic fashion, and cultivate the self. MacIntyre, on the other hand, suggests the reintroduction of a pre-Enlightenment model. Understanding the problem to be caused by the loss of natural teleology, MacIntyre's solution is to look to the past for a social and ethical model which can support teleology and traditional ways of life which have been marginalized by modernity. His diagnosis is that the loss of teleology has not only led to a loss of meaning but also led to the ethical impoverishment of modern moral discourse. Recognizing Aristotelian ethics contains a *telos*, which connects the individual and community in the pursuit of a shared good, MacIntyre's response is to revive the Aristotelian virtue ethics tradition. However, in this chapter it will be argued that this approach is untenable.

In order to illustrate the impracticality of MacIntyre's theory, this chapter will begin by addressing MacIntyre's account of modernity and where he sees the problem to have emerged from (Section 6.1). Here it will be illustrated that the consequence of the Enlightenment's failure to rationally justify morality was the emergence of emotivism which has dominated not only ethical discourse but also modern European culture. In Section 6.2, it will also be questioned whether this criticism can be extended to our socio-existential approach to authenticity; that is, we will seek to determine if MacIntyre's prognosis also underpins the ethical approach developed in this book. Having defended our concept of authenticity against any charges of emotivism, we will then turn to MacIntyre's constructive account (Section 6.3). Here we will discuss MacIntyre's proposed resolution to emotivism: to revive the virtue ethics tradition through practices, narrative and tradition and we will also discuss their resemblance to authenticity. It will also be suggested that his account of narrative unity enables us to further develop the socio-existential account of authenticity. In Section 6.4 MacIntyre's virtue theory will be critically analysed and it will be illustrated that his account of tradition is unsatisfactory for the reason that it is informed by nostalgia. Furthermore, it will be argued that the pessimistic conclusion of *After Virtue* leads to the realization that, as a means to resolve the diagnosed problem, MacIntyre's account is insufficient.

6.1 Modern culture of emotivism

MacIntyre's philosophical epic, *After Virtue*, begins with the 'disquieting suggestion' that modern European culture is akin to a post-catastrophic scientific community.[1] Within this hypothetical scenario, people believe that they are practising science when what they are engaging with are merely fragments of scientific theories. As a consequence of no longer possessing the context for these theories, MacIntyre claims that their practices are incomprehensible and unjustifiable. This, however, we are informed, is not merely a hypothetical situation, but a metaphor for the current state of modern moral philosophy. As MacIntyre himself puts it, 'what we possess [...] are the fragments of a conceptual scheme, parts which now lack those contexts from which their significance derived' (2010: 2). MacIntyre's reason for asserting this is because he notes that within modern moral discourse there is no longer any possibility of engagement to reach moral truth. That is, despite appeal to supposed 'objective standards' which are drawn from historical origins, moral differences are at their very core incommensurable.

MacIntyre inherits this argument, that modern moral philosophy is based on a conceptual scheme of which key elements are now missing, from G. E. M. Anscombe. In 'Modern Moral Philosophy', she claims secular approaches to morality are without foundation (1958). Within her influential article, Anscombe focuses her attention on utilitarianism and deontological ethics, which she claims to be misguided attempts to replace the role of God with that of a legislator.

---

[1] Within this chapter we will focus predominantly on the philosophical arguments devised within MacIntyre's magnum opus, *After Virtue*. It is in this text where MacIntyre presents his most systematic critique of modernity, and his first attempt to articulate his response to that problem. Although his resolution has been modified within subsequent publications, the general outline of his account remains unchanged. For this reason, attention will be focused on the account developed in *After Virtue*, and which will be supplemented by noting the developments which take place in his later thought.

This is made explicit through the modern usage of the terms 'ought', 'obligation' and 'right', which were previously given context and validity by God. However, Anscombe notes that within modern moral philosophy the ascription of these to an artificial legislator renders these terms incoherent.[2] The reason is because ethical values were granted validity by the authority of God, but deontology and utilitarianism take these very terms and attempt to provide a rational foundation for them. Her response is that the gap caused by this 'needs to be filled by an account of human nature, human action, that type of characteristic a virtue is, and above all of human "flourishing"'(2010: 41). MacIntyre develops Anscombe's account by suggesting that the reason why moral agreement cannot be arrived at is because the arguments have become relative to the advocate's perspectives, and as such, their standards are not objective and their rational arguments are arbitrary.

According to MacIntyre, the unrecognized catastrophe which led to these consequences was the collapse of the Enlightenment Project. MacIntyre's underlying claim is that within medieval Europe, from the twelfth century onwards, the dominating moral scheme was structurally similar to that devised by Aristotle in his *Nicomachean Ethics*. That is, medieval moral philosophy was of the same teleological structure as Aristotelianism, insofar as it begins with a theory of man-as-he-happens-to-be and advances a view of man-as-he-ought-to-be-if-he-recognized-his-telos, both of which were underpinned by a rational end. Within the theistic frameworks of Christianity, Judaism and Islam, respectively developed by Aquinas, Maimonides and Avicenna, the understanding of human *telos* was, however, extended beyond reality, becoming something which is achieved in the next life. Nevertheless, the role that ethics plays within these theoretical frameworks is to help agents achieve their natural end. Furthermore, common to each of these teleological structures is that one arrives at one's natural end through reason. This, however, was undermined by the emergence of a socio-historical event which challenged key elements of this teleological structure.

Here MacIntyre draws upon Max Weber, whom he recognizes as a major articulator of the modern condition and shares the historical diagnosis that Protestant religious denominations lie at the root of the problem.[3] However,

---

[2] There are two ways of reading 'Modern Moral Philosophy': (i) as advocating virtue ethics, and (ii) as an argument for religious based ethics, the former of which is upheld here. For the arguments surrounding these two readings, see *Virtue Ethics,* eds. Roger Crisp and Michael Slone (Oxford: Oxford University Press, 2001), 9.

[3] Their views, however, differ insofar as Weber is not troubled by that which MacIntyre has problematized. Weber believes there is no *telos* and this is something we have simply got to accept.

it is not Protestantism per se but rather the voluntarist teachings of Luther, Calvin and Pascal, as practised in Northern Europe, to which MacIntyre traces the problem. Voluntarist Christian moral theology suggests that the arbitrary will of God is the source of moral laws. This belief undermined the structure of preceding theories because it separated moral judgement from practical reasoning and denied that one could discover what is right through natural inclinations. Since the purpose of preceding approaches to ethics was to enable humans to achieve their natural end, MacIntyre claims that the rejection of any sense of human nature, and the abandonment of the notion of *telos*, leaves a moral scheme with no teleological context for its framework.

Although moral voluntarism maimed teleological ethics, MacIntyre claims that this was a fatal blow which resulted in a fundamental distortion of that which ethical and moral reasoning entails. Rather, when the theology of religious voluntarists was dismissed by the Enlightenment, secular moral philosophers mistakenly assumed that rational morality possessed this very content and form. As MacIntyre suggests, 'Kant never doubted for a moment that the maxims which he had learnt from his own virtuous parents were those which had to be vindicated by a rational test' (2010: 44). As a consequence, the task of modern moral philosophy became to devise a new *telos* or find a new categorical status for the rules of morality. Kant attempted to create a new categorical status for moral absolutes, through inviting individuals to determine their own maxims. Bentham, having arrived at the belief that the rational end of humanity was happiness, attempted to devise a new *telos* based on the principle of utility, emphasizing the greatest good for the greatest number. However, since moral positions such as deontology and utilitarianism do not possess an objective form of the good to validate their claims, MacIntyre suggests secular moral philosophy became a mere mask for arbitrary choice.

As a consequence of this flawed moral framework, eighteenth-century philosophers' task to provide a rational foundation for their moral beliefs became unachievable. As MacIntyre concisely puts it, 'they inherited incoherent fragments of a once coherent scheme of thought and action, and since they did not recognize their own peculiar historical and cultural situation, they could not recognise the impossible and quixotic character of their self-appointed task' (2010: 55). This he elucidates through the examples of Hume, Kant and Kierkegaard, who all attempted to justify morality upon

---

For an excellent analysis of Weber's influence upon MacIntyre, see Breen, *Under Weber's Shadow* (2012), Part III.

the conditions determined by the Enlightenment. Concluding that morality was not a rational process, Hume argued that it was determined by the passions. Kant, responding to Hume, and rejecting his reasoning, advocated the rational determination of the will. Recognizing both of his predecessors to be mistaken, Kierkegaard then abandoned both of these in favour of the arbitrary choice of the will.[4] Although each of these thinkers adopted the content of traditional conservative morality, MacIntyre claims that as a consequence of voluntary theology's rejection of teleology they were caught between the autonomy of the individual and the authority of moral principles. As he aptly expresses, 'the elimination of any notion of essential human nature and with it the abandonment of any notion of *telos* leaves behind a moral scheme composed of two remaining elements' (2010: 55). That which remained was (a) man as he is, and (b) moral principles. However, without *telos*, moral principles become entirely arbitrary.

In MacIntyre's account, the Enlightenment project of justifying morality therefore failed, not because of fallacious reasoning, but because ethics and action were not treated teleologically. Without a natural *telos* there was no measure to judge whether an action was good or evil. Thus, the primary challenge to morality was the religious move to voluntarianism with Luther, Calvin and Pascal denying that humans could discover their end through reason. This, however, was not the only cause of the catastrophe, but was supplemented by the secular and scientific rejection of Aristotle's natural philosophy. Focusing on the moral–ethical consequences, MacIntyre notes that, like the scientific fragments in his disquieting suggestion, moral rules have survived in absence of their teleological context. What caused this situation according to MacIntyre was therefore twofold: the secular rejection of Christian theology and the philosophical rejection of Aristotelianism.

In *Ethics in the Conflicts of Modernity*, MacIntyre refines his account of modern moral philosophy, which he terms 'morality'. He here employs this term to encompass not only philosophy but also modern moral thinking and the cultural 'institution' or framework underpinning it.[5] He employs this term to categorize a variety of moral theories which adhere to six salient characteristics. The criteria which MacIntyre sets forth is that it is a secular doctrine, universally

---

[4] MacIntyre's reading of Kierkegaard is a controversial one which has been contested by Kierkegaard scholars and dealt with extensively in *Kierkegaard After MacIntyre: Freedom, Narrative, and Virtue* (Chicago: Open Court, 2001).
[5] On this point, MacIntyre is not only indebted to Anscombe, as previously indicated but also inspired by Bernard Williams, who in understanding Morality in this way takes it to be problematic. *Ethics in Conflicts of Morality*, 158.

binding, functions as a set of constraints, is framed in abstract terms, advocated as the latest development in moral thought and whose rules ought always to be obeyed. As MacIntyre himself explains, 'it is presented as a set of impersonal rules, entitled to the assent of any rational agent whatsoever, enjoining obedience to such maxims as those that prohibit the taking of innocent life and theft and those that require at least some large degree of truthfulness and at least some significant measure of altruistic benevolence'(2016: 65). Here MacIntyre has Kantianism, utilitarianism and contractarianism in mind, which suggest that agents have a duty not to harm others, and act in a way which brings about the greatest good for all: 'in the area of theoretical debate, there are Kantian, utilitarian, and contractarian exponents of Morality and of each such view there are several versions' (2016: 117). However, unlike Aristotelianism, within which ethics, politics and economics are all connected through the pursuit of *eudaimonia*, within Morality these are all separated, unconnected spheres. This leads MacIntyre to question, 'whence then is it that the precepts of Morality are taken to derive their peculiar authority for those whom those precepts have authority?' (2016: 119). That is, presented as a universal norm, which is abstract from all other spheres of social life, what is it that justifies Morality's universal appeal?

According to MacIntyre, the consistent failure of Morality to provide a satisfactory response to this problem has resulted in emotivism.[6] This is the ethical perspective that all moral judgements are none other than expressions of preference, attitude or feeling. This moral standpoint was championed by C. L. Stevenson, according to whom 'this is good' means roughly the same as 'I approve of this; do so as well' (MacIntyre 2010: 12). Modern moral philosophy culminates in this position because it embraces the belief which preceding moral arguments have attempted to resist, that there is no rational foundation. As MacIntyre elucidates, 'what I have suggested to be the case by and large about our own culture – that in moral argument the apparent assertion of principles functions as a mask for expressions of personal preference – is what emotivism takes to be universally the case' (2010: 19). Thus, if emotivism is true, then all moral disagreement is rationally interminable. However, as a moral theory, MacIntyre illustrates that emotivism fails for three reasons.

---

[6] In *Ethics in the Conflicts of Modernity*, MacIntyre turns his attention to philosophy of mind, in order to determine how desires are orientated towards their ends. Here he determines that there are two ultimate approaches: neo-Aristotelianism and expressivism. The latter of these he refers to as a more philosophically advanced account of emotivism, and which he defines as a second order theory about the meaning and use of evaluative and normative expressions. That is, it holds that evaluative and normative judgements are the expressions of desires and passions.

First, to elucidate a sentence by its function, an essential part of the theory must provide identification and characterization of the feelings or attitudes in question. However, on this matter emotivism is circular. An emotivist would claim that moral judgements express feelings and when pressed further they would claim that these are feelings of approval, but when asked 'what kind of approval' they would be forced to remain silent or beg the question by stating 'feelings of approval'. Secondly, it conflates expressions of personal preference and evaluative preference. These, however, ought to remain separate for the reason that personal preferences derive validity from evaluative preference. As MacIntyre states, 'utterances of the first kind depend upon who utters them to whom for any reason-giving force they may have, whilst utterances of the second kind are not similarly dependent for their reason-giving force on the context of utterance' (2010: 31). Thirdly, emotivism is a theory about the meaning of sentences, but the expressions of feeling or attitude is characteristically not a function of the meaning of sentences but their use on particular occasions. To illustrate this, MacIntyre draws upon Gilbert Ryle's example of the angry schoolmaster who shouts the correct answer at the student who has made an arithmetical mistake. MacIntyre's point is that the use of this sentence to express feeling has no connection with its meaning.

Although MacIntyre's argument has thus far been concerned with abstract moral theory, he illustrates that the loss of teleology has had wider-reaching implications, impacting upon modern society as a whole. The first social implication which emerges from the loss of teleology is a lack of unified identity, and which has led to the 'compartmentalisation of the self' (2006a: 159). What MacIntyre means is that modern individuals fulfil contradictory roles because they lack a coherent identity. For example, one may assume the role of a loving partner and parent, yet simultaneously facilitate a position, such as an administrator or insurance broker, which permits one to treat others instrumentally, and as the means to monetary gain. For MacIntyre this is the consequence of the loss of an overall structure of the good with which to coordinate one's actions and life. As MacIntyre explains, 'the peculiarly modern self, the emotivist self, in acquiring sovereignty in its own realm lost its traditional boundaries provided by a social identity and a view of human life as ordered to a given end' (2010: 34). As a consequence of the fragmented and disconnected nature of modern moral discourse, supposed ethical appeals merely mask the individual's subjective preference. A further consequence of this cultural condition is that rather than enabling one to arrive at any genuine moral insights, ethical arguments simply provide a tool for manipulation.[7] It is this very outcome, of the emergence and acceptance of manipulation, which lies at the heart of the modern world for MacIntyre.

This second implication, according to MacIntyre, has led to the consequence that we now exist within a 'culture of emotivism', which permits us to treat others instrumentally. In order to make this apparent, he offers the example of modern social characters who conduct themselves according to emotivist principles, such as the 'rich aesthete', 'manager', 'therapist' and 'conservative moralist'.[8] The rich aesthete employs *schemes* to manipulate others to alleviate boredom, the manager treats their employees as a means to achieving *efficiency*, the therapist treats their patients according to their *theories*, regardless of the patient's own goals, and the conservative moralist opposes liberal politics which seek to transform society, based on their own conservative *values*. Each of these characters exhibits characteristics of emotivism insofar as none of them actually question what they do, they just do it, and judge their success by measuring the effectiveness of manipulating others into their projects. MacIntyre thus concludes that the aesthete's *schemes*, the manager's *efficiency*, the therapist's *theories* and moral conservative's *values* are merely manipulative tools.[9] Here MacIntyre can be seen to share a similar perspective of modernity to Weber, who summarizes the perverse state of modern moral culture and civilization by claiming 'of the last stage of this cultural development, it might well be truly said: "Specialists without spirit, sensualists without heart; this nullity imagines it has attained a level of civilisation never before achieved"' (2005: 124).

---

[7] In this respect, MacIntrye can be seen to be influenced by Weber's 'polytheistic disenchantment', which Habermas also address and sees the concept of expertise as perpetuating. Whilst Weber endorses this as paving the path to a meaningful vocation, MacIntyre rejects it as endorsing emotivism, that all reasons and arguments are expressions of individual preference.

[8] The fourth character, the moral conservative, was only added in the third edition of *After Virtue*, as MacIntyre himself makes explicit in the prologue 'conservative moralists, with their inflated and self-righteous unironic rhetoric, should be set alongside those figures whom I identified [. . .] as notable characters in the cultural dramas of modernity.' Ibid., xv.

[9] Although bureaucrats and managers may attempt to validate their roles in terms of the 'science of management', MacIntyre claims that they have no grounds to do so. *After Virtue*, 77. Rather, 'the concept of managerial effectiveness is after all one more contemporary moral fiction'. He argues that there is no such thing as neutral, impersonal appeals to objective facts, and since expertise also relies upon 'facts', it is thus never objective. Social scientists offer a mechanistic science of behaviour, which has been supported by bureaucracies to justify their expertise. However, although managerial expertise derives authority from social sciences, the social sciences themselves have not yet been justified as sciences. Ibid., 106–8.

6.2 Emotivism and authenticity

Having provided his prognosis of modern European culture, MacIntyre claims that Nietzsche's analysis is 'one of two genuine theoretical alternatives confronting anyone trying to analyse the moral condition of our culture' (2010: 110). In MacIntyre's account, Nietzsche makes two significant contributions to moral philosophy. First, Nietzsche recognized that the appeals to objectivity made by thinkers of the Enlightenment were none other than exercises of subjective will. Secondly, he understood the logical implications of this insight and its consequences for moral philosophy. However, although MacIntyre honours Nietzsche with this achievement, he simultaneously discredits him in dismissing what he perceives to be Nietzsche's ethical project. MacIntyre understands Nietzsche as claiming that if morality is none other than the expression of will, then morality is only what is created by one's will. Moreover, if morality is a fiction, then one ought to replace reason with will and courageously take it upon oneself to become ethically autonomous and determine one's own values. This then leads MacIntyre to make the backhanded compliment that 'it is in his relentlessly serious pursuit of the problem, not in his frivolous solutions that Nietzsche's greatness lies' (2010: 114).

In order to elucidate his view of Nietzsche's contribution, MacIntyre offers the analogy of Captain Cook's voyage to Polynesia. Upon arrival, the ship's crew noticed that the natives had strict laws on certain practices, such as the restriction on communal dining of mixed genders. However, when the Europeans questioned the reason for this peculiar cultural practice, they were offered the explanation that it was 'taboo'. Later, when Christian missionaries requested that these laws be repealed, the king, Kamehameha II, was able to do so without question or consequence. The explanation MacIntyre offers for this phenomenon is that Polynesian culture once had a set of background beliefs which had since been abandoned and forgotten. In this way, MacIntyre claims that modern morality has become equivalent to Polynesian 'taboo'. He then questions, 'why should we not think about our modern uses of *good*, *right*, and *obligatory* in any different way from that in which we think about late eighteenth century Polynesian uses of *taboo*? And why should we not think of Nietzsche as the Kamehameha II of the European tradition?' (2010: 113).

The second genuine alternative to analyse the modern condition is that provided by Aristotelianism. MacIntyre claims that Aristotle advocated the most comprehensive ethical theory – namely, living in accordance with one's nature enabled one to obtain *eudaimonia*, or human flourishing, and live the good life. Thus, it is the absence of teleology, which was present in Aristotle's virtue ethics, which has led to the problems with which MacIntyre contends. However, in a liberal democracy there can be no shared good, and as such, ethical debate can be none other than subjective preference. For MacIntyre's Nietzsche, the ultimate foundation of morality is the 'will to power'. However, MacIntyre is critical of what he conceived to be the dominating philosophical perspective, as advocated by Nietzsche's metaphysical heirs. Given the culture of emotivism, MacIntyre recognizes that the doctrine of will to power is the correct metaphysical diagnosis. This then led him to question if it 'was it right in the first place to have rejected Aristotle?' (2010: 117).

Although MacIntyre provides a compelling account of the ethical inadequacies of modern moral philosophy, one concern which arises is whether this is applicable to our socio-existential theory of authenticity. This issue arises because MacIntyre extends this criticism to Sartre and Nietzsche, from both of whom dimensions of our concept of authenticity have been derived. MacIntyre's claim is that Nietzsche's successors are the heirs to emotivism.[10] Here attention will be turned to analysing MacIntyre's exact criticism and whether this charge is correct. Since the concept of authenticity developed in this book incorporates aspects of Sartrean philosophy, and works within the Nietzschean tradition, it will be necessary to illustrate that MacIntyre's criticism cannot be extended to the concept of authenticity advocated within this book. In order to demonstrate that this is the case, we will first lay out MacIntyre's criticisms of Sartre and Nietzsche and explain the sense in which MacIntyre understands Nietzsche and Sartre to be emotivists.

MacIntyre's criticism of Sartre as perpetuating emotivist ideals is one which he has held since early in his career. In *A Short History of Ethics* MacIntyre expounds the fundamental tenants of emotivism and prescriptionism by comparing them to Sartrean existentialism. In his own words, 'like Sartre, the prescriptivist and emotivist do not trace the source of the necessity of choice, or of taking up one's own attitudes, to the moral history of our society. They ascribe it to the nature of moral concepts as such. And in so doing, like Sartre, they try to absolutize their own individualist morality' (1997: 171). Here MacIntyre is making a metaethical criticism, namely, that a key component which Sartre and emotivism share is that neither derives their ethical standpoint from an objective source. On the contrary, both approaches begin with the individual determining the

---

[10] In *After Virtue* he targets Sartre, and in *Three Rival Versions of Moral Enquiry*, Foucault and Derrida also come into his sights.

ethical through their own faculties, as opposed to appealing to external moral norms and values. Thus, according to MacIntyre, a consequence of Sartre's self-overcoming of nihilism is the denial of our intersubjectivity, believing that the individual develops themselves irrespective of moral norms or external values.

A second respect in which MacIntyre associates Sartre with emotivism is present within his recently published *Ethics in the Conflicts of Modernity*. Here MacIntyre imagines Ayer commending Sartre for his emphasis on individual independence from any system of values, unless one so chooses. As MacIntyre elucidates, 'in this rejection of any standard external to and independent of agents' feelings, concerns, commitments, and attitudes by appeal to which their normative and evaluative judgements might be justified, expressivists have on occasion found common ground with at least one version of existentialism' (2016: 23). This ethical critique is also prevalent in *After Virtue* where he compares Sartre with sociologist Erving Goffman, taking both to be advocates of emotivism in their rejection of an essential self. Comparing their concepts of subjectivity, MacIntyre claims, 'for Sartre, whatever social space it occupies it does so only accidently. And therefore he too [like Goffman] sees the self as in no way an actuality' (2010: 32). The second manner in which MacIntyre associates Sartre with emotivism is thus in regard to his rejection of ethical locatedness. That is, MacIntyre's critique is that the radical individualism of the existentialists leads to ethical relativism by suggesting that the individual determines and validates that which is ethical for themselves.

Unlike his criticisms of Sartre, which appear sporadically throughout his major texts, MacIntyre's criticism of Nietzsche is much more sustained, and one which takes central stage in *After Virtue*. However, as an adequate analysis of MacIntyre's view of Nietzsche has been presented in the preceding pages, here the focus will be restricted to the fundamental grounds of disagreement. As with his charge of subjectivity against Sartre, MacIntyre's preoccupation with Nietzsche begins in *A Short History of Ethics*, where he makes a similar meta-ethical criticism. MacIntyre's complaint is that 'Nietzschean man, the Übermensch, the man who transcends, finds his good nowhere in the social world to date, but only in that in himself which dictates his own new law and his own new table of the virtues' (1997: 257). This is problematic because it denies the shared values and norms which emerge from within intersubjective relationships. As MacIntyre elucidates, 'it is because this is so that the great-man cannot enter into relationships mediated by appeal to shared standards or virtues or goods; he is his own only authority and his relationships to others have to be exercises of that authority' (1997: 258).

In *Dependent Rational Animals*, MacIntyre praises Nietzsche both biographically and philosophically for his heroic actions in attempting to reject the external factors which impinged upon his existence. However, MacIntyre claims that the outcome of Nietzsche's rejection of external norms and values is that one cannot exist intersubjectively. As MacIntyre stresses, 'among the commitments and relationships that Nietzsche has had to reject in order to escape from what he took to be their imprisoning power are just those without which shared communal deliberation cannot take place' (1999: 165). The consequence of this is a lack of external justification, as MacIntyre continues to explain, 'Nietzsche, in a heroic series of acts isolated himself by ridding himself, so far as is humanly possible, of the commitments required by the virtues of acknowledged dependence' (1999: 162).[11] MacIntyre has in mind Nietzsche's genealogical method, which suggests that social norms are none other than the expression of domination, the recognition that one lives in conformity to the herd that allows for the ability to break free and gain ethical independence. MacIntyre thus exclaims that 'the Nietzsche of *Beyond Good and Evil*, has arguments that, if treated with adequate seriousness, force on expressivists a significant reformulation and extension of emotivism' (2016: 42). The reformulation which MacIntyre imagines would be in choosing between identifying with a pre-rational attitude or present desire, Nietzschean genealogy would then lead an emotivist to recognize the discredible nature of their judgements.

MacIntyre's criticisms of emotivism, and which he directs against the philosophical thought of both Sartre and Nietzsche, are therefore threefold. First, both approaches begin from the individual and attempt to turn their own moral standpoint into universal ideals. Secondly, that a consequence of the rejection of external norms as bad faith, or the domination of the herd, results in a lack of external justification for those values which they attempt to posit as ethical ideals. Thirdly, that their philosophies deny the centrality of intersubjectivity to ethical life and, if realized, would culminate in a perverse society wherein human interdependencies are unacknowledged or, worse, derided. MacIntyre brings these criticisms together, applying them to both Nietzsche and Sartre accusing both of extending the ethic inherent in emotivism. In his own words,

> when Nietzsche sought to indict the making of would-be objective moral judgements as the mask worn by the will-to-power of those too weak and slavish

---

[11] The virtues of acknowledged dependence are just generosity, virtues of giving (industriousness in getting, thrift in saving and discrimination in giving), and virtues of receiving (gratitude, courtesy, forbearance and truthful acknowledgement of dependence). Ibid., 121–7.

to assert themselves with archaic and aristocratic grandeur, and when Sartre tried to exhibit the bourgeois rationalist morality of the Third Republic as an exercise in bad faith by those who cannot tolerate the recognition of their own choices as the sole source of moral judgement, both conceded the substance of that for which emotivism contended. (2010: 22)

MacIntyre's criticism is, therefore, that both Nietzsche and Sartre's rejection of social relations and intersubjectivity prevents a communal good being posited, and that without a concept of the good they are unable to critique immoral action.

Now that MacIntyre's criticisms have been elucidated we may turn to analysing whether these can be extended to the concept of authenticity developed here. In devising the dimensions of a socio-existential approach to authenticity, we began with Sartrean choice. Likewise, from working within the Nietzschean tradition, rejecting the way in which social norms limit one's capacity for self-realization, our account seems susceptible to MacIntyre's charges of emotivism. However, assuming his charges against Sartre and Nietzsche are correct, it will be illustrated that this has no bearing upon our concept of authenticity.[12] The concern, then, is whether this charge of emotivism is applicable to the socio-existential approach to authenticity.

Our account of authenticity is, however, able to overcome these charges. In order to make this explicit, it will first be useful to recap on precisely that which our approach entails. In Chapter 3 it was determined that the socio-existential approach to authenticity was composed of six dimensions. These were (i) choice, (ii) commitment, (iii) maturity, (iv) becoming what one is, (v) intersubjective consciousness and (vi) heritage. The first dimension, choice, was derived from Sartrean thought and is a key component of authenticity. This, however, was criticized by Merleau-Ponty for the reason that if we can reject our choice freely then it cannot be considered to be truly meaningful. In response to this criticism we then modified this dimension through appeal to Beauvoir's concept of commitment – that choices become more meaningful the longer we are committed to them. We then considered that although one may be committed to one's choice, one may still fail to live authentically because one's project has not been carefully chosen. In order to prevent one from committing to an

---

[12] Kevin Hill has defended Nietzsche against MacIntyre's criticisms and argues that MacIntyre's Nietzsche is not the true Nietzsche. Understanding MacIntyre's critique to rest upon Nietzsche's rejection of all previous cultural frameworks, Hill argues, 'Nietzsche is neither rejecting the Enlightenment project altogether, nor the classical tradition which it superseded.' 'MacIntyre's Nietzsche: A Critique', *International Studies in Philosophy* 24, no. 2 (1992): 3–12.

unrealizable goal, we then turned to Ferrara's concept of maturity. It then became apparent that our choices cannot be groundless but must come from somewhere, and we adopted the Nietzschean dimension of becoming what one is. Although this seemed to suggest a subjective stance, that our choice was a representation of what we are, we then drew upon Taylor's horizon of intelligibility which led to the dimension of intersubjective consciousness. However, it was suggested that Taylor's account did not quite explain the historical and temporal constraints imposed upon us, and so we introduced the dimension of heritage. We then determined that through living in accordance with these dimensions one's life was imbued with meaning.

There are, therefore, two specific points in our theory to which MacIntyre's criticisms are potentially applicable. The first is the Sartrean derived dimension of choice, and the second is the Nietzschean inspired dimension of becoming what one is. With regards to the former, if we take individual choice to be the basis for ethical decisions then we arrive at a purely subjective standpoint. As for the latter, the meta-ethical explanation that choices gain intelligibility from self-affirmation appears to reject intersubjectivity and any form of external validity. These two dimensions alone are therefore susceptible to MacIntyre's ethical and meta-ethical criticisms of emotivism. However, our socio-existential approach departs significantly from Nietzsche and Sartre and avoids MacIntyre's criticism of being subjectively derived through our penultimate dimensions of intersubjective consciousness. That is, by recognizing that our choices are limited and given meaning by the context within which we exist, we gain validity from an external source.

The resolution to MacIntyre's three criticisms – the meta-ethical criticism of absolutizing individual choice, the ethical criticism of lacking an external framework to validate individual values and the social criticism that if universalized this moral approach would culminate in a perverse state – lies with the dimension of intersubjective consciousness. First, by insisting that individuals exist within a horizon of significance, we are able to circumvent MacIntyre's concern that emotivism lacks any source of validation outside the self. That is, by taking an intersubjective standpoint, one's choice is only made meaningful, and granted validity, in relation to other individuals. Secondly, the dimension of choice, which our account of authenticity began with, cannot be said to be subjective because one's choices are informed, and made meaningful, by one's social context. The socio-existential approach to authenticity, therefore, overcomes MacIntyre's charges of subjectivity, by arguing that human beings exist within a cultural horizon, and that it is from here one obtains one's possibilities of choice. Thus, we may satisfactorily claim that although Sartre and Nietzsche may be guilty of these accusations, the concept of authenticity constructed within this book is not.

6.3 Practices, narrative and tradition

Having provided an overview of MacIntyre's theory of modernity and illustrated that his criticisms of emotivism in no way impinges upon our account of authenticity, attention will now be turned to articulating MacIntyre's constructive project. His argument thus far has been to illustrate the limitations of emotivism, and to argue that, although Nietzsche believed himself to have overturned Enlightenment morality, Nietzsche himself perpetuates this position. MacIntyre's attention then turns to providing an argument why we ought to revive the virtue ethics tradition. In advocating virtue ethics, he provides an argument why Aristotle's ethical approach is the most comprehensive account of ethics and offers the means to renew the virtues within modern society through his tripartite theory of practices, narrative and tradition. In this section, MacIntyre's theory will also be compared and contrasted with the socio-existential approach to authenticity.

In order to argue that it was wrong to have rejected Aristotle, and that we ought to revive the virtues, MacIntyre offers a compressed history of the virtue tradition. He begins by appealing to recorded accounts of early human civilization from within Irish, Icelandic and Hellenic literature. The view at which he arrives is that within each of these heroic societies subjects understood themselves in relation to their community. Moreover, MacIntyre establishes that within these virtue-based communities that moral and social life was inseparable. Focusing on the various views of virtues within Athens, MacIntyre demarcates what he believes to be four competing approaches: Sophistic, Platonic, tragedian and Aristotelian. MacIntyre's account of Sophistic virtues holds that virtues are relative, insofar as they advocate that which is desirable for each particular city.[13] His analysis of Platonic virtues claims that for Plato the virtues are real, unified and crucial to one's success as a citizen.[14] MacIntyre's view of tragedian virtues

---

[13] This perspective, that the Sophists endorsed relativism, is based upon the misattribution of the term 'Sophist' to rhetoricians such as Thrasymachus and Gorgias who are never actually referred to as 'Sophists' within the Platonic dialogues within which they feature. See Corey, *The Sophists in Plato's Dialogues* (2015).
[14] Here MacIntyre can be seen to derive the Platonic conception of virtues from *Republic*, where it is argued that justice is the defining virtue of the soul, and that which presides over Spirit and desire.

focuses on Sophocles, within whose plays virtues are portrayed as objective but conflicting, that is, although human effort is judged by the gods it is shown to be ultimately futile.

MacIntyre rejects Sophistic virtues as relative, and tragedian as futile, and whilst he believes Plato's approach articulates a concise account of the virtues, in *Whose Justice? Which Rationality?* he ultimately argues that Aristotle is a more rigorous thinker (1988). In his analysis, MacIntyre notes that the Aristotelian approach addresses the question of the good life in a much more coherent manner than the previous accounts. It does so by positing the *telos* of human existence as *eudaimonia*, which loosely translates to 'human flourishing' or 'happiness', and which is achieved by the virtues. As MacIntyre's surmises, 'the virtues are precisely those qualities the possession of which will enable an individual to achieve *eudaimonia* and the lack of which will frustrate this movement towards that *telos*' (2010: 148). Within his approach, the character qualities which enable one to achieve *eudaimonia* must be recognized by the community, whilst it is the role of the community to determine the course of action which enables the individual's achievement.

The Aristotelian account thus connects both the individual and communal goal. Furthermore, human virtues and civic laws are connected, in that laws do not make sense without virtues and the development of virtues is encouraged and supported by laws. This approach, however, is in contrast to modern society, wherein the individual is an autonomous agent who understands themselves to have entered into society by choice to protect their own interests. Despite upholding Aristotle's account of the virtues in *After Virtue*, MacIntyre takes issue with several aspects. First, he rejects Aristotelian metaphysical biology, because he believed that it led to an indefensible metaphysical doctrine of nature, namely, that it justified arbitrary inequalities and was thus ideological. Secondly, he expresses the concern that particular virtues presuppose a particular *polis*. As he makes explicit, 'if a good deal of the detail of Aristotle's account of the virtues presupposes the now-long-vanished context of the social relationships of the ancient city-state, how can Aristotelianism be formulated so as to be a moral presence in a world in which there are no city-states?' (2010: 163). Thirdly, he sees the unity of the virtues as a mistake, as it does not permit tragedy or moral dilemmas. As a result of Aristotle's belief in the unity of the virtues, conflict only occurs when a hero with flaws emerges. MacIntyre, on the other hand, siding

---

However, since there is no single text devoted to ethics within Plato's oeuvre, that precisely which Plato is advocating is a contested issue. For the arguments surrounding this topic, see *Plato 2: Ethics, Politics, Religion, and the Soul*, ed. Gail Fine (Oxford: Oxford University Press, 2000).

with the Homeric and Sophoclean view that tragedy is basic to the human condition, argues that conflict is natural and necessary in order for individuals to learn and develop the virtues.[15]

Tracing the genealogical development of the virtues, MacIntyre notes that the Aristotelian tradition was continued within the cloisters of the medieval universities. The Scholastic appropriation of Aristotelianism, however, added additional virtues and modified the account of teleology.[16] For Aristotle, *telos* was something which could be achieved by living well, whereas in Christianity the end goal, of salvation, was only to be achieved in the next life. Through their modification, MacIntyre claims that the Scholastics improved Aristotelian teleology in two respects.[17] First, whereas Aristotle restricted *eudaimonia* to certain individuals, the Scholastics made it obtainable to everyone. Secondly, the medieval account of the virtues was historically aware. That is, MacIntyre claims that despite engaging with preceding accounts of ethics, Aristotle did not have a historical sense of himself as working within a particular tradition. In response to the various accounts of virtues, MacIntyre attempts to determine a 'single core conception of the virtues' (2010: 181). However, rather than the practical claims offered in the aforementioned accounts (Sophistic providing that which is desirable; Platonic, what it takes to be a successful citizen; tragedian, to understand the gods; and Aristotelian, to achieve *eudaimonia*), he focuses on that which they are doing when they define virtues. This then leads him to determine that virtues refer to excellence in practical reasoning and human action.

In defining virtues in this way, MacIntyre begins the constructive part of his approach, where he is concerned with how one can become virtuous and how the good life is attained and which he attempts to articulate through the idea of 'practices'. These refer to specific activities within which one acquires abilities which enable one to develop within a particular field. As MacIntyre himself explicates, '[practices are] any coherent and complex form of socially established cooperative human activity through which goods internal to that form of activity are realised in the course of trying to achieve those standards of excellence which are appropriate to [. . .] that form of activity' (2010: 118). What

---

[15] MacIntyre concedes these points in his later work. In his subsequent writings, beginning with *Three Rival Versions of Moral Inquiry*, he comes to embrace Aristotle's metaphysical biology through his endorsement of Thomism. He also revokes his critique of the unity of the virtues in *Whose Justice? Which Rationality?*

[16] What Christian thinkers such as St Augustine and St Aquinas considered to be theological virtues were faith, hope and charity, and which were derived from 1 Corinthians 13.

[17] St Augustine and St Aquinas used the Latin term *beatitudes* and although MacIntyre takes these two terms to be equivocal, there is a significant difference. Namely, that *eudaimonia* is happiness attained through natural means, whilst *beatitūdō* is that derived through supernatural union with God.

he is suggesting is that in order to be considered a practice it is necessary that the field in question is (i) complex, (ii) possesses a standard of excellence and (iii) leads to internal goods. In order to elucidate, MacIntyre offers the concrete examples of farming, football and chess. Each of these cases is complex in the sense that they are constituted by various components. For example, farming is not a simple matter of growing vegetables, but requires various techniques in order to be successful within that field. There are also standards by which it is possible to determine the ability of a farmer, footballer or chess player. That is, it is possible to objectively claim that someone is a bad farmer if their crops fail to flourish, a poor footballer if they fail to score or a poor chess player if they lack the foresight to determine the outcomes of their moves.

Fundamental to the notion of practices are what MacIntyre refers to as 'internal goods'. These refer to the good that is unique to the practice and which is only attainable by engagement in that practice, and are contrasted with external goods such as financial or material gain and social status. MacIntyre explains the relationship between internal goods and practices through the example of teaching a child how to play chess (2010: 188). Initially, one could motivate the child to play by rewarding them with the external good of sweets. However, since the child perceives the practice of chess merely as a means to achieving the sweets, it makes sense for them to cheat. If, on the other hand, the child was motivated by the internal good of becoming a skilled player within the practice of chess, then they would conceive of cheating as counterproductive. The notion of practices therefore possesses a moral dimension insofar as it implies acting towards an end in order to obtain excellence, as opposed to instrumentally perceiving practices as a means to obtain an external good. In recognizing this internal feature, that it is through practices that we learn the virtues initially, MacIntyre makes the claim that morality ought to be conceived of as practice based. The reason is because realizing internal goods requires acting in virtuous ways, such as being honest, courageous, just and by acting with integrity.

MacIntyre's emphasis on, and development of, internal goods distinguishes between appropriate and inappropriate activities within practices. That is, he determines that internal goods, which are an end in themselves, offer the appropriate moral action, whereas external goods, which are acquired through treating practices as a means to an end, lead to inappropriate actions. Here MacIntyre can be seen to advocate an ethical approach similar to the concept of authenticity upheld in this book, in that it makes a distinction between authentic and inauthentic choices. That is, like internal goods, authentic actions are those which are enacted as an end in itself for the individual's own good, whereas inauthentic actions, like external goods, are those which are conducted to achieve an end through treating something else as a means. MacIntyre's notion of practices can therefore be seen to provide an ethical guide to action which divides actions into two categories: those which enable one to act ethically and those which do not. This leads MacIntyre to offer the preliminary definition of virtues as that which 'enables us to achieve those goods which are internal to practices and the lack of which effectively prevents us from achieving any such goods' (2010: 191).

The second aspect of MacIntyre's theory of virtues emerges as a consequence of his rejection of certain components of Aristotelianism.[18] As he himself notes, 'if we reject [Aristotle's metaphysical] biology, as we must, is there any way in which that teleology can be preserved?' (2010: 162). In order to overcome this problem, and supplement his account of practices, he substitutes Aristotle's concept of natural teleology with a sociological account. MacIntyre's alternative is to suggest that individuals ought to understand themselves in terms of self-narrative. What is meant by this is that whenever one has a concept of self, understanding their life from beginning to middle to end, that concept and understanding takes a narrative form. That is, 'the unity of an individual life is the unity of a narrative embodied in a single life' (2010: 218). Narrative involves a search for who one is, and what one ought to do. This then incorporates an element of the individual determining their *telos* for themselves, by questioning, 'what is good for me?' It is then for this reason that MacIntyre claims, 'the unity of human life is the human of a narrative quest' (2010: 203). The goal which the individual sees in their future and is pursued through action then serves as the *telos* for their acts. Not only does narrative provide a *telos*, insofar as it posits a goal for the future, but it also circumvents compartmentalization, that is, the fragmentation of one's identity, which underpins emotivism. This leads MacIntyre to claim that narrative is in fact the correct way of understanding identity, and as such, compartmentalization, is contrary to our proper mode of understanding ourselves.

Through the imperative of embarking upon a narrative quest to reclaim unity, MacIntyre seems to be articulating something similar to the concept of authenticity devised in this book. Both MacIntyre's approach and socio-

---

[18] MacIntyre makes his reason explicit in *Ethics in the Conflicts of Modernity*, where he states 'his [Aristotle's] conception of the natural slave as one who can act in accordance with reason only as the instrument of another and his claim that women are unlike men in their inability to control their passions as reason dictates are both wrongheaded in themselves and symptoms of something more deeply wrong', 85.

existential authenticity are premised on the recognition that without teleology human existence lacks unity. Whilst authenticity is a response to the loss of natural teleology, and argues that the individual can, to a certain extent, determine the meaning of their life for themselves, MacIntyre also offers an alternative to the natural teleology offered by Aristotle's metaphysical biology and argues that unity can be obtained through understanding one's existence in terms of a narrative quest. More than this, he argues that this is the correct way of understanding human agency. This approach is given in contrast to the existentialist conception that the individual is able to choose their existence for themselves; instead, MacIntyre argues that the concept of person is given in advance of any choice. That is, 'the key question for men is not about authorship; I can only answer the question "What am I to do?" if I can answer the prior question "Of what story or stories do I find myself a part?"' (2010: 201).

MacIntyre further develops the concept of narratives in *Ethics in the Conflicts of Modernity*. Responding to Strawson's critique, that narrative is the wrong way to conceive of one's life, MacIntyre claims that humans do not always consciously conceive of their lives in terms of narrative.[19] On the contrary, MacIntyre claims,

> we generally become aware of the narrative structure of our lives infrequently and in either of two ways, when we reflect upon how to make ourselves intelligible to others by telling them the relevant parts of our story or when we have some particular reason to ask 'How has my life gone so far?' and 'How must I ask if it is to go well in future?'. (2016: 241)

Thus far, MacIntyre's theory of virtues has presented an account of how one ought to act, through practices, and the means to readdress the loss of natural teleology through narrative quest, both of these, however, focus exclusively on the individual. In order to defend his account against the same charges of subjectivity as he levies against emotivism, MacIntyre supplements his account with the concept of 'tradition'.

Tradition is applied in the normal sense of a cultural tradition which shapes one's identity. As MacIntyre himself explains, 'what I am, therefore, is in key part what I inherit, a specific past that is present to some degree in my present. I find myself part of a history and that is generally to say, whether I like it or not, whether I recognize it or not, one of the bearers of a tradition' (2010: 221).

---

[19] Strawson's approach is instead to advocate 'the truly happy-go-lucky, see-what-comes-along-lives are among the best there are, vivid, blessed, profound . . . a gift for friendship is shown in how one is in the present'. However, MacIntyre questions, 'what are the happy-go-lucky able to say in explaining and justifying their lives, when they are called to account by those others? What has Strawson to say on their behalf?' (2016: 240).

This goes along with that which the existentialists referred to as 'facticity' (Heidegger 2010: 82; Sartre 2013: 79). However, whilst they believed that this was not something essential which defines one, for MacIntyre it is a necessary component of self-understanding. He also uses the concept of 'tradition' in a more technical sense, which suggests that traditions are not simply cultural frameworks within which we exist, but also are preserved or surpassed through sustained dialogue. As he makes evident, 'a living tradition is a historically extended, socially embodied argument, and an argument precisely in part about the goods which constitute that tradition. Within a tradition the pursuit of goods extends through generations, sometimes through many generations' (2010: 222). It is thus through the virtues that traditions are extended and developed. In this sense, traditions frame practices, and it is the historical development of these which increases the complexity and raises the standards of excellence. More than this, however, they provide a rational account of how societies develop historically.

Thus, contrary to abstract universal norms, natural rights and individual choice, as exemplified in modern moral debate, for MacIntyre, ethical theory ought to be contended and capable of developing through dialogue. Understanding virtues in terms of practice and narrative is only satisfactory when considered in relation to the historical contexts to which they belong. This leads MacIntyre to offer a further definition of virtues:

> The virtues find their point and purpose not only in sustaining those relationships necessary if the variety of goods internal to practices are to be achieved and not only in sustaining the form of an individual life in which that individual may seek out his or her good as the good of his or her whole life, but also in sustaining those traditions which provide both practices and individual lives with their necessary historical context. (2010: 223)

Within the publications which succeed *After Virtue*, it is the notion of tradition which MacIntyre focuses on and attempts to develop. The primary reason was because his emphasis on particular traditions raises the question of whether values are relative to those traditions.[20] In order to contest this charge of relativism, MacIntyre develops the idea that rationality is tradition-guided enquiry in *Whose Justice? Which Rationality?* As Jean Porter explains, 'what had

---

[20] Although MacIntyre argues that tradition can provide a rational means of moral discourse, in *Three Rival Versions of Moral Enquiry*, he attempts to demonstrate the manner in which rival traditions can enter into dialogue. Here he distinguishes between tradition, which he sees as championed by Aquinas, with the encyclopaedic approach which he associates with the Enlightenment, and the genealogical mode of moral inquiry which is indicative of Nietzsche's successors.

initially been suggested as a moral concept, a part of the necessary framework for developing the idea of virtue, has now been transformed into an epistemic and linguistic concept, which plays a central role in explicating the meaning of truth and rationality' (2003: 50). Akin to the concept of authenticity, MacIntyre suggests that since we exist within a cultural framework this framework provides us with our possibilities. That is, in forming a narrative one does so from within a historical context and social setting. Moreover, MacIntyre claims that Morality, understood in the Williamsian sense, is social and constituted by human relationships.

Having defined virtue, MacIntyre then turns his attention to determining the way in which virtue-based ethics could be reintroduced into modern society. In order to achieve this, he first offers an analysis of the modern use and understanding of virtues. In doing so he notes that there has been a shift in culture from emphasis on virtues to the 'virtue of rule following' (2010: 235). That is, rather than attempting to develop those virtues which enable one to live well, the concept of duty has been upheld as the fundamental virtue which individuals ought to embrace. Furthermore, individuals no longer pursue excellence in practices, but attempt to understand and advance morality through art and literature.[21] The Victorians in particular perpetuated this practice, offering moral tales which offer advice on how to conduct oneself. As a consequence of the loss of natural teleology and a shared natural good, 'the tradition of the virtues became an empty shell in the dominant culture of modernity. Yet, the language of virtue has remained a central part of Western moral vocabulary' (Lutz 2012: 131).

However, he notes that there are two approaches which have attempted to reintroduce the tradition of virtues to modernity. The first of which was suggested by William Cobbett, who attempted to achieve political change and looked back in history to identify the ideal circumstances for the development of virtues. The second emerged within the novels of Jane Austen, whose characters live private lives of virtue even when the world makes it difficult for them to do so. However, having shown that Cobbett attempted to radically reform society but with no lasting consequences, MacIntyre determines that Cobbett's 'public political work' cannot provide an adequate model (2010: 239). Rather, it is Austen's account, which attempts to develop the virtues within the enclaves

---

[21] Oscar Wilde's exclamation 'There is no such thing as a moral or an immoral book. Books are well written or badly written. That is all', which was given in response to the criticism of *The Picture of Dorian Gray* that it was immoral and would corrupt those who read it, can be seen to be a reproach against this moralized view of art.

that society overlooks, to which MacIntyre turns for inspiration on how to re-implement the virtues. For him, Austen's novels 'teach us to observe that both in her own time and afterwards the life of the virtues is necessarily afforded a very restricted social and cultural space' (2010: 243). Recognizing that the same conditions within which Austen devised her characters are those which confront the modern individual, MacIntyre suggests the only way forward is 'the construction of local forms of community within which the intellectual and moral life can be sustained through the new dark ages which are already upon us' (2010: 263).

Comparing modernity to the dark ages, MacIntyre notes that the virtues survived the fall of Rome. However, he also arrives at the stark realization that this time the barbarians are not waiting at the gates, but that they have been governing us for a long time. What MacIntyre is inferring is that although he has articulated the theoretical method to revive the virtue ethic tradition within modern society, the conditions by which to do so are no longer present. MacIntyre arrives at the rather sobering realization that 'we must seek an architect for this model of social life that will enable communities to embody the tradition of the virtues to flourish in the midst of a social and political culture that rejects its tradition' (2010: 243). In reference to Samuel Beckett's *Waiting for Godot*, within which the protagonists wait in vain for an unknown reason, MacIntyre concludes *After Virtue* with the pessimistic claim that the only hope is to wait for a new St Benedict.[22]

6.4 Criticisms of MacIntyre's virtue ethics

Now that MacIntyre's theory of the virtues has been discussed, attention will be turned to critically analysing the components of practices, narrative and tradition. Here we will discuss the possibility of evil practices, the practicalities of narrative quest and the charge of nostalgia as informing his concept of tradition. It will be argued that there is an inherent problem with his dimension of practices, insofar as it potentially permits one to cultivate cruel actions. The dimension of narrative, however, will be defended and shown to be beneficial

---

[22] MacIntyre's choice is made apparent by John Henry Newman, according to whom, 'St Benedict found the world, physical and social, in ruins, and his mission was to restore it in the way not of science, but of nature, not as if setting about to do it, not professing to do it by any set time, or by any rare specific, or by any series of strokes, but so quietly, patiently, gradually, that often till the work was done, it was not known to be doing', referenced in Christopher Dawson's *Religion and the Rise of Western Culture* (New York: Image Books, 2001), 53.

to the development of our theory of socio-existential authenticity. The concept of tradition, on the other hand, will be shown to be steeped in nostalgia, and as such creates a distorted image of ethical reality. Furthermore, it will be argued that his pessimistic conclusion reinforces the claim that virtue theory is unable to provide a practical resolution to the problems of modernity.

One major criticism of the theory of practices is that many forms of sexual violence, such as rape, meet the criteria which MacIntyre devised in order to determine what constitutes as a practice. According to Elizabeth Frazer and Nichola Lacey, rape is complex in that there are various components, there is a standard as to what constitutes rape and the act itself is the realization of that good which is internal to it. As they themselves put it, 'masculine dominance and the symbolic and material subjugation of femininity can be uniquely realised through the penetration of a woman, with the phallus, against her will' (1996: 274). Their claim is that MacIntyre's definition of practices prior to the good, and his neglect of power relations is what permits 'evil practices'. They suggest that this can be resolved in two respects. First, MacIntyre could redefine his concept to include such practices as football, but exclude sexual violence, though it would be difficult to do so without arbitrary appeals. Secondly, he could develop an account of power relations and a theory of power. This would enable him to avoid including sexual violence within practices by arguing that rape cannot be considered a practice because it is a manifestation of power.

This argument, however, is not entirely convincing. First, because the purpose of sexual assault is always an internal good, such as sexual gratification or power, both of which MacIntyre would define as external goods. Secondly, sexual assault is a vicious act and one which any rational agent would define as a vice, as opposed to a virtue. Moreover, MacIntyre himself personally responds to this criticism, rejecting the claim that it is necessary to supplement his conception with an account of power relations, and that if he were to do so his account would become incoherent. Furthermore, MacIntyre claims there is already a conception of justice inherent within practices which defends against deformation and prejudice. As he explicitly states, 'the conception of justice as a virtue which is required if the goods internal to practices are to be achieved, let alone the goods of individuals lives and of communities, is itself sufficient to provide a standard for identifying and condemning the deformations and distortions to which practices may be subjected, and the consequent injustices to women and others' (1996: 290).

However, although MacIntyre can dismiss sexual violence, his account nevertheless seems susceptible to the inclusion of 'evil' practices. Let us imagine, for example, a community of assassins within which the inhabitants revere and advocate the execution of their targets with increasingly cruel techniques. In such an example, the more sadistic and savage the act, the more the assassin is respected and the greater their reputation becomes. Within this community, assassination can be conceived of as complex in that it incorporates various techniques and actions. There is also a standard of excellence involved which develops with the invention and implementation of more barbaric and efficient means to dispose of one's victim. For this reason, practices may be said to permit immoral acts, and in this respect MacIntyre's account is flawed. Since practices are fundamental to MacIntyre's ethical theory, insofar as they possess internal goods, and are capable of determining the good life, it would seem that MacIntyre cannot provide a sufficient reconfiguration of the Aristotelian virtue ethics tradition.

With regard to narrative, the second part of MacIntyre's theory of virtues, Bernard Williams claims that it comes up short on two grounds (2009). First, he questions how it is possible to identify the narrative of a person's life unless one possesses a prior conception of a person's life. Secondly, continuing this line of argument, he asks how narrative can contain the possibility of coherence without possessing an antecedent idea of the coherence of a person's life. Williams argues that both of these problems can be resolved through making concessions. First, MacIntyre could claim that narrative does not need to explain the most elementary levels of what a person is. Rather, we begin with a basic understanding of a person and simple actions and can explain the more complex aspects and actions through narrative. Secondly, MacIntyre could claim that the coherence of life is not recognized in advance of its narrative interpretation, but rather we are given material about which questions of coherence can be asked and answered in terms of narrative.

However, Williams recognizes that these concessions raise doubts concerning the sources of these interpretations, their standing and their relations to fictions. He quotes Kierkegaard, who claims it is not possible to interpret one's own life because one can never be in a position to retrospectively analyse it. This then appears to undermine MacIntyre's account, since he states that it is essential to discover who one is in order to decide what one should do, and if one cannot reflect on who one is, then one will not be able to decide what to do. One way of resolving this issue would be to permit that others could interpret our lives on our behalf. This seems to be inferred by MacIntyre's example of the various interpretations of the life of Thomas Becket (2010: 198). If this is indeed the case, then the unity of an actual life is the unity of a fictional life. Furthermore,

Williams claims, that MacIntyre must believe 'unity is found first in life, and is carried over from life to the construction of fiction' (1996: 310). Williams, however, argues that such a position is indefensible, and that we cannot understand our lives as analogous to fictional characters for the simple reason that they do not possess unrealized possibilities. That is, fictional characters' entire lives are already set out within a novel. As Williams concisely explains, 'it is essential to fictional lives that their wholeness is always already there, and essential to ours that it is not' (1996: 311).

These concerns then create problems for MacIntyre's concept of narrative – namely, if a narrative is retrospectively applied to one by another, and the person in question was not aware of the narrative which they are supposed to embody, then where does that narrative come from? Williams suggests two possible responses. The first is that even if one cannot consciously aim towards embodying a particular narrative, it could be claimed that their considerations were nevertheless drawn from a repertoire of stories which define recognizable lives. The second is that the considerations which shape one's life are not ordered into a unified whole and that the narrative which gives unity to one's life is a fiction. Williams, however, sides with the latter, believing 'we have a much greater interest in living a life that is our own and in having an adequate grasp of the considerations that at various stages direct it, than we do in the ambition that it should genuinely present a well-shaped tale to potential narrators of it' (1996: 313). Thus, for Williams, it is more important to live a fragmented, but authentic life, than one which conforms to a coherent narrative which has been determined by someone else.[23]

Williams's criticisms are quite accurate, and if MacIntyre had intended the concept of narrative quest in a literal sense, then these would be much more damning. However, MacIntyre's intention was to employ this as a metaphor, albeit one which he took too far. As Michael Bell makes apparent, 'MacIntyre's use of narrative as a model of the moral life seems to me to be justified for its purposes. But the need for this metaphor to be so deep and subliminal as not to appear metaphorical at all leaves it with a slippery and potentially misleading value when extrapolated from its context' (1992: 172). That which is truly important for MacIntyre, and which he is attempting to elucidate, is personal intelligibility and the idea of trying to lead a life of integrity, of not being a mass of contradictions or, worse, an unreflective mass of contradictions unaware of

---

[23] Although MacIntyre deals extensively with Bernard Williams's philosophical approach within in *Ethics in the Conflicts of Modernity*, in which he argues that it is a response to expressivism, he does not address William's criticisms of narrative.

the tensions in one's life. The concept inherent within narrative is an important one, and one which we do regularly employ in order to make sense of our lives. It also seems accurate to claim that such retrospective self-interpretation enables us to question the meaning of our individual lives. Thus, that which is necessary in order to maintain this concept is to remind ourselves that narrative is merely a metaphor of how we arrive at self-understanding. This metaphor of narrative is also beneficial to the development of our own understanding of authenticity. By conceiving of authenticity in these terms, we can provide a unified understanding of our own lives. This line of argument, however, will be further discussed in Chapter 7.

Thus far, we have discussed the major criticisms of the concepts of practices and narrative. We have illustrated that although there are flaws inherent within practices, which prevent MacIntyre from excluding evil acts, his concept of narrative is beneficial to our concept of socio-existential authenticity. With regard to his concept of tradition, however, it will be claimed that the primary problem, that it is grounded on the desire to revive a bygone era, negatively impacts upon MacIntyre's entire project. MacIntyre himself pre-empts this criticism in his discussion of traditions where he claims that 'this virtue is not to be confused with any form of conservative antiquarianism; I am not praising those who choose the conventional conservative role of *laudator temporis act*. It is rather the case that an adequate sense of tradition manifests itself in a grasp of those future possibilities which the past has made available to the present' (2010: 223). Here he attempts to differentiate his own position from that of conservativism. However, the charge of nostalgia more specifically suggests that MacIntyre arbitrarily favours and attempts to revive a moral framework which was indicative of pre-modernity.

The attempt to revive a pre-modern theory is supposed through his pessimistic view of modernity which simultaneously undermines his account. The conclusion that we are living within a new dark age suggests that modern individuals are worse off than their predecessors, and his claim that modernity has dismantled the means to reintroduce virtue ethics expresses a deep pessimism regarding the success of his project. This perspective is further expressed by John Horton who emphasizes that 'given the importance which MacIntyre attaches to the social embeddedness of thought and enquiry, his largely negative views of modernity continually threatens to undermine any attempt to root his positive proposals in the contemporary world' (1996: 14). Thus, it would seem that the consequence of MacIntyre's nostalgia, to return to and revive the trajectory set by the Aristotelian tradition, leads to the pessimistic conclusion that the reimplementation of virtue ethics is not something which can be easily achieved, for the reason that the necessary social conditions have been rejected by modern European society. The pessimistic overtones of *After Virtue* thus lead to the perspective that it is, as Benjamin Barber dramatically puts it, 'a sermon of despair' (1988: 190).

Terry Pinkard accurately pinpoints this charge of nostalgia against MacIntyre when he states that '[his] sustained attack on the notion that "the present is progress" has fuelled that idea that he must be some kind of nostalgic pre-modern thinker, a kind of Irish-Scottish Heidegger, wishing, as it has been unkindly said, for all of us to return to some vanquished Catholic world within which the cacophony of the modern condition is absent' (2003: 180–1). Pinkard, however, argues that the charge of nostalgia is not a legitimate one. He attempts to do so by demonstrating that MacIntyre's disdain for modernity does not stem from a romantic longing for a pre-modern existence, but rather from within the influences exercised upon him by Karl Polanyi and Max Weber. Granted neither of these theorists held romantic sympathies, Pinkard further argues that MacIntyre's recognition of rights for women and minorities prevents one from categorizing him as a pre-modern thinker. Pinkard thus defends MacIntyre against this charge of nostalgia, on the grounds that those with whom he developed in dialogue did not idealize the past and that MacIntyre himself was a staunch defender of modern rights. MacIntyre himself makes this second claim explicit in *Ethics in the Conflicts of Modernity* where he states that there has been genuine historical progress in political liberation, and artistic and scientific achievements. As he puts it, 'the history of modernity, insofar as it has been a series of social and political liberations and emancipations from arbitrary and oppressive rule, is indeed in key respects a history of genuine and admirable progress' (2016: 123). However, although he recognizes the positive contributions of modernity, his outlook still remains relatively negative, for as he continues, 'yet it is this very same modernity in which new forms of oppressive inequality, new types of material and intellectual impoverishment, and new frustrations and misdirections of desire have been recurrently generated' (2016: 124). Thus, although MacIntyre's does recognize that there has been a certain degree of progress within modernity, he is still nevertheless quite sceptical.

In terms of romantically praising pre-modernity, we can claim that MacIntyre's approach is a lot more nuanced than first anticipated. However, a further charge of nostalgia is made against MacIntyre by Martha Nussbaum in her review of *Whose Justice? Which Rationality?* Here Nussbaum claims that MacIntyre longs 'nostalgically for a unanimity that human life has never really had' (1989: 41). Thus, rather than ascribing a general romanticism as motivating MacIntyre's emphasis on tradition, Nussbaum's claim is that the form of virtue which MacIntyre prescribes is one which has never before existed. To reiterate MacIntyre's pessimistic conclusion, modernity cannot sustain the virtues because it lacks the practices which give the virtues determinate content. However, although MacIntyre believed that this unanimity was inherent within pre-modernity and lost with the onset of modernity, this belief can be challenged on two grounds.

First, although MacIntyre takes practices to be fundamental to the virtues, and claims that the conditions for the virtues, including practices, are no longer present, it can be objected that not all pre-modern work was practice based. That is, it is a myth that all pre-modern people acquired the good by participating in practices. As Keith Breen makes explicit, 'it is certainly true that some forms of work [. . .] once had a practice-like character, but it is also true that whole categories of people – women, serfs, the poor – were denied access to them by institutions such as the medieval guild' (2016: 148). MacIntyre himself recognized this problem as inherent within Aristotle's metaphysical biology, and it was for this reason that he initially rejected Aristotle's account of natural teleology. That is, for Aristotle, only autonomous, male citizens could achieve *eudaimonia*. Thus, whilst we can claim that the practices did exist in pre-modernity, they were only accessible to a limited group of autonomous citizens.

Secondly, MacIntyre's belief that only pre-modernity enabled us to engage in practices is also mistaken. Following on from the previous point, that not all pre-modern life was practice based, David Miller argues 'MacIntyre's decline-and-fall-of-the-practices thesis is at best a gross exaggeration, and it follows that there are many contemporary forms of human activity within which different conceptions of justice apply' (1994: 259). Focusing on the concept of justice, which all practices have at their core, Miller contends that there are internal goods to achieve and standards of excellence to comply with within modern economic activities. And although modern society may not possess the same concept of justice as pre-modernity, there are competing conceptions of what is just within modern society, and which adhere to the conditions of practices. Moreover, in this way, Miller claims 'for the first time, perhaps, almost everyone can aspire to a state of affairs in which their merits are recognised and duly rewarded' (1994: 259). Thus, although many traditional practices have become redundant, we can nevertheless conceive of new practices which emerged with modernity and which have become accessible to a greater number of people. Furthermore, we can claim that the unanimity which MacIntyre believed to be present within pre-modernity, and which leads to his pessimistic conclusion, is a fiction.

As we saw, MacIntyre ends *After Virtue* with the pessimistic conclusion that the necessary conditions with which to revive the virtue ethics tradition no longer exist. However, if we accept Nussbaum's line of argument, then the conditions which MacIntyre envisages never truly existed, and his own narrative quest, to revive this pre-modern framework, is the search for Novalis's blue flower.[24] In the closing sentence of *After Virtue*, MacIntyre suggests that instead of Godot, we are waiting for a new St Benedict. However, as a consequence of his nostalgia, this metaphor is a little too apt, for if the conditions which he depends upon never existed, then like Beckett's Godot, the new St Benedict will never arrive. In his disdain towards modernity and desire to revive a pre-modern framework, a quote from Max Weber seems appropriate: 'to the person who cannot bear the fate of the times like a man, one must say: may he rather return silently, without the usual publicity build-up of renegades, but simply and plainly. The arms of the old churches are opened widely and compassionately for him' (1991: 155).

Weber's criticism entails that traditional values remain present for those who wish to remain in the shade, for those who delude themselves into believing that the past was better than the present, and that this traditional framework can be restored. A similar criticism can be made from our socio-existential perspective. Namely, rather than deceiving oneself with regards to the restriction of freedom and loss of meaning, the socio-existential attitude is to acknowledge that we must courageously confront our existential predicament. The necessity to avoid nostalgia, on our account, is to ensure we maintain a realistic approach. If we delude ourselves into believing a sense of unanimity exists this would prevent one from living an authentic existence, as our choice would not be a mature one. Thus, by resisting nostalgia, and taking a realistic approach, by embracing one's fate, we can avoid descending into an inauthentic existence.

6.4 Summary

We began this chapter with MacIntyre's analysis of modernity and the claim that modern moral discourse and society has been dominated by emotivism.

---

[24] Within Novalis's unfinished novel, *Heinrich von Ofterdingen*, the protagonist dreams of the most beautiful flower he has ever perceived, however, as he reaches out to pluck it he awakens from his dream and spends the rest of his life searching for it in vain. The blue flower thus became a symbol of romanticism and the nostalgic longing for the unobtainable.

Although he had applied this criticism to Sartre and Nietzsche, we defended our concept of authenticity by illustrating that the dimensions of intersubjective consciousness and heritage enabled us to circumvent this charge. Having discussed MacIntyre's suggestion to revive the virtue ethics tradition, we then critically analysed his proposal which was constituted of practices, narrative and tradition. Here we argued that whilst the concept of narrative was beneficial to our own account, MacIntyre's account of practices appears to permit the flourishing of evil acts. Moreover, tradition, which was based on a nostalgic sense of unity, which did not exist, led to his pessimistic conclusion. However, throughout this enquiry it was determined that although MacIntyre's virtue ethics does not provide a satisfactory theory, our engagement was not entirely negative, but led to the further development of our concept of authenticity. This has been our aim within the last three chapters – to further develop the socio-existential ethic of authenticity. Having derived various aspects from each alternative approach to modernity, we will now revisit these and draw out the implications for our concept of authenticity.

7

Finding meaning in freedom

Throughout the course of our enquiry we have been concerned with the problems of freedom and meaning. In particular, our attention was fixed on how the Enlightenment's pursuit of progress problematized freedom and led to a loss of meaning. In response to this problem, it was claimed that a bulwark to nihilism was present within the ethical ideal of authenticity. This argument was first posited in Chapter 3, where we offered an initial explanation as to how living authentically provides us with purpose. In order to illustrate that authenticity was best suited to this role, we considered alternative responses as posed by modern, postmodern and pre-modern advocates. Each of the respective theorists whom we considered was shown to construct an ethical ideal in response to the intellectual fallout of the Enlightenment. Having considered these three alternative approaches, and shown them to be wanting with regard to the problem of meaning, our aim will be to draw upon these encounters and develop the socio-existential approach to authenticity in relation to each. The primary purpose of this chapter, however, will be to bring our investigation to a close and justify our claim regarding the importance of authenticity. The aim, therefore, will be to further develop our concept and demonstrate the manner in which authenticity offers a satisfactory resolution to the problem, enabling us to find meaning in freedom.

The first section of this chapter (Section 7.1) will begin with an overview of the alternative responses to the problems of freedom and meaning, as explicated within the previous three chapters. We will then discuss the ways in which our concept of authenticity has developed through engagement with the aforementioned theorists. Here we will reiterate the aspects which we incorporated and further develop these in relation to our concept of socio-existential authenticity. In Section 7.2, we will turn to address the opening question of this book (can authenticity provide a compelling resolution to the problems of freedom and meaning which pervade modern existence?)

by explaining how we can find meaning within the freedom created by the Enlightenment. Having provided a defence of our theory, we will then consider some practical problems with authenticity in Section 7.3. Here we will discuss the concern that authenticity has become commodified, and that the pursuit of such an ideal can only end in disillusion or disappointment. A further problem which we will consider is caused by our increased dependence on technology. Namely, as a large percentage of communication is conducted through social media, it will be questioned whether the internet provides an alternative domain within which to achieve authenticity. We will then offer some concluding remarks in Section 7.4, where we will evaluate the success of our socio-existential concept of authenticity and elucidate that which we have determined through our enquiry.

7.1 Picking up the spear

In the previous three chapters, we considered alternative explanations as to that which caused the problems of freedom and meaning and their proposed resolution. The first alternative was Habermas's modernist approach, which diagnosed the problems to be a consequence of the colonization of the lifeworld. Habermas's proposal to reverse the encroachment of systems imperatives upon the lifeworld was to increase communicative action through the ethical ideals of self-determination and self-realization. Next, we analysed Foucault's postmodern account, which claimed discourses of power had come to impinge upon and diminish the autonomy of the individual. His response to such social domination was to engage in self-creation and cultivate the ideal of care. Finally, we addressed MacIntyre's pre-modern perspective, which offered an ethical post-mortem, claiming that the breakdown of hierarchies has led to the rise of manipulation and the emergence of a culture of emotivism. His suggestion was that the ills of modernity could be overcome through reviving the virtue ethics tradition. However, in each of the aforementioned accounts, we found that although they offered compelling arguments to address the problems of freedom and meaning, their approaches nevertheless left something to be desired.

Habermas was taken to be a representative of modernism for the obvious reason that he sought to continue the Enlightenment's 'project of modernity'. His means to achieve this was through increased communicative action, which he believed to be an underdeveloped form of rationality. Through the realization of this strand of rationality, Habermas believed that greater autonomy could be achieved. However, although he recognized unbalanced rationalization had led to decreased freedom and the loss of meaning, his resolution to these problems was shown to be inadequate. Habermas's attempt to address the colonization of the lifeworld was to increase communicative rationality. This, however, relied upon an unrealistic dualism of system and lifeworld. The problem was that Habermas believed power could be restricted to systems. Furthermore, his emphasis on the priority of the right over the good was shown to be inconsistent and led to a performative contradiction, as any concept of right necessarily depends upon a preconceived notion of good. As a consequence, if good has precedence, and Habermas attempts to form his conception of the good through the notion of 'right', then this results in the situation that his notion of 'right' is unfounded and incapable of setting the limits for self-realization. Thus, not only is Habermas's account subject to a performative contradiction but it is also unable to directly address the problems of freedom and meaning.

Foucault's account was viewed as postmodern, for the reason that he rejected the project of modernity and attempted to go beyond it, attempting to overcome the problems it produced. Although the Enlightenment's aim was to increase freedom through rationalization, Foucault argued that those very institutions which were built upon a rational foundation have ironically come to dominate subjects through the discourse of power. The ultra-radical conception of power, which he was shown to espouse, not only 'subjected' agents but consequently also stifled their ability to live a meaningful existence. Although Foucault suggested the Stoic-inspired 'care of the self' as a resolution to this form of social control, his response did not provide a substantial account of how one can live a meaningful life. His resolution, rather, is to engage in the aesthetic practice of self-creation, crafting our lives into a work of art. This ideal, however, was argued to be but an empty aesthetic, which, devised entirely by the subject, was devoid of intersubjective meaning.

MacIntyre offered a pre-modern response to the extent that he attempted to revive a philosophical framework which existed prior to the Enlightenment. In his account, modern moral discourse has become unintelligible because thinkers of the Enlightenment deconstructed the frameworks within which ethical concepts made sense. Furthermore, the loss of a shared good has led to a culture of emotivism and the rise of instrumental reasoning. That is, as a consequence of lacking a universal good, our moral decisions have become based on our emotions, and we consciously, and without moral quandary, treat others as a means to an end, rather than as an end in themselves. MacIntyre's solution to these problems was to revive the virtue tradition and re-imbue society with a new *telos*. In order to provide a new shared social standard, his suggestion was to reintroduce virtue ethics through the notions of practices, narrative and tradition. This would address the problem of freedom by restoring teleology, the loss of which led to these problems. With regard to the problem of meaning, MacIntyre enables the individual to find fulfilment through the concept of narrative quest. Out of the three considered theorists, he offers the most fully developed response to the problem of meaning. However, his approach was deemed to be ultimately unrealistic. The reason why MacIntyre's account is incapable of being enacted is because it rests upon an inaccurate account of the distinction between pre-modernity and modernity. Furthermore, his concept of tradition, which underpins his virtue theory, leads to the pessimistic conclusion that the necessary conditions are no longer present.

Having discussed the three alternative resolutions to the modern problems of freedom and meaning, we are now in a better position to address the question which motivated this enquiry: Does appeal to the ideal of authenticity provide a satisfactory response to the problems of modernity? Before addressing this question, it will be necessary to first expand on that which we have learnt through our engagement. Although we have argued that each of the alternative accounts offers an insufficient response to the problems of freedom and meaning, our analysis is not to be entirely negative. On the contrary, there are lessons to be learnt and benefits to be derived from each of our encounters. The greatest concepts are not those which develop in isolation, but those which are forged and tempered through external engagement. As Nietzsche aptly puts it, 'the very reason [the Greeks] got so far is that they knew how to pick up the spear and throw it onward from the point where others had left it' (1998: 30). The aspects which we have drawn out, and intend to integrate, are Habermas's engagement with the colonization thesis, Foucault's concept of social domination in terms of power and MacIntyre's notion of narrative quest. Having made our intentions explicit, we shall now turn to explicating these positive experiences and to illustrating how they help to develop our concept of authenticity.

From engagement with Habermas it was claimed that his attempt to reverse the colonization of the lifeworld would provide us with the continued possibility to live authentically. In particular, we will focus on his 'colonization thesis', which diagnosed a central concern of contemporary capitalist society. This was the suggestion that economic and administrative models of the systems sphere have begun to colonize the public and private realms of the lifeworld sphere. As Habermas explains, 'in the end, systemic mechanisms suppress forms of social integration even in those areas where a consensus-dependent coordination of action cannot be replaced, that is, where the symbolic reproduction of the lifeworld is at stake' (1987: 196). Put simply, institutions and practices which were not previously economically orientated have become dominated by, and directed towards, the acquisition of capital. This problem is one which is all too familiar to anyone involved within the arts and humanities, where practices which ought to be pursued for their own end have been restricted by and subjected to bureaucratic 'blue sky thinking'.[1]

This insight is valuable insofar as it has conceptualized a phenomenon which many of us can recognize yet may be unable to articulate. In what way, however, can this be said to contribute towards our concept of authenticity? Habermas's insight, that various aspects of public and private life are being transformed by economic and managerial imperatives, enables us to preserve the domains within which authenticity can be realized. It also leads us to take the criticism seriously, that authenticity as an ideal has become commoditized. As mentioned earlier, colonization entails that those practices which ought to be pursed for their own good have been subjected to economic and bureaucratic standards. This then raises the question of whether our concept of authenticity is also subject to these very demands. Although Habermas's account offers a resolution to this problem, our rebuttal of his response requires that we demonstrate how the account of authenticity developed here is capable of circumventing this issue. This concern, however, will be taken up in the following section, where sufficient space can be dedicated to such an undertaking.

Through our analysis of Foucault, we determined that the most beneficial aspect of his account is his treatment of power, which, unlike Habermas, accepts that power is to be found within all spheres. Foucault's perspective entails that institutions exert their influence through discourse, and that this acts as an external force which simultaneously produces the subject. As he himself puts it, 'Power produces; it produces reality; it produces domains of objects and rituals of truth. The individual and the knowledge that may be gained of him belong to this production' (1991a: 194). Our analysis of Foucault argued that although his early work offers an ultra-radical concept of power, within which the subject is dominated and produced, within his later work he employs a subtler concept of power. Attempting to overcome the subjection which discourse impinges upon agents, Foucault argues that we can do so through care of the self. However, the concept of power which he operates under is not ultra-radical, but, as Lukes

---

[1] This problem is the focus on Boltanski and Chiapello's excellent study, *The New Spirit of Capitalism*, and which will be elucidated in Section 7.3.

claims, ideological power. In what way, then, can this understanding of power be beneficial to our concept of authenticity?

This understanding of power relations enables us to better understand those externally imposed values which we associate with inauthentic existence. That is, we can understand the social subjugation/pressure to conform perpetuated by *das Man* as a form of ideological power exercised over us. Thus, rather than simply 'inauthentic', we can more accurately claim that the inability to achieve self-actualization is a consequence of externally applied power. Aside from a diagnostic tool, by which we can determine why one's existence is inauthentic, what other benefits are there of endorsing this concept of power? Thinking of authenticity in terms of power also permits us to conceive of the self beyond our immediate, concrete social situation. In particular, it allows us to better understand how we conduct ourselves and are shaped online. In contemporary society, many of our social interactions and communication are conducted through social media. And as the internet provides an alternative platform for social interaction, it also exists as a potential platform for domination. We will, however, reserve this discussion until Section 7.3, where we will address the question of how power shapes social media, and consequently, our virtual selves.

The aspect which we shall derive from our engagement with MacIntyre is his concept of narrative. According to this idea, whenever we attempt to make sense of our lives, we do so through the construction of narratives. In this way, our previous actions and achievements are incorporated into and interpreted as a unified whole which contributes towards our current understanding of our selves. Everything we have done in our life seems to point towards our current project. What if our project fails? Do we lose our identity? According to MacIntyre, this failed project is assimilated into our next narrative; that is, 'the narrative in terms of which he or she at first understood and order experiences is itself now made into the subject of an enlarged narrative' (2006a: 5). Thus, when we engage in self-reflection, we always do so within a narrative framework. Through this manner of understanding, we come to think of our lives as directed towards a particular end, which MacIntyre terms 'narrative quest'. However, for MacIntyre, the end which one pursues is not previously known. Rather, it is only through the quest that one comes to understand oneself. As he explains, 'it is in the course of the quest and only through encountering and coping with the various particular harms, dangers, temptations and distractions which provide any quest with its episodes and incidents that the goal of the quest is finally to be understood' (2010: 219).

What is it, in particular, that we intend to integrate into our own approach from MacIntyre's account? MacIntyre's concept of narrative unity offers us a valuable metaphor by which to understand one's authentic self. That is, through the notion of narrative one can explain how one gives unity to one's past projects, by interpreting them as contributing towards one's current project. With our example of the authentic academic, it was not taken to be one's individual essence. That is, we do not introspect and discover our attributes as an academic; rather, we interpret our past choices and various projects retrospectively and form them into one intelligible whole. MacIntyre's account of narrative quest also correlates with the dimension of 'becoming what one is', insofar as one does not necessarily know what one is to become, and in this way avoids arbitrary choice. That is, one's choice is not arbitrary because it is not chosen in a vacuum but arises out of circumstance. The concept of narrative can thus further explain where our understanding of ourselves comes from.

7.2 Finding meaning in freedom

Now that we have illustrated why the alternative approaches are insufficient, and the manner in which these encounters have helped shape our concept of authenticity, we may continue to address the question raised at the outset of our intellectual voyage. Namely, we will proceed to demonstrate that the concept of authenticity provides a satisfactory resolution to the problem of meaning. The problem was that increased freedom, which was pursued by the Enlightenment, not only liberated one from metaphysical and social restraints but simultaneously also diminished any prior sense of purpose. The increase of rationality then confined us within a Weberian iron cage, restricting our freedom and ability to exist in any genuine sense. Regardless of narrative – whether through loss of social goals or natural *telos* – meaning is not externally offered, but must be subjectively sought within our intersubjective context. Before we address this question, by determining the means by which we achieve purpose, it will be beneficial to first recap on our concept of authenticity.

Thus far construed, our concept of socio-existential authenticity is comprised of six dimensions. Insofar as we rejected possession of an inner essence to be discovered through introspection, we determined that the first dimension to offer the means of attaining authenticity was *choice*. After discussing the implications of choice, it was illustrated that in order for one's choice to be meaningful, that a second necessary condition was that of *commitment*. The third dimension arose in response to the problem that one might choose and commit to a project which one is incapable of realizing, here it was claimed that this could be avoided through *maturity*. To address the problem of arbitrary choice of projects, it was upheld that 'what we are' emerges immanently, and that we choose to accept or reject this by *becoming what one is*. This choice of acceptance or rejection is determined by the fact that our choices are only meaningful within intersubjective horizons of significance, and this adds an ethical dimension which we achieve through *intersubjective consciousness*. Following from this, it was claimed that our possibilities are shaped by historical factors and that authenticity is temporal insofar as it is not a permanently attained state, but is in fact determined by our *heritage*. As a consequence of adhering to these six dimensions, it was then determined that the individual can conceive of their life as a unified whole, and by thinking of it as possessing an end provides our lives with *meaning*.

In what way then can our concept of socio-existential authenticity be said to respond to the problems of freedom and meaning? With regard to freedom, within a liberal democracy a new good, which offers a substantive way of life, cannot be posited as a political ideal all should adhere to. The reason is because we ought to respect everyone's individual autonomy, and to uphold one world view would doubtless lead to oppression. That is, were we to posit a singular substantive good, this would discriminate against those who do not hold the same cultural values, have a different national identity or lack the capacities to realize such an ideal. In a liberal democracy we ought to respect difference and esteem everyone according to their own abilities. As Taylor concisely explains, 'democracy has ushered in a politics of equal recognition, which has taken various forms over the years, and has now returned in the form of demands for the equal status of cultures and of genders' (1994: 27). As a consequence, the only guide to action is that which we ourselves ascertain.

That is, because we lack a singular, unified, objective good, which orders our behaviour, there is no external guide, but rather we ought to turn inwards. We are thus confronted with ethical responsibility for our lives, and authenticity provides the most realistic approach to this problem. Thus, although we cannot posit a substantive vision of the good (that one ought to be pious, rational, etc.), we can offer a set of formal conditions, or dimensions, which presents an ethical ideal whilst preserving the individual's freedom to choose. That is, through living an authentic existence we can achieve freedom, rejecting the social shackles imposed upon us, and determine our values for ourselves.

As for the problem of meaning, in Chapter 3 a preliminary account was given to explain the manner in which our socio-existential approach could address this problem. Here we claimed that these combined dimensions led to a unified sense of self which brought one's projects together. Offering the example of an authentic academic, we claimed that through the dimension of *choice* we do not have to accept a way of life which others have determined for us. With regard to *commitment*, our project must be that which we are committed to achieving. As for *maturity*, we must be physically and mentally capable of achieving our goal. By *becoming what one is*, we are then capable of avoiding arbitrary choice. *Intersubjective consciousness* prevents us from forming a project which is ethically undesirable. Through *heritage* our choices are historically bound. A consequence of adhering to each of these dimensions is that our project becomes meaningful. However, we have since supplemented our account with the additional dimension of MacIntyre's concept of narrative unity, which enables us to further articulate the notion of unity inherent within authenticity. Understood in this way, the example of an authentic academic is a consequence of narrative; that is, we have interpreted our choices, heritage, what we are, etc., to point to this particular project.

Our concept of socio-existential authenticity is therefore capable of addressing the problem of freedom and meaning. We can engage with the loss of freedom by rejecting externally applied values and conceptions of the good imposed upon us. That is, rather than living in accordance with tradition or convention, for no other reason than it is socially endorsed, we ought to critically analyse such values. Our concept of authenticity also offers a satisfactory response to the loss of meaning, which was induced by the loss of natural teleology, by advocating the construction of individual projects. That is, rather than offering an objective good which everyone can adhere to, we claimed that the individual is tasked with determining the good for themselves. Having explicated the way in which our modified concept of socio-existential authenticity addresses the problem of freedom and meaning, we will now consider it in relation to the alternative theories considered in the preceding chapters. Here we will illustrate the manner in which authenticity overcomes the problems the previous three approaches encountered, and the way in which authenticity can be said to offer a better approach to the problems of freedom and meaning.

In our analysis of Habermas, it was illustrated that he acknowledges the problems caused by the failure of the Enlightenment and actively attempts to resolve them by developing communicative rationality. However, although he acknowledges that freedom and meaning have been problematized by modernity, it is the loss of autonomy which maintains his focus. One consequence of prioritizing the loss of autonomy, caused by the colonization of the lifeworld, at the expense of the loss of meaning, is that he attempts to posit a rational foundation for morality, as opposed to focusing on a concept of the good. However, it was determined that his theory depends upon a prior conception of the good. A further implication is that his discourse ethics fails to address the problem of meaning. Our concept of authenticity, however, did not encounter this problem. Rather than beginning with a context-less, rational-based, moral theory, authenticity instead offers a new good, insofar as it implores the individual to realize their life for themselves. In this way, we prioritized ethics, and since ethics is an intersubjective, collaborative endeavour, which is bound by social norms, we realize our authentic self through our interactions with others.

In engagement with Foucault, it was determined that he rejected the Enlightenment as a failed project, and that the rational institutions it established had ironically limited freedom. To recover a sense of subjectivity, he emphasized the reintroduction of the ethic of 'care' as a way of responding to the problem of power. Although Foucault offers an ethical ideal in response to the loss of freedom, his ethic of care lacks the context to make choice meaningful. That is, despite his injunction to cultivate oneself into a work of art, which provides a sense of unity, the grounds of one's choice are still ultimately arbitrary. Thus, although he could be considered to address the problem of meaning through turning one's life into an oeuvre, the choice of how to construct one's life is one which is fundamentally meaningless. Our theory of authenticity, on the other hand, offers unity through the Nietzschean ideal of 'becoming what one is' and narrative. That is, because choice is something which arises unconsciously and which we ourselves give shape to through interpretation, it is not an arbitrary action. The dimension of intersubjective consciousness ensures one's choice does not negatively impinge upon other's attempts to attain authenticity, which Foucault's aesthetic approach is unable to prevent.

MacIntyre provides the most formidable challenge to authenticity in that his account adequately addresses the problems of freedom and meaning. Recognizing that the Enlightenment led to a loss of natural teleology, MacIntyre attempts to construct a new *telos* to remedy the negative implications caused by the pursuit of autonomy. In order to develop his social teleology, he relies upon a tripartite concept of virtue (practices, narrative and tradition). However, it was demonstrated that his concept of tradition is ultimately informed by nostalgia. Rather, than attempting to restore teleology, our approach was instead to accept our socio-existential condition and to face the consequences. That is, the authentic approach was to recognize that a single, objective conception of the good cannot be restored, and to do so would impinge upon the democratic right to equality, and the subsequent ability to freely choose one's mode of existence. Although the most ideal resolution may be to reinstate an objective goal, this is simply something which cannot be achieved within our current cultural climate. Thus, what we can conclude is that our concept of authenticity provides the best response to the problem of freedom and meaning out of those considered.

7.3 Can one be authentic within contemporary society?

Although we have defended our theory, and demonstrated the manner in which our concept of authenticity is capable of addressing the problems of freedom and meaning, we will now turn to address some practical problems which do not need to be solved, but do pose problems. That is, we will consider concrete problems which are not necessary for the maintenance of our socio-existential approach, but which deserve attention. Two particular problems will be raised: (i) whether authenticity has been commodified and (ii) whether the internet provides us with an alternative domain to realize our authentic selves. We will begin this section by readdressing a concern first raised in Chapter 3, that authenticity, which was initially a reaction against the commodification of society, has itself been subjected to this very form of commodification.

In the previous section, we stated that a potential problem of the colonization of the lifeworld was that authenticity itself had become commodified. The argument that authenticity has been assimilated into capitalism has also been made by Luc Boltanski and Eve Chiapello.[2] In *The New Spirit of Capitalism*, Boltanski and Chiapello argue that the reciprocal shaping of authenticity and capitalism is evident within managerial literature. More generally, they analyse the dynamic relation between capitalism and critique and determine that recent transformations in capitalism have been accompanied by ideological changes. These changes led to the emergence of new 'spirits' which are comprised of alternative configurations of autonomy, authenticity, security and the common good.[3] Through their analysis of managerial texts, they determine that capitalism has to date taken three particular forms.

---

[2] Boltanski and Chiapello employ the concept of authenticity in a very general sense, incorporating both the subjective self-realization and the genuineness of material objects, as opposed to any specific concept.

[3] Hugh Willmott notes that despite developing Weber's concept of capitalism, as is evident in the title of their text, Boltanski and Chiapello's concept of 'spirit' offers a very different formulation of the same term. See 'Spirited Away: When Political Economy Becomes Culturalized', in *New Spirits*

The first spirit of capitalism that Boltanski and Chiapello present was prevalent in the late nineteenth century and was epitomized by the bourgeois entrepreneur and the family business. The form of the common good and sense of security which were espoused centred on economic propensities, including avarice, saving and the tendency to rationalize daily life, and traditional domestic predispositions, such as lineage, and patriarchal relations with employees to ensure subordination (2005: 17). However, the critique of bourgeois morality – good manners and doing what was done – and the domination of cultural institutions led to the development of the second spirit of capitalism. In the 1930s the family business and entrepreneur came to be replaced by the bureaucratized industrial firm and the character of the manager. The common good of the industrial firm was achieved through the solidarity of the institution and pursuit of social justice through collaboration between large firms and the state. Workers were afforded security in the second spirit through the emphasis on long-term planning and the very size of the organization, which offered job security and career prospects (2005: 18).

The third spirit which emerged was that of 'network capitalism', and which was fuelled by a 'connexionist' logic: that professional development is to be achieved through connections. In reaction to authoritarian, unadaptable and attached employees who prefer security, network capitalism instead favours enthusiastic, flexible, autonomous workers who can lead authentic lives by engaging in projects and maintaining networks (2005: 112–19). The ideal which modern individuals are expected to cultivate is accurately encapsulated by Hans J. Pongratz and G. Günter Voß's concept of the 'entreployee' (*Arbeitskraftunternehmer*) (2003: 239–54). What the concept of entreployee entails is an employee who is required to understand their abilities as commodities which require entrepreneurial development. Whilst the previous two spirits offered security, the third instead offers freedom to pursue one's own end. Instead of a hierarchy there is an emphasis on working with others in projects, making connections and acquiring abilities to improve one's employability as a form of personal capital.

The emergence of this 'new spirit of capitalism', we are told, was a consequence of the aesthetic critiques of capitalism's massification of the subject.[4] This criticism

---

of Capitalism?: Crises, Justifications, and Dynamics, ed. Paul du Gay and Glenn Morgan (Oxford: Oxford University Press, 2013).

[4] This demand for liberation and individuality was manifested in the visual criticisms of bohemian and avant-garde artists, who reacted against the loss of difference by turning their lives into artwork. The Bloomsbury Group, for example, opposed convention and offended Victorian sensibilities through their rejection of sexual taboos. Rather than simply painting or writing about that which was prohibited they instead lived in commune with multiple lovers. Their 'transgressive' lifestyle, or

entails that material reproduction led to a mass society bereft of difference. The consequence is that 'human beings are standardized and lose all particularity, all difference, when they are assembled in a crowd' (2005: 439). Thus, it is not only products which have become mass-produced but human beings have also been subjected to these same conditions through the externally cultivated desire for consumption. As Boltanski and Chiapello explain, there is no longer any relevant distance between my desire for some particular object and someone else's desire for an identical object' (2005: 439). This concern of massification can also be illustrated through the examples of workers on a production line, or infantry soldiers on the front line, each of whom fulfils the same role as their colleagues and can be easily replaced.

The new spirit of capitalism, however, responded to this demand for differentiation and demassification by internalizing this critique. Capitalism achieved this by incorporating the demand for authenticity into its own specific mechanisms through commodification. As Boltanski and Chiapello explain, 'hearing the demand expressed by the critique, entrepreneurs seek to create products and services which will satisfy it, and which they will be able to sell' (2005: 441–2). The intended outcome, then, was to dispel massification by producing and providing products and services which are not mass-produced, but possess difference and are deemed 'authentic'. In order to achieve this aim, entrepreneurs turned their attention to certain qualities of human beings and goods that had hitherto remained outside of the commodity sphere. Furthermore, they employed a method of codification which involves discovering and reproducing the distinctive features which make a product authentic. The consequence of this search for authentic products then led to the commodification of tourism, cultural activities, personal services and leisure, as can be seen through the anti-tourism movement.[5]

---

unifying every aspect of their life into one whole, became the ideal, and was incorporated as a cog into the capitalist machine.

[5] Citizens in Venice have objected on the grounds that tourism is eroding the quality of their life. The main complaint is that the surge in B&B's, to accommodate tourists, has made it difficult for residents to find homes to rent on a long-term contract. Angela Giuffrida. '"Imagine Living with This Crap": Tempers in Venice Boil over in Tourist High Season', *The Guardian*. https://www.theguardian.com/world/2017/jul/23/venice-tempers-boil-over-tourist-high-season (accessed 30 January 2018).

Opposition to tourism is also premised on the basis that it leads to the impoverishment of the local working class. Although one may conjecture that tourism boosts the local economy, 'tourist-prices' in Catalonia and Barcelona have not only increased the cost of living but also led to increased rent which many blue-collar workers are unable to afford. Laurence Peter. '"Tourists Go Home": Leftists Resist Spain's Influx', BBC News. http://www.bbc.co.uk/news/world-europe-40826257 (accessed 30 January 2018).

Thus far, Boltanski and Chiapello's diagnosis seems to correlate with Habermas's colonization thesis, that certain relationships with others and other's very mode of being has been assimilated into capitalism. However, Boltanski and Chiapello argue that the commodification of authenticity possesses a paradoxical character. Namely, in order to profit from human qualities, products have to be manufactured in a way which removes them from the context which made them authentic in the first place. As they explain, 'on the one hand, to earn the label "authentic" these goods must be drawn from outside the commodity sphere, from what might be called "sources of authenticity"' (2005: 443). This, however, is problematic because once an instrumental end is introduced, such as profit, then the phenomenon no longer continues to be authentic.

Furthermore, since consumers demand authentic products, and commodities which are offered fail to be authentic as soon as they are introduced into the commodity sphere, any such attempt can only result in failure for the producer and discontent for the consumer. As Boltanski and Chiapello elucidate, 'simply by virtue of the fact that to ensure their commodification these goods must be reproduced and copied, while undergoing a process of coding and calculation of profitability, they are bound to disappoint' (2005: 445). The failure of this attempted assimilation then casts a shadow of suspicion over authenticity. Namely, 'how can we know if some particular thing, event or feeling is the expression of the spontaneity of existence, or the result of a premeditated process aimed at transforming an "authentic" good into a commodity? Similarly, how can we tell if a particular author is an "authentic" rebel or an "editorial" product?' (2005: 446).

As a consequence of the failure of capitalism to fully incorporate authenticity, a deep seated distrust of authenticity has ensued. One can no longer tell if public figures are truly how they present themselves, or whether their marketing team has determined that the persona they portray is one which resonates with the youth, and as such, is capable of acquiring a greater fan base and thus profit. Furthermore, due to the emphasis on making connections and networking, one is unable to decidedly determine whether a colleague or client is a true friend or simply seeking to increase their contacts. The consequence, in Boltanski and Chiapello's account, is that the attempt to assimilate these criticisms has led to high levels of anxiety and frequent cycles of enchantment and disenchantment regarding the authenticity of individuals and products.

Susanne Ekman takes Boltanski and Chiapello's argument one step further by arguing that authenticity is exploited not only by management and organizations but also by the employees. Agreeing that the demand for authenticity heightens anxiety and worker vulnerability, Ekman claims employees also exploit the connexionist logic as a means of pursing authenticity. In her own words, 'while managers emphasized that employees should provide personal authenticity to serve commercial concerns, the employees emphasized, in turn, that they would only pursue commercial concerns in a context of authenticity' (2013: 307). This leaves mangers and organizations vulnerable because they are required to accommodate workers whom they depend upon for their competitive advantage.

Although authenticity has been assimilated into the capitalist engine, even if it has not been fully incorporated, it nevertheless raises concerns whether individuals are indeed authentic. However, Ekman's extension of this enquiry could be seen to provide a counter-argument to the claim that authenticity has been commodified. By illustrating that employees put self-development before commercial concerns, Ekman's analysis suggests a resistance to commodification. That is, the refusal of employees to relegate their pursuit of authenticity to commercial ends demonstrates the importance of authenticity in their lives. Thus, although Boltanski and Chiapello's position stresses that authenticity has been hollowed out, Ekman illustrates that people nevertheless pursue it. A further criticism of Boltanski and Chiapello's analysis, made by Armand Hatchuel, is that its focus on managerial literature is too narrow. Hatchuel's criticism is that it does not tell us anything about capitalism itself, but simply demonstrates what people who write about management literature think about management (Leca and Naccche 2008: 616).

This second argument could be challenged by Somogy Varga's extension of Boltanski and Chiapello's argument, that capitalism has appropriated authenticity, and which he develops in line with Charles Guignon's focus on self-help literature. Varga agrees with Boltanski and Chiapello to the extent that authenticity, 'an idea once used to question the legitimacy of hierarchical institutions and to critique the power of capitalistic requirements, now seems to function as an institutionalized demand on subjects that matches the systematic demands of contemporary capitalism' (2012: 127–8). For Varga the relationship between authenticity and capitalism has become paradoxical because 'the same intentional process of institutional realisation that has led to normative progress now runs counter to its original aim' (2012: 147). Thus, although the concept of authenticity initially provided a critical response to hierarchical institutions and capitalist requirements, it no longer appears to fulfil this function.

The problem for Varga is that the reciprocal shaping of capitalism and authenticity has led to the development of a 'performative model' of authenticity, within which employability is a by-product of self-fashioning. As he explains, 'in the performative model of authenticity, difference is not the by-product of an autonomous life but the primary source of both authenticity and market value' (2012: 134). Focusing on self-help guides, Varga illustrates how these motivational manuals combined the quest for authenticity with management strategies.[6] Namely, we are urged to 'take stock of our assets' and taught to employ techniques of self-marketing and personal branding to achieve authenticity. Here, however, the narrative is maintained that adherence to these ideals does not change our character but leads to a discovery of who we truly are. That is, 'creating an authentic "personal brand" is not considered an adjustment of one's personality to external market requirements but as a part of oneself' (2012: 134). Moreover, we are assured that distinction is the reason for success, since it makes us stand out from the competition. In this way, then, authenticity becomes bound to performance, since it is in performing the act of differentiation that our authentic self supposedly lies.

However, this 'performative model' of authenticity which emerged contains an inner tension because it was developed by combining two competing means of achieving authenticity. As Varga explains, 'both the idea of being true to something given – detected by introspection – and the productionist idea of choosing from different identities from a pool of possibilities have become moulded into the performative model of authenticity' (2012: 135). This tension between introspection and self-creation turns the performative model into something which is not only contradictory but also impossible to achieve, and which Varga claims leads to mental fatigue. As he exclaims, 'the attempt to fulfil the institutional demand for authenticity (to permanently perform and to put the self and emotions to work in order to secure employability) creates the social preconditions which lead to the exhaustion of the self' (2012: 149). One's authentic self only exists in the performance of difference, and as such, one's authentic self must be continuously created. 'If it is the performance of the uniqueness of my self that confers worth to my self, and if the significance of my uniqueness comes from being performed by me at my will, then my strategy of authenticity is self-defeating' (2012: 151). The reason why it is self-defeating is because the very attempt to perform by creating difference not only leads to exhaustion but also leads to depression, which Varga suggests has become the *other* of the contemporary demand for authenticity.

---

[6] The self-help guides which Varga appeals to include William Arruda's *An Introduction to Personal Branding: A Revolution in the Way We Manage Our Carriers* (2003); Peter Horn's *Personal Branding* (2004), Christiane Gierke"s *Persönlichkeitsmarketing* (2005); and Gitte Härter and Christiane Öttl"s *Selbstmarketing* (2005).

Varga's analysis could be challenged on the grounds that he focuses upon a popular concept of authenticity as developed within self-help books. This is problematic because, as argued in Section 3.2, the notion of 'authenticity' which these propose is a generic approach which is designed to appeal to a mass audience. Whilst adherence to this concept can account for rises in diagnosed cases of depression, the performative model goes against one of the defining features of authenticity, that it is an end in itself. Thus, although this concept may have been endogenized by capitalism, it seeks the end of employability through performance, as opposed to living an authentic existence. As with Boltanski and Chiapello's analysis, any attempt to commoditize authenticity ultimately ends in inauthenticity. As for the concern of exhaustion through performance, on our account, which is aligned with self-creation, one does not necessarily need to engage in constant recalibration of character to remain authentic. Rather, it is only necessary to engage in self-adjustment when social circumstances change and the conditions which permitted one to be authentic in the first place have been eroded.

A further response to Varga would be to suggest that his approach is overly critical. That is, the constant critique of commodification leads to a perspective of doom and gloom, that it is a problem which can never be resolved. In the analysis that commodification is constantly attempting to assimilate authenticity, one could simply respond that everything can be commodified, and that is just how commodification works. We must acknowledge that at this stage in history, commodification is a problem which modernity sensitizes us to. However, whilst commodification is a potent danger – we can claim, as Ekman has illustrated, that authenticity provides a counterweight. Thus, rather than remain constantly critical as Varga's position entails, we ought to remain eternally vigilant. That is, although commodification is not a fundamental problem, it still poses a persistent threat, and as such, we simply need to be aware of the dangers.

Although we cannot claim that authenticity has been successfully incorporated into capitalism, the problem of commodification nevertheless remains. The consequence of the role of authenticity within a connexionist world leads to anxiety and a general distrust of authenticity, and from an emphasis on the performance of difference the threat of exhaustion and depression emerges. Thus, through Boltanski and Chiapello, and Varga's analysis of attempts to assimilate authenticity into capitalism, as reflected within managerial literature and self-help guides, we have been led to the understanding of the dangers which authenticity is vulnerable to. In order for our socio-existential concept of authenticity to be successful, we must be able to avoid these concerns. However, since the emphasis on networking and performance is something which is beyond our control, the best we can do is to acknowledge these problems so that we ourselves do not fall prey to them.

If authenticity is subjected to systems imperatives and capitalism's demands, then perhaps we ought to seek out an alternative domain within which to live authentically? Within contemporary society, an increasing amount of communication and social interaction is conducted virtually. That is, relationship building and networking is established and developed outside of the classroom and the office, though not in physical locations, but online through social media.[7] And as technology develops, it could be speculated that a great deal more of our socializing will be relocated to virtual space. With this in mind, the internet, and in particular, social media could potentially provide us with a commodification-free space to live authentically. Thus, in order to determine whether this is the case, we will now turn our attention to discussing the possibilities of living authentically online through social media.

One interesting feature of social media is that it appears to provide the ideal platform for self-development. This is made explicit by psychologist, Sherry Turkle, in *Life on the Screen*, where she claims that 'the Internet has become a significant social laboratory for experimenting with the constructions and reconstructions of self that characterize postmodern life' (1995: 180). Turkle offers the case study of sixteen-year-old, American student, Audrey, who experiments with different aspects of her personality online. 'Audrey tries out a "flirty" style. She gets a good response from Facebook friends, and so she ramps up the flirtatious tone. She tries out an "ironic, witty" tone in her wall posts. The response is not so good, so she retreats' (1995: 192). In Turkle's account, the internet exemplifies the postmodern phenomenon of multiple identities. This, however, is problematic for our account, as discussed in Section 5.4, since postmodernism emphasizes fragmentation instead of unity. Furthermore, Rahel Jaeggi questions Turkle's claim regarding the creation of multiple identities and instead argues that the internet does not lead to new kinds of identity formation. Instead, Jaeggi claims that 'what takes place is not a multiplication of selves but playing with various aspects of an identity' (2014: 107).

---

[7] This is made evident by Shannon Vallor who notes, 'LinkedIn encourages social relations organized around our professional lives, Twitter is useful for creating lines of communication between ordinary individuals and figures of public interest, MySpace was for a time a popular way for musicians to promote themselves and communicate with their fans, and Facebook, which began as a way to link university cohorts and now connects people across the globe, has seen a surge in business profiles aimed at establishing links to existing and future customers'. See 'Social Networking and Ethics', in *The Stanford Encyclopaedia of Philosophy*. https://plato.stanford.edu/archives/win2016/entries/ethics-social-networking.' (accessed 14 January 2018)

Thus, the supposed reconstruction of life which Turkle associates with the internet, does not necessarily lead to a plurality of selves, but a multitude of possibilities to realize one's self. Given that this is the case, one ought to question whether it is possible to portray an authentic virtual self. One problem which may appear to hinder such self-projection is whether our online selves are shaped by others' demands of us, or by ourselves. To extend Foucault's conception of power to virtual communities, the internet has become a 'virtual panopticon' where individuals are constantly observed and regulate their online footprint to conform to popular consensus. As it has been argued that authenticity offers a way beyond the discourses of power which society produces, it seems reasonable to assume that one can also express one's authentic self on the internet. That is, as social media sites provide a vehicle for creative self-development, it should be possible to cultivate an authentic self online, irrespective of constant surveillance.

Discussion which relates to this question arises within Turkle's *Alone Together*, where it is argued that social media sites cause us to perform to an audience. Turkle's claim is that through social media the self is becoming increasingly externally manufactured, as opposed to internally developed. In Turkle's account, a consequence of creating something for other's consumption leads to us playing to an audience, and especially in ways which we imagine our audience to desire. Thus, rather than presenting our true selves, our online presence instead becomes a performance (2010). This, however, differs from Varga's claim regarding the performative model of authenticity. In Varga's account, the emphasis is upon performing difference, which emphasizes employability as a by-product of self-fashioning. For Turkle, on the other hand, the notion of performance instead suggests individuals do not portray who they truly are, but what others expect from them.

This issue of performance is not merely problematic in terms of achieving authenticity but, like the performative model in Varga's account, these attempts to realize one's true self also lead to psychological deprivation. The reason is because, like Weber's critique of science, there is no end to the internet, but instead, a perpetual present. The internet presents more possibilities and opportunities to promote ourselves and network with others, but we cannot utilize all of these possibilities. As Mark Dooley elucidates, 'it is a culture of immediacy in which only the present moment matters. There is no past or future in cyberspace, only a perpetual 'now' in which all desires must be instantaneously gratified. It is a no man's land devoid of the public-private distinction, a spectral sphere where no one can hide, a domain where no one ever sleeps' (2015: 2). Thus, whilst there are infinite opportunities to develop ourselves, the attempt to keep up with these can only end in fatigue. The internet never rests, but we must.

Our online interactions thus appear to be, for the most part, shaped and determined by others' expectations of us. By making such demands online, this influences how we conduct ourselves in reality. That is, we document our experiences and attempt to live lives which exceed standard expectations, so that we may convey them to others. In this way, social media produces a new dimension of social and physical reality. Although social media profiles appear to be externally constructed by other's criticisms and demands, on the socio-existential approach this does not inhibit one from developing an authentic self. The dimension of intersubjective consciousness recognizes that we do not develop in monologue, but that we are shaped by our interactions with others. Thus, the fact that we may develop our virtual selves in accordance with other's demands is not problematic. What is important is that one does not allow these demands to entirely consume and control one's virtual self, as with the example of Audrey downplaying her wit to conform to the one-dimensional image which others expect of her.

The primary benefit of the internet is that it allows us to experiment. As Hubert Dreyfus makes explicit, '[the internet presents] a new medium for exploring other ways of life, virtual worlds may enable people to learn through safe experimentation which sort of life works best for them' (2009: 98). Focusing on the virtual world *Second Life*, Dreyfus enquires into the possibilities of experimentation. Here he determines that there are less consequences to one's action, and as such, fewer risks. Dreyfus offers the example of virtual relationships, noting that if one breaks up, one does not have to face the person again: 'one doesn't have to clean up the mess one leaves. You can always just walk away' (2009: 100).[8] He compares *Second Life* to a masquerade to the extent that 'people are disguised and are allowed to do normally forbidden things without adverse consequences for their everyday lives' (2009: 100). However, Dreyfus determines that although risk-free experimentation may be more exciting, it does not provide serious satisfaction (2009: 101). The reason is precisely because in order to derive true satisfaction, risk must be involved. On the internet, however, where there is nothing ventured, there is nothing to be gained.

---

[8] Contrary to Dreyfus, Vallor argues that 'Facebook, LinkedIn and Google+ would shift away from the earlier online norms of anonymity and identity play, instead giving real-world identities an online presence'. However, Dreyfus's claim regarding experimentation remains pertinent. See 'Social Networking and Ethics', in *The Stanford Encyclopaedia of Philosophy*. https://plato.stanford.edu/arc hives/win2016/entries/ethics-social-networking (accessed 14 January 2018).

Moreover, it could be argued that the benefit of online experimentation is simultaneously its downfall. Namely, the internet encourages us to act without thinking of the consequences. Whilst this permits us to pursue any lifestyle we can conceive of, no matter how deviant, this is only possible because there are no moral boundaries online. As Dooley attests, 'it is, moreover, a pleasure paradise which facilitates any and all "experiments in living" irrespective of the moral repercussions for those still rooted to the real' (2015: 3). It is perhaps for this reason that people on social media behave in ways which they would not in real social interactions. We can see the dark side of online experimentation when we conceive of those who, like MacIntyre's rich aesthetes, manipulate others for their own entertainment, through trolling and cyber-bulling.

Such behaviour is exemplified in the case of Brenda Leyland who 'trolled' Madeleine McCann's family on Twitter. Leyland, a 63-year-old, university-educated mother of two, posted or reposted more than four hundred messages about the McCanns, referring to them as 'liars' and 'profiting from tragedy' (2018). However, after her information was anonymously passed to a Sky news reporter, who turned up on her doorstep and broadcast her image on television, Leyland took her own life, illustrating remorse regarding her behaviour. A further high-profile case is that of Peter Nunn, a 33-year-old, who aspired to study law at university and was jailed for threatening to rape Stella Creasy MP and Caroline Criado-Perez. Nunn targeted Creasy and Criado-Perez for the trivial reason that they campaigned to have Jane Austen's image on the Bank of England ten pound note. Nunn directly threatened Creasy: 'You better watch your back, I'm going to rape your arse at 8pm and put the video all over.' He also referred to Creasy and Criado-Perez as 'witches' and posted appalling tweets such as 'Best way to rape a witch, try and drown her first then just when she's gagging for air that's when you enter' (2018).

The sort of behaviour elicited within these two examples is certainly not something which could be considered acceptable in any social circumstance. Nevertheless, behind the protection of an anonymous username, people feel free to engage in ethically appalling behaviour, irrespective of the psychological effects which it may have upon others. As Andrew Potter makes explicit, 'in a sense, what we're seeing is a great sociological experiment in the slow but steadily corrosive effects of information technology on the private sphere. For all their benefits, digital communications technologies work as a sort of social acid, eating away at the boundaries between public and private and eliminating the established norms of discretion, courtesy, and common sense' (2010: 162). Thus, whilst social media may provide us with a platform for experimentation to discover our authentic selves, it is subject to the same criticism as we levelled against Foucault's ethic of care: it is morally bereft. Thus, whilst we can engage in aesthetic cultivation online through self-expression and experimentation, the internet cannot be held morally responsible.

Moral issues aside, it could also be claimed that the attempt to live authentically online is also not free from commodification. The economic impingement upon authenticity can be said to be continued through algorithms which depend upon us accurately portraying who we are online.[9] Amazon, for example, makes suggestions based on the products we view and purchase, to entice us into making further purchases. Search engines and social media websites are also connected: if we search for a product on Google, the item then appears advertised in our news feed on Facebook. In these ways, the information which we input enables companies to access their target audience directly. The act of expressing our authentic selves on the internet thus not only leads to increased sales but also provides extremely efficient market research. Here we can see further evidence of Boltanski and Chiapello's claim that capitalism is adapting the ideal of authenticity. Thus, whilst we may feel motivated to live authentically on the internet, the more we reveal about our true selves, the greater the opportunity for companies to generate profit.

We initially turned to the internet as a domain in which to pursue authenticity and evade commodification. However, it has been determined that the commodification of authenticity is continued through internet-based algorithms. Moreover, not only was it suggested that commodification cannot be evaded online but the conditions for living authentically are actually worse as well. The internet thus seems to pose the same problems of performance of difference, and commodification, but without the reward of risk, and the issue that online behaviour is often morally devoid. Thus, whilst the internet may provide us with a platform for self-discovery and to experiment, it does not appear to be a domain through which to attain authenticity.

In this section, we raised some practical problems which theories of authenticity must contend. Specifically, we considered the problems induced by commodification and the increasing dependence upon social media. However, we have only hinted towards the extent of these issues, and in order to offer a conclusive account, a much more sustained analysis is required. From what

---

[9] The extent to which algorithms affect authenticity has been explored by Wendy Hui Kyong Chun who argues that 'the imperative "be true to yourself", or more simply "be true", makes our data valuable – that is, recognizable – across the many media platforms we use', *Twitter.com* https://twitter.com/joannekcheung/status/932041231160561665 (accessed 22 November 2017).

our brief survey has suggested, Boltanski and Chiapello, and Varga point out real dangers which all concepts of authenticity are vulnerable to, that commodification does pose a genuine threat to authenticity. However, the realization that any attempt to live a meaningful existence may be impinged upon by capitalism should not be interpreted as a passive response. On the contrary, to confront reality is to cultivate a state of preparedness and a willingness to accept the inevitable. The benefit of heeding these concerns then enables us to live an authentic existence within contemporary modern society, by being aware of the dangers and actively resisting the subordination of authenticity to commercial ends. Thus, whilst we do recognize dangers, which require further engagement, our initial reaction is to remain eternally vigilant.

7.4 Concluding remarks

This investigation began with the aim of addressing two specific research questions. First, we set out to determine the manner in which modernity has come to problematize freedom and meaning. Here it was discovered that the unforeseen consequences of the Enlightenment's pursuit of progress was the loss of objective meaning. Furthermore, that the rational foundations which many modern institutions were built upon have ironically led to decreased freedom. The second research question which we aimed to address was to determine whether the phenomenon of authenticity can provide a satisfactory response to the problems of freedom and meaning. Noting the competing accounts of authenticity, we reviewed contemporary approaches, their contributions and defects, and constructed a socio-existential approach which incorporated aspects from the two major approaches. Having provided a full account of authenticity, we then offered a provisional explanation as to how our concept of authenticity could address the problems of freedom and meaning. This account suggested that one could operate within restricted freedom and acquire intersubjective meaning through pursuit of a maturely conceived project. Although we demonstrated that our concept of authenticity can respond to the problems of freedom and meaning, we then considered three alternative approaches which could be said to address the same concern.

The three approaches we analysed were Habermas's modernist approach, Foucault's postmodern perspective and MacIntyre's pre-modern response to the problems of freedom and meaning. Habermas attempted to resolve these issues by completing the Enlightenment project, Foucault saw rationality as problematic and suggested turning inwards to avoid subjection caused by discourse, and MacIntyre understood modernity as ethically impoverished and attempted to revive the virtue ethics tradition. Each of these accounts, however, was shown to provide insufficient resolutions to the problems of freedom and meaning induced by the Enlightenment. Habermas's account was shown to be dependent on a preconceived conception of the good, Foucault's ethic of care lacked a moral filter and MacIntyre's nostalgia led to an obscured view of modernity and an overly pessimistic position. And although these were deemed to be deficient in terms of meaning, we nevertheless learnt from our engagement. We adopted MacIntyre's notion of narrative quest and used it to supplement our account; influenced by Habermas, we drew out the implications of the colonization thesis for authenticity, and demonstrated that commodification does appear to pose a threat; and from Foucault, we considered authenticity in terms of power relations, which led us to the realization that the question of identity within a digital age is one which will eventually require further engagement.

What we have determined from our enquiry is that the concept of authenticity is tremendously important to modern individuals, insofar as it provides an ethical ideal by which to orientate our actions and derive a sense of purpose. And although the problems of freedom and meaning could be relinquished by imposing a unified conception of the good, this is simply an unrealistic and unachievable aim, as illustrated by our discussion of MacIntyre's nostalgic-pessimistic approach. Furthermore, the attempt to continue down the path paved by the Enlightenment, as demonstrated by Habermas's focus on autonomy and his relegation of ethics, is likewise impeded because it is necessary to possess a prior conception of the good, which this approach is unable to provide us with. We must also attempt to offer an intersubjective account of ethics in order to avoid descending into aestheticism and subjectivism. We do need a conception of the good, though this conception cannot be coercively imposed, but can only be realized by people in plural and individual ways. Insofar as our approach does not deceive itself into engaging in the impossible task of presenting a singular substantive vision of the good, or continuing the failed project of modernity, our socio-existential approach, therefore, provides the most comprehensive account out of those considered.

We have therefore achieved our aim, insofar as we defended our theory, and illustrated how it can respond to the problems of freedom and meaning. However, it was also demonstrated that capitalism and the internet provide practical and social challenges to living authentically. And whilst it is not necessary to resolve these problems to support our theory, these are important issues which require further consideration. With regard to capitalism, the extent to which commodification impedes our ability to live an authentic existence remains to be seen. As for the internet, we merely scratched the surface with regard to whether it makes it easier to be ourselves, and whether we ought to understand it in more positive terms. Both of these issues are wide avenues of enquiry, which deserve further investigation, and whilst we do not have the space or necessity to fully address them here, we have provided a good foundation for future research.

Bibliography

Abbey, Ruth. (2000). *Charles Taylor*. Teddington: Acumen.

Allen, Amy. (2013). 'Power and the Subject', in *A Companion to Foucault*, edited by Christoper Falzon, Timothy O'Leary and Jana Sawicki. Chichester: Blackwell.

Anderson, Thomas. (1993). *Sartre's Two Ethics: From Authenticity to Integral Humanity*. Chicago: Open Court.

Anscombe, G. E. M. (1958). 'Modern Moral Philosophy', *Philosophy* 33: 1–19.

Arendt, Hannah. (1989). *Lectures on Kant's Political Philosophy*. Chicago: University of Chicago Press.

Bacon, Francis. (2009). *The New Organon*, edited by Lisa Jardine and Michael Silverthorne. Cambridge: Cambridge University Press.

Baehr, Peter. (2001). 'The "Iron Cage" and the "Shell as Hard as Steel": Parsons, Weber, and the *Stahlhartes Gehäuse* Metaphor in the Protestant Ethic and the Spirit of Capitalism', *History and Theory* 40 (2): 153–69.

Barber, Benjamin. (1988). *The Conquest of Politics: Liberal Philosophy in Democratic Times*. Princeton: Princeton University Press.

Beauvoir, Simone. (1962). *The Ethics of Ambiguity*, translated by Bernard Frechtman New York: Citadel Press.

Beauvoir, Simone. (1965). *Force of Circumstance*, translated by Richard Howard. New York: Penguin.

Beauvoir, Simone. (2004a). *A Review of The Phenomenology of Perception*, by Maurice Merleau-Ponty, in *Simone de Beauvoir: Philosophical Writings*, edited by Margaret A. Simons. Urbana: University of Illinois Press.

Beauvoir, Simone. (2004b). *Existentialism and Popular Wisdom* in *Simone de Beauvoir: Philosophical Writings*, edited by Margaret A. Simmons. Urbana and Chicago: University of Illinois Press.

Beauvoir, Simone. (2006). *She Came to Stay*, translated by Yvonne Moyse and Roger Senhouse. New York: Harper Perennial.

Beauvoir, Simone. (2010). *The Second Sex*, translated by Constance Borde and Sheila Malovany-Chevallier. London: Vintage.

Bell, Michael. (1992). 'How Primordial Is Narrative?', in *Narrative in Culture*, edited by Cris Nash. London and New York: Routledge.

Benjamin, Walter. (1999). 'The Work of Art in the Age of Mechanical Reproduction', in *Illuminations*, translated by Harry Zohn. New York: Schocken.

Benjamin, Walter. (2002). *The Arcades Project*, translated by Howard Eiland and Kevin McLaughlin. Harvard: Harvard University Press.

Benhabib, Seyla and Passerin d'Entrèves, Maurizio. (1996). *Habermas and the Unfinished Project of Modernity: Critical Essays on The Philosophical Discourse of Modernity*. Cambridge: Polity.

Berlin, Isaiah. (1976). *Vico and Herder: Two Studies in the History of Ideas*. London: Hogarth Press.

Bernstein, J. M. (1995). *Recovering Ethical Life: Jürgen Habermas and the Future of Critical Theory*. London: Routledge.

Blair, Dierdre. (1990). *Simone de Beauvoir: A Biography*. London: Cape.

Boltanski, Luc and Chiapello, Ève. (2005). *The New Spirit of Capitalism*, translated by Gregory Elliott. London: Verso.

Bowler, Peter J. and Morris, Rhys. (2005). *Making Modern Science: A Historical Survey*. Chicago: University of Chicago Press.

Boyle, David. (2004). *Authenticity: Brands, Fakes, Spin and the Lust for Real Life*. London: Harper Perennial.

Bronner, Stephen Eric. (2004). *Reclaiming the Enlightenment: Toward a Politics of Radical Engagement*. Columbia: Columbia University Press.

Breen, Keith Gerard. (2012). *Under Weber's Shadow: Modernity, Subjectivity and Politics in the Work of Habermas, Arendt and MacIntyre*. Farnham: Ashgate.

Breen, Keith Gerard. (2016). 'In Defence of Meaningful Work as a Public Policy Concern', in *Philosophy and Political Engagement: Reflection in the Public Sphere*, edited by Keith Breen and Allyn Fives. London: Palgrave Macmillan.

Buber, Martin. (1937). *I and Thou*, translated by Ronald Gregor Smith. Edinburgh: T.&T. Smith.

Camus, Albert. (2004). 'The Rebel: An Essay on Man in Revolt', in *Plague, Fall, Exile and the Kingdom and Selected Essays*, translated by Stuart Gilbert and Justin O'Brien. New York: Random House.

Chidester, David. (2005). *Authentic Fakes: Religion and American Popular Culture*. Berkeley: University of California Press.

Chomsky, Noam. (2011). 'Academic Freedom and the Corporatization of Universities', Presented at University of Toronto, Scarborough. Transcript accessed at https://chomsky.info/20110406/

Chomsky, Noam. (2014). 'On Academic Labor', Presented Adjunct Faculty Association of the United Steelworkers in Pittsburgh, Pennsylvania. Transcript accessed at https://www.counterpunch.org/2014/02/28/on-academic-labor/

Cooke, Maeve. (1992). 'Habermas, Autonomy and the Identity of the Self', *Philosophy and Social Criticism* 18 (3): 269–91.

Cooke, Maeve. (1997). *Language and Pragmatics: Study of Habermas' Pragmatics*. Cambridge, MA: MIT Press.

Cooke, Maeve. (1999). 'Habermas, Feminism and the Question of Autonomy', in *Habermas: A Critical Reader*, edited by Peter Dews. Oxford: Blackwell.

Crawford, Michael H. and Whitehead, David. (2010). *Archaic and Classical Greece: A Selection of Ancient Sources in Translation*. Cambridge: Cambridge University Press.

Crisp, Roger and Slone, Michael. (2001). *Virtue Ethics*. Oxford: Oxford University Press.
Davenport, John J. and Rudd, Anthony. (2001). *Kierkegaard After MacIntyre: Freedom, Narrative, and Virtue*. Chicago: Open Court.
Dawson, Christopher. (2001). *Religion and the Rise of Western Culture*. New York: Image Books.
Dooley, Mark. (2015). *Moral Matters: Philosophy of Homecoming*. London: Bloomsbury.
Dreyfus, Hubert. (2009). *On the Internet*. New York: Routledge.
Ekman, Susanne. (2013). 'Authenticity at Work: Questioning the New Spirit of Capitalism from a Micro-sociological Perspective', in *New Spirits of Capitalism?: Crises, Justifications, and Dynamics*, edited by Paul du Gay and Glenn Morgan. Oxford: Oxford University Press.
Finlayson, Gordon. (2005). *Habermas: A Short Introduction*. Oxford: Oxford University Press.
Ferrara, Alesandro. (1993). *Modernity and Authenticity: A Study of the Social and Ethical Thought of Rousseau*. Albany: State University of New York.
Ferrara, Alesandro. (1998). *Reflective Authenticity: Rethinking the Project of Modernity*. London: Routledge.
Ferrara, Alesandro. (2012). *The Force of the Example: Explorations in the Paradigm of Judgement*. Columbia: Columbia University Press.
Ferber, Michael. (2005). *A Companion to European Romanticism*, edited by Michael Ferber. Oxford: Blackwell.
Foucault, Michel. (1977). *Power/Knowledge: Selected Interviews and Other Writings from Trillin -1977*, translated by Colin Gordon. New York: Pantheon Books.
Foucault, Michel. (1980). *The History of Sexuality: Volume One*, translated by Robert Hurley. New York: Random House.
Foucault, Michel. (1988). *An Aesthetics of Existence* in *Michel Foucault: Politics, Philosophy, Culture. Interviews and Other Writings 1977–1984*, edited by Lawrence D. Kritzman. New York: Routledge.
Foucault, Michel. (1990). *Care of the Self: The History of Sexuality: Volume Three*, translated by Robert Hurley. London: Penguin.
Foucault, Michel. (1991a). *Discipline and Punish: The Birth of the Prison*, translated by Alan Sheridan. New York: Vintage Books.
Foucault, Michel. (1991b). *What Is Enlightenment* in *the Foucault Reader*, edited by Paul Rabinow. London: Penguin.
Foucault, Michel. (1991c). 'Nietzsche, Genealogy, History', in *The Foucault Reader*, edited by Paul Rabinow. London: Penguin.
Foucault, Michel. (1992). *The Use of Pleasure: The History of Sexuality: Volume Two*, translated by Robert Hurley. London: Penguin.
Foucault, Michel. (2000a). 'The Ethic of Care for the Self as a Practice of Freedom: An Interview with Michael Foucault on January 1984', in *Ethics: Subjectivity and Truth; Essential Works of Michel Foucault 1954–1984*, edited by Paul Rabinow. London: Penguin.

Foucault, Michel. (2000b). 'The Hermeneutic of the Subject', in *Ethics: Subjectivity and Truth; Essential Works of Michel Foucault 1954–1984*, edited by Paul Rabinow. London: Penguin.

Foucault, Michel. (2000c). *On the Genealogy of Ethics: An Overview of Work in Progress* in *Ethics: Subjectivity and Truth; Essential Works of Michel Foucault 1954–1984*, edited by Paul Rabinow. London: Penguin.

Foucault, Michel. (2000d). 'Technologies of the Self', in *Ethics: Subjectivity and Truth; Essential Works of Michel Foucault 1954–1984*, edited by Paul Rabinow. London: Penguin.

Foucault, Michel. (2001a). 'Subject and Power', in *Power: Essential Works of Foucault* Vol.3, edited by James D. Faubion. London: The New Press.

Foucault, Michel. (2001b). 'Truth and Power', in *Power: Essential Works of Foucault*, Vol. 3, edited by James D. Faubion. London: The New Press.

Foucault, Michel. (2011). *The Order of Things: An Archaeology of the Human Sciences*, translated by Don Idhe. New York: Routledge.

Frankfurt, Harry. (1971). 'Freedom of the Will and the Concept of Person', *Journal of Philosophy* 68 (1): 5–20.

Fraser, Elisabeth. (1996). 'MacIntyre, Feminism and the Concept of Practice', *After MacIntyre: Critical Perspectives on the Work of Alasdair MacIntyre*, edited by John Horton and Susan Mendus. Cambridge: Polity Press.

Fraser, Nancy. (1989). *Unruly Practices: Power, Discourse and Gender in Contemporary Social Theory*. Cambridge: Polity Press.

Gadamer, Hans Georg. (2004). *Truth and Method*, translated by Joel Weinsheimer and Donald G. Marshall. New York: Continuum.

Garrard, Graeme. (2008). 'Nietzsche For and Against the Enlightenment', *The Review of Politics* 70 (4): 595–608.

Gemes, Ken. (2001). 'Postmodernism's Use and Abuse of Nietzsche', *Philosophy and Phenomenological Research* 62 (2): 337–60.

Gibson, Catrin. 2017. 'Authentic Love', *Sartre Studies International* 23 (1): 60–79.

Giuffrida, Angela. (2018). '"Imagine Living with This Crap": Tempers in Venice Boil over in Tourist High Season'. *The Guardian*. https://www.theguardian.com/world/2017/jul/23/venice-tempers-boil-over-tourist-high-season, accessed 30 January 2018.

Golomb, Jacob. (1995). *Authenticity: From Kierkegaard to Camus*. New York: Routledge.

Grene, Marjorie. (1948). *Dreadful Freedom: A Critique of Existentialism*. Chicago: Chicago University Press.

Grene, Marjorie. (1952). 'Authenticity: An Existential Virtue', *Ethics* 62 (4): 266–73.

The Guardian. (2018). '"Twitter Troll" Bombarded Labour MP Stella Creasy with Abuse, Court Hears'. *The Guardian*. https://www.theguardian.com/uk-news/2014/may/19/twitter-labour-mp-stella-creasy-court, accessed 06 January 2018.

Guignon, Charles. (2004). *On Being Authentic*. London and New York: Routledge.

Guignon, Charles. (2008). 'Authenticity', *Philosophy Compass* 3 (2): 277–90.

Habermas, Jürgen. (1984). *The Theory of Communicative Action Vol.1 Reason and the Rationalisation of Society*, translated by Thomas McCarthy. Boston: Beacon Press.
Habermas, Jürgen. (1987a). *The Theory of Communicative Action Vol.2 Lifeworld and System: A Critique of Functionalist Reason*, translated by Thomas McCarthy. Boston: Beacon Press.
Habermas, Jürgen. (1987b). *Philosophical Discourse of Modernity: Twelve Lectures*, translated by Frederick Lawrence. Cambridge: Polity.
Habermas, Jürgen. (1989). *The Structural Transformation of the Public Sphere*, translated by Thomas Burger. Cambridge: Polity Press.
Habermas, Jürgen. (1990). *Moral Consciousness and Communicative Action*, translated by Christian Lenhardt and Shierry Weber Nicholsen. Cambridge, MA: MIT Press.
Habermas, Jürgen. (1992a). *Justification and Application: Remarks on Discourse Ethics*, translated by Ciaran P. Cronin. Cambridge, MA: MIT Press.
Habermas, Jürgen. (1992b). *Postmetaphysical Thinking: Philosophical Essays*, translated by William Mark Hohengarten. Cambridge, MA: MIT Press.
Habermas, Jürgen. (1996). *Between Facts and Norms: Contributions to a Discourse Theory of Law and Democracy*, translated by William Rehg. Cambridge, Massachusetts: MIT Press.
Hall, Eric. (2015). *The Paradox of Authenticity*. Tübingen: Mohr Siebeck.
Hampson, Norman. (1990). *The Enlightenment: An Evaluation of Its Assumptions, Attitudes and Values*. London: Penguin Books.
Heidegger, Martin. (1993). *Letter on Humanism in Basic Writings*, translated by David Farrell Krell. New York: Harper Collins.
Heidegger, Martin. (2010). *Being and Time*, translated by John Macquairie and Edward Robinson. London: Blackwell.
Hegel, Georg Friedrich. (2001). *Philosophy of History*, translated by J. Sibree. Kitchener, ON: Batoche Books.
Hegel, Georg Friedrich. (2008a). *Outlines of the Philosophy of Right*, translated by T. M. Knok. Oxford: Oxford University Press.
Hegel, Georg Friedrich. (2008b). *Phenomenology of Spirit* in *The Hegel Reader*, edited by Stephen Houlgate. Oxford: Blackwell.
Heller, Agnes. (1982). 'Habermas and Marxism', in *Habermas: Critical Debates*, edited by Thomas B. Thomas and David Held. London: Macmillan.
Heter, T. Storm. (2006). *Jean-Paul Sartre's Ethic of Engagement*. New York: Continuum.
Hill, Kevin. (1992). 'MacIntyre's Nietzsche: A Critique', *International Studies in Philosophy* 24 (2): 3–12.
Hölderlin, Friedrich. (2010). *Hyperion*, translated by Ross Benjamin. New York: Archipelago Books.
Honneth, Axel. (1991). *The Critique of Power: Reflective Stages in a Critical Social Theory*, translated by Kenneth Baynes. Cambridge MA: MIT Press.
Hook, Derek and Rienstra, Byron. (2006). 'Weakening Habermas: The Undoing of Communicative Rationality', *Politikon* 33 (3): 313–39.

Horton, John. (1996). 'Alasdair MacIntyre: *After Virtue* and After', in *After MacIntyre: Critical Perspectives on the Work of Alasdair MacIntyre*, edited by John Horton and Susan Mendus. Cambridge: Polity Press.
Horton, John. (2005). *Political Obligation*, Basingstoke: Palgrave Macmillan.
Houlgate, Stephen. (2005). *Opening Hegel's Logic: From Being to Infinity*. West Lafayette: Purdue University Press.
Houlgate, Stephen (ed.). (2008). *The Hegel Reader*. Oxford: Blackwell.
Ice Cube (1991). 'No Vaseline'. In *Death Certificate*. Priority Records.
Israel, Jonathan. (2009). *A Revolution of the Mind: Radical Enlightenment and the Intellectual Origins of Modern Democracy*. Princeton: Princeton University Press.
Israel, Jonathan. (2013). *Democratic Enlightenment: Philosophy, Revolution, and Human Rights 1750-1790*. Oxford: Oxford University Press.
Jaeggi, Rahel. (2014). *Alienation*, translated by Frederick Neuhouser and Alan E. Smith. New York: Columbia University Press.
Jaspers, Karl. (1956). *Reason and Existenz*, translated by William Earle. London: Anchor.
Johnson, James. 'Arguing for Deliberation: Some Skeptical Considerations', *Deliberative Democracy*, edited by Jon Elster. Cambridge: Cambridge University Press, 1998.
Jütten, Timo. (2013). 'Habermas and Markets', *Constellations* 20 (4): 587-603.
Kalberg, Stephen. (1980). 'Max Weber's Types of Rationality: Cornerstones for the Analysis of Rationalisation Processes in History', *American Journal of Sociology* 85 (5): 1145-79.
Kant, Immanuel. (1993). *The Grounding for the Metaphysics of Morals*, translated by James Ellington. London: Hackett.
Kant, Immanuel. (2009). *An Answer to the Question: What Is Enlightenment?* translated by H. B. Nisbit. London: Penguin.
Kaufmann, Walter. (1989). *Existentialism: From Dostoyevsky to Sartre*. New York: Plume.
Kaufmann, Walter. (2017). *Nietzsche: Philosopher, Psychologist, Antichrist*. Princeton: Princeton University Press.
Kasulis, Thomas. (2002). *Integrity and Intimacy: Philosophy and Cultural Difference*. Honolulu: University of Hawaii Press.
Keats, Jonathan. (2013). *Forged: Why Fakes Are the Great Art of Our Age*. Oxford: Oxford University Press.
Kierkegaard, Soren. (1968). *The Concept of Dread*, translated by Walter Lowie. Princeton: Princeton University Press.
Kierkegaard, Soren. (1987). *Either/Or Part II*, translated by Howard V. Hong and Edna H. Hong. Princeton: Princeton University Press.
Kierkegaard, Soren. (2009). *Concluding Unscientific Postscript*, translated by Alastair Hannay. Cambridge, Cambridge University Press.
Kierkegaard, Soren. (2015). *Kierkegaard's Journals and Notebooks: Volume I Journals AA-DD*, edited by Bruce H. Kirmmse. Princeton: Princeton University Press.

Kitchen, Ruth. (2013). 'From Shame Towards an Ethics of Ambiguity', *Sartre Studies International* 19 (1): 55–70.

Koopman, Colin. (2013). 'The Formation and Self-Transformation of the Subject in Foucault's Ethics', in *A Companion to Foucault*, edited by Christoper Falzon, Timothy O'Leary and Jana Sawicki. Chichester: Blackwell.

Laterius, Diogenes. (1948). *Lives of Eminent Philosophers*, translated by R. D. Hicks. London: W. Heinemann.

Leca, B. and Naccache, P. (2008). 'Book Review: Le Nouvel Esprit du Capitalisme: Some Reflections from France', *Organization* 15 (4): 614–20.

Löwith, Karl. (1995). *Martin Heidegger and European Nihilism*, edited by R. Wolin. New York: Columbia University Press.

Lukes, Stephen. (1989). 'Of Gods and Demons: Habermas and Practical Reason', in *Habermas: Critical Debates*, edited by John B. Thompson and David Held. Cambridge, MA: MIT Press

Lukes, Stephen. (2005). *Power: A Radical View*. London: Palgrave Macmillan.

Lundgren-Gothlin, Eva. (1996). *Sex and Existence*, translated by Linda Schenck. London: The Athlone Press.

Luther, Timothy C. (2009). *Hegel's Critique of Modernity: Reconciling Individual Freedom and the Community*. New York: Lexington Books.

Lutz, Christopher. (2012). *Reading Alasdair MacIntyre's After Virtue*. New York: Continuum.

MacIntyre, Alasdair. (1988). *Whose Justice? Which Rationality?*. Notre Dame: Notre Dame University Press.

MacIntyre, Alasdair. (1991). *Three Rival Versions of Moral Enquiry: Encyclopaedia, Genealogy, and Tradition*. Notre Dame: Notre Dame University Press.

MacIntyre, Alasdair. (1996). 'A Partial Response to My Critics', in *After MacIntyre: Critical Perspectives on the Work of Alasdair MacIntyre*, edited by John Horton and Susan Mendus. Cambridge: Polity Press.

MacIntyre, Alasdair. (1997). *A Short History of Ethics: A History of Moral Philosophy from the Homeric Age to the Twentieth Century*. London: Routledge.

MacIntyre, Alasdair. (1999). *Dependent Rational Animals: Why Human Beings Need the Virtues*. Chicago: Open Court.

MacIntyre, Alasdair. (2006a). *Social Structures and Their Threat to Moral Agency* in *Ethics and Politics*: Volume 2. Cambridge: Cambridge University Press.

MacIntyre, Alasdair. (2006b). 'Epistemological Crises, Dramatic Narrative, and the Philosophy of Science', in *The Tasks of Philosophy: Selected Essays, Volume 1*. Cambridge: Cambridge University Press.

MacIntyre, Alasdair. (2010). *After Virtue: A Study in Moral Theory*. Notre Dame, IN: University of Notre Dame Press.

MacIntyre, Alasdair. (2016). *Ethics in the Conflicts of Modernity: An Essay on Desire, Practical Reasoning, and Narrative*. Cambridge: Cambridge University Press.

Mah, Harold. (1990). 'The French Revolution and the Problem of German Modernity', *New German Critique* 50: 3–20.

Maly, Ico and Varis, Piia. (2015). 'The 21st-Century Hipster: On Micro-Populations in Times of Superdiversity', *European Journal of Cultural Studies*, 69 (6): 637–53

Maslow, Abraham. (1987). *Motivation and Personality*. New York: Pearsons.

Maslow, Abraham. (1990). 'A Theory of Human Motivation', *Psychological Review* 50: 370–96.

McBride, Cillian. (2013). *Recognition*. Cambridge: Polity Press.

McCarthy, Thomas. (1985). 'Complexity and Democracy: Or the Seducements of Systems Theory', *New German Critique* 35: 27–53.

McLeod, Kembrew. (1999). 'Authenticity Within Hip-Hop and Other Cultures Threatened with Assimilation', *Journal of Communication* 49 (4): 134–50.

McFall, Lynn. (1987). 'Integrity', *Ethics* 98 (1): 5–20.

Merleau-Ponty, Maurice. (2012). *Phenomenology of Perception*, translated by Donald A. Landes. London: Routledge.

Miller, David. (1994). 'Virtues, Practices and Justice', in *After MacIntyre: Critical perspectives on the work of Alasdair MacIntyre*, edited by J. Horton and S. Mendus. Cambridge: Polity.

Mishima, Yukio. (1979). *Mishima on Hagakure: The Samurai Ethic and Modern Japan*, translated by K. Sparling. London: Penguin.

Mishima, Yukio. (2003). *Sun and Steel*, translated by John Bester. New York: Kodansha.

Nehamas, Alexander. (1983). 'How to Become What One Is', *The Philosophical Review* 92: 385–417.

Newton, Isaac. (1999). *The Principia: Mathematical Principles of Natural Philosophy*, edited by I. Bernard Cohen and Anne Whitman. Berkeley, CA: University of California Press.

Nietzsche, Friedrich. (1968). *The Will to Power*, translated by Walter Kaufmann and R. J. Hollingdale. New York: Random House.

Nietzsche, Friedrich. (1971). *Twilight of the Idols*, translated by R. J. Hollingdale. London: Penguin Books.

Nietzsche, Friedrich. (1991). *The Gay Science: With a Prelude in German Rhymes and an Appendix of Songs*, translated by Walter Kaufmann. London: Random House.

Nietzsche, Friedrich. (1996a). *Human, All Too Human: A Book for Free Spirits*, translated by R. J. Hollingdale Cambridge: Cambridge University Press.

Nietzsche, Friedrich. (1996b). *Thus Spoke Zarathustra: A Book for All and None*, translated by Walter Kaufmann. New York: Random House.

Nietzsche, Friedrich. (1998). *Philosophy in the Tragic Age of the Greeks*. Translated by Marieanne Cowan. Chicago, IL: Regnery Gateway.

Nietzsche, Friedrich. (2000a). *Beyond Good and Evil: Prelude to a Philosophy of the Future* in *the Basic Writings of Nietzsche*, translated by Walter Kaufmann. New York: Random House.

Nietzsche, Friedrich. (2000b). *The Case of Wagner* in *The Basic Writings of Nietzsche*, translated by Walter Kaufmann. New York: Random House.

Nietzsche, Friedrich. (2007). *Ecce Homo: How To Become What You Are*, translated by Duncan Large. Oxford: Oxford University Press.

Nietzsche, Friedrich. (2008). *On the Genealogy of Morals*, translated by Keith Ansel-Pearson. Cambridge: Cambridge University Press.

Nussbaum, Martha. (1989). 'Recoiling from Reason', Review of *Whose Justice? Which Rationality?* by Alasdair MacIntyre. *The New York Review of Books* 36 (19): 36–41.

Ortega Y. Gasset, José. (1994). *Revolt of the Masses*. New York: W. W. Norton & Company.

Owen, David. (1997). *Maturity and Modernity: Nietzsche, Weber, Foucault and the Ambivalence of Reason*. London: Routledge.

Patten, Alan. (2002). *Hegel's Idea of Freedom*. Oxford: Oxford University Press.

Peter, Laurence. (2018). '"Tourists Go Home": Leftists Resist Spain's Influx'. *BBC News*. http://www.bbc.co.uk/news/world-europe-40826257, accessed 30 January 2018.

Pinkard, Terry. (2003). 'MacIntyre's Critique of Modernity', in *Alasdair MacIntyre*, edited by Mark C. Murphy. Cambridge: Cambridge University Press.

Pippen, Robert. (1991). *Modernism as a Philosophical Problem: On the Dissatisfactions of European High Culture*. Oxford: Basil Blackwell.

Pongratz, Hans J. and Voß, G. Günter. (2003). 'From Employee to "Entreployee". Towards a Self-Entrepreneurial' Work Force?' *Concepts and Transformation* 8 (3): 239–54.

Porter, Jean. (2003). 'Tradition in the Recent Work of Alasdair MacIntyre', in *Alasdair MacIntyre*, edited by Mark C. Murphy. Cambridge: Cambridge University Press.

Potter, Andrew. (2010). *The Authenticity Hoax: How We Got Lost Finding Ourselves*. New York: Harper Collins.

Plato. (2003). *The Last Days of Socrates*, translated by Hugh Tredennick. London: Penguin.

Plato. (2008). *Republic*, translated by Robin Waterfield. Oxford: Oxford University Press.

Rehg, William. (1997). *Insight & Solidarity: The Discourse Ethics of Jürgen Habermas*. Berkeley: University of California Press.

Ridley, Aaron. (1997). 'Nietzsche's Greatest Weight', *Journal of Nietzsche Studies* 14: 19–25.

Rorty, Richard. (1991). 'Moral Identity and Private Autonomy: The Case of Foucault', in *Richard Rorty, Essays on Heidegger and Others*: Philosophical Papers 2. Cambridge: Cambridge University Press.

Rousseau, Jean-Jacques. (1983). *Emile*, translated by Peter Jimack. London: Grant & Cutler.

Rousseau, Jean-Jacques. (1997). *The New Heloise: Letters of Two Lovers Who Live in a Small Town at the Foot of the Alps*, translated by Philip Stewart and Jean Vaché. London: University Press of New England.

Rowley, Hazel. (2005). *Tete-a-tete: Simone de Beauvoir and Jean-Paul Sartre*. New York: Harper Colins.

Sartre, Jean-Paul. (1989). *No Exit and Three Other Plays*, translated by S. Gilbert. London: Random House.

Sartre, Jean-Paul. (2007). *Existentialism Is a Humanism*, translated by Carol Macomber. New Haven; Yale University Press.

Sartre, Jean-Paul. (2013). *Being and Nothingness: An Essay on Phenomenological Ontology*, translated by Hazel E. Barnes. Oxford: Routledge.

Schecter, Darrow. (2010). *Critique of Instrumental Reason from Weber to Habermas*. New York: Continuum.

Scheuerman, William. (1999). 'Between Radicalism and Realism: Democratic Theory in Habermas' Between Facts and Norms', in *Habermas: Critical Reader*, edited by Peter Dews. Oxford: Blackwell.

Schrift, Alan. (1995). *Nietzsche's French Legacy: A Genealogy of Poststructuralism*. London: Routledge.

Schrift, Alan. (2013). 'Discipline and Power', in *A Companion to Foucault*, edited by Christoper Falzon, Timothy O'Leary and Jana Sawicki. Chichester: Blackwell.

Seidman, Steven. (1983). 'Modernity, Meaning, and Cultural Pessimism in Max Weber', *Sociological Analysis* 44 (4): 267–78.

Shuttleworth, K. M. J. (2012). 'The Role of Death Within the Phenomenologies of Hegel and Heidegger', in *The Yearbook of the Irish Philosophical Society*, 137–51. Dublin: Mullen Print.

Shuttleworth, K. M. J. (2019a). 'An Existential Interpretation of the Picture of Dorian Gray: A Heideggerian Perspective', *Yearbook of the Irish Philosophical Society*: 181–99.

Shuttleworth, K. M. J. (2019b). 'Watsuji Tetsurō's Concept of Authenticity'. *Comparative Continental Philosophy* 11 (3): 235–50.

Smith, Patrick. (2018). 'Read the Deleted Tweets Brenda Leyland Sent About The McCanns Before She Died.' *Buzzfeed*. https://www.buzzfeed.com/patricksmith/read-the-deleted-tweets-brenda-leyland-sent-the-mccanns?utm_term=.ftpaWqJ3k#.ivvDLP2d0, accessed 6 January 2018.

Stern, J. P. (2014). *Understanding Moral Obligation: Kant, Hegel, Kierkegaard*. Cambridge: Cambridge University Press.

Taylor, Charles. (1975). *Hegel*. Cambridge: Cambridge University Press.

Taylor, Charles. (1983). *Liberalism and the Origins of European Social Theory*. Berkeley: University of California Press.

Taylor, Charles. (1985). *Philosophical Papers 1: Human Agency and Language*. Cambridge: Cambridge University Press.

Taylor, Charles. (1989a). 'The Liberal-Communitarian Debate', in *Liberalism and the Moral Life*, edited by N. Rosenblum. Cambridge, MA: Harvard University Press.

Taylor, Charles. (1989b). *Sources of the Self: The Making of Modern Identity*. Harvard: Harvard University Press.

Taylor, Charles. (1992). *The Ethic of Authenticity*. London: Harvard University Press.

Taylor, Charles. (1994). *The Politics of Recognition* in *Multiculturalism*, edited by Amy Gutmann. Princeton: Princeton University Press.

Tolstoy, Leo. (2006). *The Death of Ivan Ilych*, translated by Anthony Briggs. London: Penguin.

Trilling, Lionel. (2009). *Sincerity and Authenticity*. Oxford: Oxford University Press.
Turkle, Sherry. (1995). *Life on the Screen: Identity in the Age of the Internet*. New York, Simon and Schuster.
Turkle, Sherry. (2010). *Alone Together: Why We Expect More from Technology and Less from Each Other*. New York: Basic Books.
Ure, Michael. (2009). 'Nietzsche's Free Spirit Trilogy and Stoic Therapy', in *Journal of Nietzsche Studies* 38: 60–84.
Vallor, Shannon. (2018). 'Social Networking and Ethics', *Stanford Encyclopaedia of Philosophy*. https://plato.stanford.edu/archives/win2016/entries/ethics-social-networking, accessed 14 January 2018.
Varga, Somogy. (2012). *Authenticity as an Ethical Ideal*. New York: Routledge.
Wahl, Jean. (2016). *Transcendence and the Concrete: A Selection of Essays*, translated by Alan D Schrift and Ian Moore. New York: Fordham University Press.
Warnke, Georgia. (1995). 'Communicative Rationality and Cultural Values', in *The Cambridge Companion to Habermas*, edited by Stephen K. White Cambridge, Cambridge University Press.
Warnock, Mary. (1970). *Existentialist Ethics*. London: Macmillan.
Watsuji, Tetsurō. (1996). *Watsuji Tetsurō's Rinrigaku: Ethics in Japan*, translated by Seiksaku Yamamoto and Robert Carter. Albany: State University New York Press.
Webber, Jonathan. (2009). *The Existentialism of Jean-Paul Sartre*. London: Routledge.
Webber, Jonathan. (2018). *Rethinking Existentialism*. Oxford: Oxford University Press.
Weber, Max. (1991). 'Science as Vocation', in *From Max Weber: Essays in Sociology*, translated by H.H Gerth and C. Wright Mills. Oxford: Oxford University Press.
Weber, Max. (2005). *The Protestant Ethic and the Spirit of Capitalism*, translated by Talcott Parsons. London: Routledge.
Welborn, Guy. (1975). *The Buddhist Nirvana and Its Western Interpreters*. Chicago: University of Chicago Press.
Wilde, Oscar. (1991a). *The Picture of Dorian Gray* in *Plays, Prose Writings and Poems*. London: Random House.
Wilde, Oscar. (1991b). *The Soul of Man Under Socialism* in *Plays, Prose Writings and Poems*. London: Random House.
Williams, Bernard. (1981). *Moral Luck*: Philosophical Papers 1973-1980. Cambridge: Cambridge University Press.
Williams, Bernard. (2009). 'Life as Narrative', *European Journal of Philosophy* 17 (2): 305–14.
Willmott, Hugh. (2013). 'Spirited Away: When Political Economy Becomes Culturalized', in *New Spirits of Capitalism?: Crises, Justifications, and Dynamics*, edited by Paul du Gay and Glenn Morgan. Oxford: Oxford University Press.
White, Stephen K. (1988). *The Recent Work of Jürgen Habermas: Reason, Justice and Modernity*. Cambridge: Cambridge University Press.
Whitehead, Alfred North. (1978). *Process and Reality: An Essay in Cosmology*. New York: Free Press.

Yasuo, Yuasa. (1987). 'Modern Japanese Philosophy and Heidegger', in *Heidegger and Asian Thought*, edited by Graham Parkes. Honolulu: University of Hawaii Press.
York, Peter. (2014). *Authenticity Is a Con*. London: Bite Back Publishing.
Young, Julian. (2007). *The Death of God and the Meaning of Life*. New York: Routledge.

Index

Abraham 33
absolute freedom 25, 61–2, 64
absolute spirit 21
academic 79–80, 89
Achilles 76
administrative power 102–3
Adorno, Theodor 86
After Virtue 138, 147, 152, 157, 159, 164, 166
Alcibiades 124, 127
Alone Together 186
Amor fati 36
anxiety 51, 62, 181
architecture 117
Aristotelian 8, 11, 17, 61, 94, 137, 151–3, 161
áskēsis 125–7
asylums 115, 117, 132
Augustine of Hippo 41, 153
Aurelius, Marcus 125
autonomy 7–9, 11, 15, 21, 26, 30, 44–6, 48, 100, 103, 106–7, 109, 111, 112, 128–9, 169, 175–8, 191

Bacon, Francis 17–18, 27
bad faith 43, 51–2, 62, 72, 148–9
Battle of Marathon 23
Beauvoir, Simone 47, 64–5, 78–9, 81, 149
becoming what one is 10, 61, 69–81, 149–50, 174–7
Being and Nothingness 50–3, 57
being-for-itself 50–2, 62
being-in-itself 50–1, 54
being true to oneself 5, 40–3, 46, 59
Benjamin, Walter 1–2, 117
Berlin, Issiah 48
Between Facts and Norms 101
The Birth of Tragedy 132
blue flower 49, 166
Boltanski, Luc and Ève Chiapello 119, 178–82, 184, 189–90
Breen, Keith 33, 96, 111, 165

Buddhist 37, 74, 77
bureaucracy 31–2, 102
Byzantine Empire 24

call of conscience 73
Camus, Albert 28, 46, 78
capitalism 4–5, 30–2, 67, 91, 178–82, 184–5, 189–92
capital punishment 118
care for self 11, 113–14, 121–5, 127–30, 135–6, 169–70, 172, 177, 189, 191
categorical imperative 46, 106
Catholic Church 14, 18
China 22
choice 10, 19, 35, 47, 51, 53–4, 56, 58, 60–6, 68–71, 76, 79, 81, 109–10, 112, 129–30, 135–6, 140–1, 149–51, 154, 157, 166, 174–7
Christianity 23–4, 28–9, 31–2, 132, 139, 153
colonization 10–12, 85–6, 88, 90, 92–3, 102, 104, 169–72, 176, 178, 181, 191
commitment 10, 44–6, 60–1, 65–6, 75, 80–1, 129–30, 147–9, 174, 176
commodification 178, 180–2, 184, 189–92
communicative action 86, 89, 96–100, 104–5, 107, 109, 111, 112, 169
communitarianism 108
compartmentalisation 32, 34, 79–80, 143, 155
connexionist 179, 182, 184
consciousness 21–4, 27, 51–2, 65, 69, 86, 89, 91, 96, 122–3, 133
contemptus mundi 31, 79
counter-discourse 9, 15, 26, 95
coup d'état 68
critical theory 91, 93
cultural impoverishment 85, 88–91, 111
culture 2–4, 28, 30, 32–4, 39, 48, 54–5, 57, 60, 73–4, 76, 87, 88–9, 91, 95, 129, 137–8, 142, 144–6, 158–9, 169–70, 175

culture of narcissism   54
cunning of reason   22

Dasein   72–4, 78
das Man   41, 73–4, 121, 173
David, Friedrich Casper   35
death   33, 63, 73, 125
death of God   27–8, 34, 130, 133–4
The Death of Ivan Illych   63, 81
decisionism   68, 71
Deleuze, Gilles   119
democracy   57, 94, 101–3, 146, 175
deontology   110, 125, 139, 140
depression   67, 183–4
Derrida, Jacques   95
Descarte, Renes   96, 124
dialectical   22, 60
dialogical   57, 75, 81, 129
Diderot, Denis   18
difference   56–8, 175, 180, 182–4, 186, 189
Diogenes of Sinope   41
Dionysus   132
discipline   114–18, 120–1, 133
Discipline and Punish   115–16, 120
discourse principle   105, 110
discourses of power   113–23, 127, 129, 160, 170, 186
disenchantment   16, 30, 32–4, 38, 79, 87, 93, 104
distinctly modern   9, 39–40, 42, 46, 59
docile bodies   116–17, 133
Dooley, Mark   186, 188
double negation   74
Dreyfus, Hubert   187

Ecce Homo   69, 120
Eigentlichkeit   72
Emile   47
emotivism   11, 137–8, 142–51, 155–6, 166, 169–70
employees   144, 179, 181–2
encroachment of systems   90, 93, 102, 169
end in itself   21, 31, 46, 59, 125, 127, 154, 184
Enlightenment   8–11, 15–21, 25–30, 34–8, 44, 48, 78, 85–9, 91–2, 94–6, 113–15, 135, 137, 139–41, 145, 151, 168–70, 174, 176–7, 190–1

entreployee   179
entrepreneur   179
Epictetus   126–7
Epicurean   23, 124–5, 127
essence   6, 37, 48–50, 52, 54, 60–3, 69, 71, 75, 174
eternal recurrence   37, 70
ethical ideal   28, 42–3, 49, 53–6, 58, 72, 78, 81, 104, 109, 111–12, 130, 168, 175, 177, 191
The Ethics of Authenticity   54
European morality   28, 34
examination   118, 125
existence precedes essence   37, 61
existentialism   39, 46–7, 49, 72, 146–7
Existentialism is a Humanism   53

false consciousness   91, 122–3
fate   31–2, 36, 38, 70, 78, 112, 166
fear   20, 31, 51, 63, 71, 125
Ferrara, Alessandro   45, 47, 67, 75, 100, 150
field of freedom   64
formal rationality   30, 32
Foucault, Michel   10–11, 36, 112, 113–37, 170, 172, 177, 190, 191
fragmented consciousness   89, 91
Frankfurt School   91
Fraser, Nancy   100–1
freedom   6–10, 12, 15–17, 19–26, 28–31, 33–9, 45, 51–2, 60–5, 70–1, 79, 85–6, 88–90, 92–4, 102–4, 107–0, 111–14, 119, 121–3, 127–8, 130, 135–7, 141, 166, 168–71, 173–8, 190–1
freedom and meaning   7, 9–10, 12, 15–17, 34–6, 38, 60–1, 79, 85–6, 93–4, 103–4, 111–12, 135, 137, 168–71, 175–8, 190–1
free will   25
French Revolution   18, 20, 25

The Gay Science   27
genealogical   32, 34, 42, 116, 120–1, 123, 127, 134, 148, 153
Genealogy of Morals   29, 131
Ghost Dog   76
Goethe, Johann Wolfgang von   31, 132
Golomb, Jacob   41

the good   11, 55, 76, 86, 94, 96, 102, 104, 106–12, 140, 143, 149, 152–4, 157, 160–1, 165, 170, 175–7, 191
greatest weight   70
Greeks   22–3, 41, 124, 127, 171
Grene, Marjorie   61, 72
guardians   19–20
Guignon, Charles   41, 48, 66–9

Habermas, Jürgen   10–11, 36, 85–114, 119, 124, 169–72, 176, 190–1
Hall, Eric   58
Hamlet   42
Haussmann, Baron   117
Heidegger, Martin   41, 46, 51, 72–4, 78, 95, 121, 157, 164
hell is other people   63
Heller, Agnes   91, 100
Henrich von Oftendingen   49
the herd   40, 131–2, 148
Herder, Johann Gottfried von   48–9, 54–5, 57
heritage   10, 61, 78, 81, 149–50, 167, 175–6
Heter, T Storm   53
hierarchical observation   117
Hip-Hop   2–3
hipsters   3–4
History of Madness   120
The History of Sexuality   115, 123
Hölderlin, Friedrich   48–9, 54
Honneth, Axel   101
horizon of significance   56, 58, 75, 98, 129, 150
horizon of the infinite   36
Horton   76, 163
hospitals   117–18
Houlgate, Stephen   21–2, 28
human condition   61–3, 153
hyper-goods   109–11
Hyperion   48

ideological   66, 89, 122–3, 152, 173, 178
immaturity   19–20, 67, 115
inauthenticity   6, 9, 11, 40, 43, 59, 63, 73–4, 101, 121, 123, 136, 184
India   22
individuality   3, 9, 23, 35, 40–2, 59, 74, 113, 123, 129–30

institutions   7, 16, 18, 22, 24–5, 87, 89, 91, 93, 102, 113, 115–19, 128, 130, 132–3, 135, 165, 170, 172, 177, 179, 182, 190
instrumental reason   10, 90, 92, 102–3, 170
integrity   9, 39, 42–6, 59, 90, 154, 162
internet   169, 173, 178, 185–9, 191–2
intersubjective   56, 63, 74–5, 85, 97–9, 106, 108, 111, 130, 147, 150, 170, 174, 177, 190–1
intersubjective consciousness   10, 61, 77, 81, 149–50, 167, 175–7, 187
introspection   6, 49, 54, 60, 96, 174, 183
iron cage   31–2, 34, 90, 174

Jaeggi, Rahel   129, 185
Jaspers, Karl   46, 100, 131
Jesus   24
Joan of Arc   76
Justification and Application   106

Kasulis, Thomas   44
Kierkegaard, Søren   26, 40, 46, 51, 63, 140–1, 161
knockers and boosters   54
know thyself   123–4
Koopman, Colin   120–1

Last Man   133
last men   29, 37
Letter to Menoeceus   125
liberalism of neutrality   55
Life on the Screen   185
lifeworld   10–11, 85–90, 92–4, 96, 98–104, 107–9, 111–12, 169–72, 176, 178
loss of freedom   33, 88–90, 92, 104, 130, 176–7
Lukács, György   91–2
Lukes, Steven   100, 121–2, 136, 172
Luther, Martin   24, 140–1

McCarthy, Thomas   100–1
McFall, Lynn   43–4
MacIntyre, Alasdair   10–12, 15, 36, 137–67, 170–1, 173, 177, 191
the Madman   27–8
Madness and Civilisation   115

man is condemned to be free   62
The Mandarins   78
Marcel, Gabriel   46–7
Marxist   91, 93
mass society   3–5, 67, 77, 180
maturity   10, 15, 19, 21–2, 24, 26, 28, 38, 61, 67–8, 77, 81, 110, 149, 175–6
meaning   5–12, 15–17, 26, 29–30, 33–9, 49, 56, 58, 60–1, 63–4, 70, 78–81, 85–9, 91, 93–4, 97, 103–4, 109, 111–14, 119, 130–1, 133–7, 143, 150, 156, 163, 166, 168–71, 173–7, 190–1
meaninglessness   29, 33, 47, 85, 135
mechanised petrification   31, 85
Merleau-Ponty, Maurice   4, 64–5, 149
military   19, 68, 115–18
Mishima, Yukio   68, 76, 81
modern ideal   41–2, 46
modernity   7–10, 15–16, 19, 26–7, 29–30, 33–4, 36–9, 42, 47, 81, 85–7, 90–1, 93–6, 112–15, 119–21, 123, 128, 135, 137, 144, 151, 158–60, 162–7, 169–76, 184, 190–1
Modernity and Authenticity   47
Moral Consciousness and Communicative Action   104, 107
moral discourse   104–5, 108, 111, 137–8, 143, 166, 170
moral integrity   43–4

narrative   12, 16, 25, 69–70, 96, 137–8, 151, 155–9, 161–3, 166, 167, 171, 173–4, 176–7, 183, 191
Nathan Barley   3
natural teleology   29, 35, 38, 61, 79–81, 94, 137, 155–6, 158, 165, 176–7
Nausea   79
network capitalism   179
Newton, Issac   17–18
nihilism   15, 16, 28–30, 33–4, 38, 80, 93, 132–3, 147, 168
non-being   50
normalizing judgement   117–18
Notebook for Ethics   52–3
nothingness   49, 50–4, 57, 62, 74
Novalis   49, 166
N.W.A   2

Occidental   7, 30, 32, 34, 55
On the Use and Abuse of History for Life   134

ontological freedom   51, 93
ontology   53, 72
Oriental world   22
Outlines of a Philosophy of the History of Man   48
Overman   133
own-most possibility   73

panopticon   116–17, 186
performance   67, 98, 183–6, 189
performative model   67, 182–4, 186
Persia   22–3
personal integrity   43–4, 46
philosophical discourse   95, 124
The Philosophical Discourse of Modernity   95
philosophical midwifery   41
Philosophy of History   21, 25
phronesis   67
The Picture of Dorian Gray   70–1, 81
Pippen, Robert   16, 21, 26, 36
Plato   7, 20, 29, 124–7, 151–3
Plutarch   126
polis   23, 41, 76
political sphere   101–2
Polonius   42
polytheism   33, 34
popular culture   3
post-metaphysical   7, 60, 74
postmodern   11, 15, 36, 95, 96, 119, 130–1, 133–4, 136–7, 168–70, 185, 190
power   10–12, 23–4, 52, 86, 88, 92, 94, 96, 100–3, 131–6, 170–3, 191
practices   4, 16, 30, 32, 34, 40, 57, 119, 121, 123, 126, 128, 137, 151, 153–61, 163, 165, 167, 171–2, 177
premodern   15, 36, 41, 42, 118, 123, 164, 168–70
principle of universalization   105–6
prisons   115–17, 132
progress   4, 7–8, 15, 17–18, 20–2, 24, 26–7, 30, 33–4, 86, 91, 164, 168, 190
project of modernity   7, 9, 26, 36, 38, 86–7, 95, 169–70, 191
Protestant   24, 31, 139
Protestant Ethic and the Spirit of Capitalism   30, 32
public shaming   118
punishment   116–18, 124
Punk Rock   2–3, 76
Puritans   31–2

radical choice   47, 53–4, 56, 58
radical freedom   66
Raphael   1
rationality   25, 30–2, 34, 79, 85, 88, 92, 94, 96, 99, 103, 112–13, 152, 157–8, 164, 169, 170, 174, 176, 190
rationalization   11, 16, 18–19, 24, 30–2, 34, 38, 48, 85, 87–8, 91–2, 96, 112, 135, 169–70
rationalization of the lifeworld   85, 88, 92
recognition (concept of)   53, 57, 58, 63, 175
reification   90–3
relative   40, 42, 73, 107, 139, 151–2, 157
remission of sins   24
reproduction   2, 88, 99, 111, 171, 180
responsibility   20–1, 35, 65, 67, 71, 175
Revolutionary Terror   25
rights   23, 102–3, 108, 157, 164
Roman Empire   24, 125, 127
Romantic   35–6, 48–9, 54, 56, 58, 65, 68, 164
Rousseau, Jean Jacques   18, 47–9, 54–5, 57, 74

samurai   68, 76
Sapere aude   20
Sarto, Andrea del   1
Sartre, Jean-Paul   39, 43, 47, 49–58, 61–5, 72, 98, 128–31, 146–51, 157, 167
Sceptics   23
schools   117–18, 124
Schopenhauer, Arthur   132–3
science   16–19, 29–30, 32–3, 79, 86, 89, 91, 115, 138, 186
Science as Vocation   32, 37
Second Life   187
secularization   28, 34, 37
sedimentation   64–5, 80
self-actualization   5, 8, 77, 173
self-care   121, 123
self-creation   6, 47, 54, 98, 113, 130–1, 134, 169, 170, 183–4
self-determination   96, 106–7, 109, 111–13, 169
self-discovery   13, 56, 69, 189
self-fashioning   69, 182
self-help   5, 66–7, 182–4
self-indulgence   6, 47, 54, 56, 135
self-realization   5, 39, 47, 93, 96, 104, 106–9, 111–12, 169–70

Seneca   126–7
sentiment of being   47
seppukku   68
The Sex Pistols   2
She Came to Stay   65, 81
sincerity   9, 39, 42–3, 45–6, 59, 99
Sincerity and Authenticity   42
social media   12, 169, 173, 185–9
socio-existential   10, 12, 60–1, 78–9, 93, 98, 114, 129, 135, 137–8, 146, 149–51, 160, 163–9, 174–8, 184, 190–1
Socrates   23, 41, 124, 127, 132
Sources of the Self   109
spirit of capitalism   179–80
Stoic   11, 23, 113, 114, 124–8, 136–7, 170
strategic action   99–101
subject   11, 23, 47, 71, 93–7, 107, 109, 115–16, 119–22, 125–6, 129–31, 134, 172–3, 179
subjection   113–15, 119–21, 123, 127–8, 135–6, 172, 191
surveillance   115–18, 121, 186
systems   8, 10, 85–94, 100–3, 112, 118, 169–71, 185

Taylor, Charles   10, 40, 47–9, 53–8, 60, 75, 87, 98, 108–12, 129, 150, 175
techne   125, 127
technologies of self   129, 135
teleology   1, 29, 35, 38, 61, 79–81, 94, 137, 141, 143, 146, 153, 155–6, 158, 165, 171, 176–7
telos   8, 21, 50, 99, 103, 137, 139–41, 152–3, 155, 170, 174, 177
The Theory of Communicative Action   97
Thus Spoke Zarathustra   29
Tolstoy, Leo   63
tradition   7, 11–12, 16, 19, 26, 45, 49, 54, 58, 86–7, 89, 91, 107–8, 124, 137–8, 145–6, 149, 151, 153, 156–61, 163, 165–7, 169–71, 176–7, 191
tragedy   132, 152–3, 188
Trilling, Lionel   42–3, 47
truth   17, 23, 29, 40–1, 70, 97–9, 113, 118, 124, 126, 128, 133, 138, 158, 172
Turkle, Sherry   185–6
Twilight of the Idols   28

ultra-radical   121–2, 170, 172
unified self   44, 80, 134

unity   3, 11–12, 20, 30, 32, 37, 43, 48, 49, 80, 130–6, 138, 152, 155–6, 161–2, 167, 174, 176–7, 185
utilitarianism   110, 125, 138–40, 142

Varga, Somogy   48–9, 66–7, 74–5, 182–4, 186, 190
vereinmensch   37
virtue ethics   11–12, 137, 139, 146, 151, 161, 163–4, 166–7, 169, 171, 191
vocation   32, 79, 144
voice of nature   48
Voltaire   18

Wagner, Richard   133
waiter (Sartre's)   52, 62
Wanderer Above the Sea of Fog   35
Warnock, Mary   52, 72

Watsuji, Tetsurō   73–5
Webber, Jonathan   52, 64–5
Weber, Max   9, 16, 18, 30–4, 36–8, 79, 85, 87–92, 96, 114, 139, 144, 164, 166
What is Enlightenment   19, 114
wholeness   48–9, 162
Wilde, Oscar   70, 158
Williams, Bernard   44, 141, 158, 161–2
will-to-power   132–3, 146, 148
The Will to Power   29
work of art   1–2, 114, 128, 130–1, 135–6, 170, 177
world historical individuals   22, 24, 26
world Spirit   21, 23–4, 26, 127

Zarathustra   29
Zoroaster   22

www.ingramcontent.com/pod-product-compliance
Lightning Source LLC
Chambersburg PA
CBHW072235290426
44111CB00012B/2098